Praise for *T*

'In Shakespeare's *Richard II*, John o   .
this England" speech. This vivid histo., ~.....,~ .~ .... ~ ....s
and passion.'

The Times, Best Books of 2021

'Helen Carr has captured the drama of [John of Gaunt's] life and the tensions inherent in it in a compelling portrait. In so doing, she reminds us of the contradictions of a period remote from our own, not just in time but in values and beliefs too... Carr has brought to life one of the major figures of medieval England.'

Linda Porter, *Literary Review*

'*The Red Prince* is not...just a book of battles and wars... it is the towering figure of John of Gaunt, a thoroughly European Englishman, who takes centre stage and it's a stirring and memorable performance.'

Leanda de Lisle, *The Times*

'Helen Carr is a really exciting new talent in the world of history writing, whose work strikes a perfect balance between lucidity and scholarship. Her debut, *The Red Prince*, is a beautifully nuanced portrait of an oft misunderstood man.'

Rebecca Rideal, author of *1666: Plague, War and Hellfire*

'A long overdue reappraisal of one of medieval England's greatest but most enigmatic figures. *The Red Prince* announces Helen Carr as one of the most exciting new voices in narrative history.'

Dan Jones, author of *The Plantagenets* and *The Hollow Crown*

'Superb, gripping and fascinating, here is John of Gaunt and a cast of kings, killers and queens brought blazingly, sensitively and swashbucklingly to life. An outstanding debut.'

Simon Sebag Montefiore, bestselling author of *Jerusalem: The Biography*

THE RED PRINCE

The Life of John of Gaunt,
the Duke of Lancaster

HELEN CARR

ONEWORLD

A Oneworld Book

First published by Oneworld Publications, 2021
This paperback edition published 2022
Reprinted twice in 2022

ISBN 978-0-86154-318-2
eISBN 978-0-86154-083-9

Typeset in Minion by Hewer Text UK Ltd, Edinburgh
Printed and bound in Great Britain by Clays Ltd, Elcograf S.p.A.

Plate section illustration credits: Portrait of John of Gaunt © Bridgeman Images; The gold
noble of Edward III courtesy of the Metropolitan Museum of Art; Effigy of Edward the
Black Prince © Bridgeman Images; Blanche of Lancaster courtesy of Wikimedia Commons;
Constance of Castile with John of Gaunt from *Froissart's Chronicles*, courtesy of Wikimedia
Commons; Geoffrey Chaucer portrait by Thomas Hoccleve, courtesy of the British Library,
Harley MS 4866; Map of London 1300 by William Shepherd from *Historical Atlas* (1926),
courtesy of Wikimedia Commons; Pontefract Castle by Michael Taylor licensed under
Creative Commons Attribution-Share Alike 4.0 International; Kenilworth Castle by J.D.
Forrester licensed under Creative Commons Attribution-Share Alike 4.0; Richard II
Westminster Portrait © The Dean and Chapter of Westminster; John of Gaunt Tomb Effigy
Drawing courtesy of Wikimedia Commons; Lancastrian Livery Collar © The Museum of
London; Seals before and after change of arms to King of Castile, John of Gaunt's Register
© National Archives; Rothwell jacket courtesy of Rothwell Church; Battle of Nájera,
Battle of Sluys and Peasants' Revolt from *Froissart's Chronicles* courtesy of Wikimedia
Commons; *The Trial of John Wycliffe* by Ford Madox Brown courtesy of Wikimedia
Commons; John of Gaunt's Cellar © Helen Carr; John of Gaunt from the St Cuthbert
window in York Minster © Chapter of York; Tomb of Katherine Swynford © Nathan Amin

Maps © Erica Milwain

Oneworld Publications
10 Bloomsbury Street
London WC1B 3SR
England

Stay up to date with the latest books,
special offers, and exclusive content from
Oneworld with our newsletter

Sign up on our website
oneworld-publications.com

MIX
Paper from
responsible sources
FSC
www.fsc.org   FSC® C018072

For my Pa.

Contents

Money

In order to demonstrate the value of fourteenth-century sums, I have on occasion used a currency converter, courtesy of the National Archives. This has helped to draw comparisons, though of course any present-day equivalents are open to debate.

I have tried to keep references to currency simple, using pounds where possible. In the fourteenth century, coinage was valued in pounds, shillings and pence. In the case of the Peasants' Revolt, I refer to groats. One groat equates to a value of four pence.

The only reference to French money is the *écu*, in regard to the King of France, John II's, ransom. The word *écu* means 'shield' and the coins are decorated with a series of shields. It is the oldest French gold coin and an abbreviation for the predecessor of the euro (European Currency Unit). From the fourteenth to the seventeenth century, the *écu* was the most important European gold coin.

Introduction

JOHN OF GAUNT – 'WHAT NAME ON THE ROLL OF ENGLISH princes is more familiar?' When Sydney Armitage-Smith wrote the first complete biography of John of Gaunt in 1904, his rhetorical question would have had the effect intended: John of Gaunt was, then, a famous, familiar figure, central to English history. Yet in the more than a hundred years since Armitage-Smith's book, Gaunt's position in popular consciousness has waned. Though his impact on the destiny of the English crown is undeniable, his character, motivations and story are often marginalised. The Black Prince needs no introduction . . . not so the younger brother whose achievements – political, military, dynastic, cultural – were arguably all more significant.

During his life, John of Ghent, or 'Gaunt' – his name dictated by his birthplace – would witness plague, war, victory and revolt, a decades-long schism in the Catholic Church between rival Popes in Rome and Avignon and the popularising of the English language in poetry and literature. He would father a future English King, become a regent in all but name and claim the kingship of Castile, where his daughter would later reign.

The first Earl of Lancaster, Edmund Crouchback, planted red roses in the gardens of the Savoy Palace. These roses became the emblem of the House of Lancaster. When King Henry VI, John of Gaunt's great-grand-son, plunged the country into civil war, red rose badges were worn by combatants in some of the bloodiest battles ever to take place on English soil. Another Lancastrian, Henry Tudor, would finally end the war in 1485, landing at Mill Bay in Pembrokeshire, clutching the sand in his fingers and claiming legitimacy as King of England. The red rose Henry proudly wore as a Lancastrian King was eventually merged with the Yorkist white of his wife, creating the famous united Tudor Rose.

John of Gaunt fits uncomfortably in the historical narrative: the son of a famous King, the brother of a famous war hero. That brother, the Black Prince, is renowned for his victories on the battlefield yet Gaunt – the Red Prince – is marginalised for his. John of Gaunt has stood in the wings, but not taken centre stage: his life has been the sub-plot, yet it laid the foundations for the sequel. Historians continue to contest John of Gaunt's legacy, helped and hindered by the polarising, conflicting accounts of his life offered by contemporary chroniclers. Where he is the righteous hero in one chronicle, he is the villain of another. To one historian he is a haughty politician, to another, a fair feudal magnate.

The novelist L.P. Hartley wrote, 'the past is a foreign country; they do things differently there'. This is particularly the case for the Middle Ages and there are limited sources that provide enough detail to piece together even fragments of his life. An existing catalogue of administrative sources relating to John of Gaunt survives mainly at the National Archives, with some additional information at the British Library and the Bodleian in Oxford. These sources – largely land grants, indentures (a type of contract), records of employment and charters – shed some light on Gaunt's life as a leading magnate in the realm, and are best read alongside the chronicle accounts which provide colour and narrative. Medieval chronicle accounts, however, are inevitably flawed. The sources for the fourteenth century are fragments of the truth, interpretations often as a result of rumour, bound together to create an 'idea' rather than a linear explanation of how things were. With many lacunae in the records of the period, medievalists – even more than historians of later periods – are forced to be subjective and interpretive. The Reformation, the Great Fire of London, war and time have resulted in a massive loss of evidence, so historians rely on the fragments that are available to them – often contemporary interpretations.

England, France and Spain are littered with legends and rumours of John of Gaunt and the times he lived. In prose, poetry or stone, his legacy endures. He was the 'cat of the court' in *Piers Plowman*, the Black Knight in Chaucer's *Book of the Duchess*, and Old Gaunt, the bereft, ageing uncle in Shakespeare's history play, *Richard II*: it is thought that Shakespeare himself played the role of John of Gaunt in the early seventeenth century. Gaunt not only featured in literature but patronised it. He was known to have supported, even befriended, Chaucer – who late in life became his brother-in-law – keeping him employed by the royal household during both Edward III's and Richard II's reigns, and it is possible that the epic poem *Sir Gawain and the Green Knight* was commissioned by Gaunt around 1375. The astrologer Nicholas of Lynn dedicated his 'Kalendarium' to John of Gaunt in 1386, suggesting an interest in science and astrology, as well as literature and art.

Like many before me, I have found John of Gaunt intriguing. Forward-thinking, ambitious, honourable and loyal, yet deeply flawed; impulsive, arrogant and impatient. His ambition, motivation, familial care and emotions suggest a deeply complex character. His experiences were some of the most revolutionary, ground-breaking and dramatic moments in history. It is these experiences – war, revolution, politics and human relationships – that I have focused on to tell the life story of John of Gaunt, the Red Prince.

Prologue

'Though the man is almost a stranger to us, his name is a household word'.

Sydney Armitage-Smith

JUST OFF THE M1, EN ROUTE TO LEEDS, LIES THE SMALL industrial town of Rothwell. In the early 1980s Rothwell was well known for its coal-mining industry and community. Six local collieries employed most of the townspeople and the community thrived off a tradition that spanned six centuries, beginning in the early fifteenth century. Margaret Thatcher's Conservative government shut down the mines in favour of cheap coal exports from abroad in the early 1980s. People sought employment elsewhere, making the most of the motor-ways that wrap around the town and account for the hum of traffic audible in the town centre today.

Rothwell is steeped in history and has, until fairly recently, been an important place on the map of England. As a settlement, listed in the Domesday Book, Rothwell was valued at £8, more than nearby Leeds. In the later Middle Ages it became an established royal hunting ground, known for fertile land and wildlife. Echoes of the medieval town remain – the market cross and street layout. However, the principal architectural feature to resist the vast concrete motorway expansion and the Industrial Revolution is Rothwell's church. Holy Trinity is situated on a rise and it looms over the town. The building we see today is the result of years of restoration and repair, and is largely a Victorian edifice, but its foundations date to before the Conquest.

Filled with crafts, toys for children, advertisements for groups and committees and polished pews, filled on Sundays with local worshippers, the inside is typical of most churches today. However, at the back of the nave stands a unique relic: a clear case contains the waistcoat, or 'jack' (jacket) of John of Gaunt, Duke of Lancaster.

John of Gaunt spent considerable time in Rothwell. It was where he came to hunt, to enjoy the simple pleasures of sport, woodland and time absent from the pressures of his prominent position. His waistcoat is large, quilted and has mostly disintegrated over time. It is similar to one that belonged to his brother, the Black Prince – held at Canterbury Cathedral as a significant tourist attraction – yet is not presented with quite the same grandeur. Staring through the thick glass of the cabinet one tries to conjure up an image of the man who possibly wore it more than six centuries ago.

Gaunt was fond of the town and the church and patronised it, even building a covered walkway from the manor house in which he would stay to the church. During one stint in Rothwell, a story goes, John of Gaunt found himself embroiled in a furious duel with a local man, John de Rothwell, over a serving girl in the castle. It is also rumoured that on Stybank Hill, which overlooks the church, he personally killed the last wild boar in England. This is probably a myth, though the story endures and his reputation has become part of local folklore.

John of Gaunt's surcoat is his surviving legacy in Rothwell, but if you head south on the M1 to London, you'll find much more. The Savoy Hotel with its glittering green facade, an icon of luxury, takes its name from the Savoy Palace, Gaunt's property in London, a byword for splendour, wealth and power. The streets around the Savoy Hotel lie on the original site of the palace – Savoy Street, Savoy Place, Savoy Court; there is even a pub called the Savoy Tap and another pub a few doors down which hangs Gaunt's portrait from its door. The Savoy Palace is an indelible part of the fabric of London, yet the palace itself no longer exists. Lancaster has more references to John of Gaunt: streets, hotels and Ye Olde John O'Gaunt pub. Leicester has a hidden cellar that is dubbed 'John of Gaunt's cellar', once part of the expansive Leicester Castle, the centre of Lancastrian Duchy administration. Hampshire, Hungerford, Cambridgeshire, Yorkshire . . . England is peppered with unassuming reminders of John of Gaunt, but the Rothwell waistcoat is personal and human. His relics may not hang in a museum, cathedral or famous castle, but they are woven into the fabric of our everyday lives in the same manner as his historic legacy.

The roots of John of Gaunt's family tree are deeply intertwined with our monarchal history. Centuries after his death, contenders for the throne harked back to their famous ancestor Gaunt to endorse their righteous inheritance of the Crown. The Tudor dynasty was born out of John of Gaunt's adultery. Prince Arthur and Catherine of Aragon were united as mutual descendants of John of Gaunt. A seemingly insignificant, crumbling relic in a small, unassuming English town holds a deeper and far more significant history – overlooked for far too long.

France in the Fourteenth Century

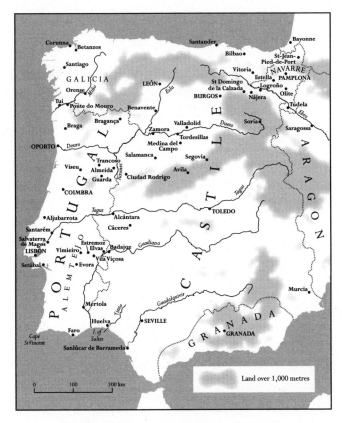

The Iberian Peninsula in the Fourteenth Century

ONE

THIS ENGLAND

This royal throne of Kings, this sceptered isle,
This earth of majesty, this seat of Mars,
This other Eden, demi-paradise,
This fortress built by Nature for herself
Against infection and the hand of war,
This happy breed of men, this little world,
This precious stone set in the silver sea,
Which serves it in the office of a wall
Or as a moat defensive to a house,
Against the envy of less happier lands,
This blessed plot, this earth, this realm, this England.

John of Gaunt in *Richard II*, Act II, Scene I

IN THE MID-FOURTEENTH CENTURY, THE CHANNEL WAS A dangerous stretch of water. French ships patrolled the sea, attacking English coastal towns in an attempt to destroy the lucrative wool trade between England and Flanders. In 1340, England and France were three years into a political, dynastic and territorial struggle – a war of succession – that would become known as the Hundred Years War. By summer 1340, both sides were yet to engage in full battle. On 24 June 1340, a 'Great Army of the Sea' dropped anchor outside the port of

Sluys, the inlet between Zeeland and Flanders, and prepared for combat. The ships were filled with French and Genoese warriors and their intimidating presence incited mass panic along the coastal towns of the Low Countries. Local people either feared attack and fled their homes, or flocked to the coastline to see the spectacle for themselves.

As French ships floated outside Sluys, the King of England, Edward III, led a fleet across the Channel, intending to land an army ashore in Flanders and oust the French who had infiltrated the country in his absence. Two months earlier, Edward had left his heavily pregnant Queen, Philippa of Hainault, in the Flemish town of Ghent where he spent months trying to make an alliance with Flanders. To secure the terms, he was forced to sail back to England, promising to return with an army and money. Philippa – expecting her sixth child – stayed behind as collateral for the enormous loan the Flemish had given the English King to begin his war.

The French King, Philip VI – the first of the Valois family – anticipated Edward's return to Flanders and mustered a fleet so vast that it would not only block Edward's landing but threaten the total annihilation of the English naval force. In May 1340, news of this mighty French fleet, floating off the coast of Flanders, reached Edward III as he held a Royal Council at Westminster. Senior members of the English nobility and clergy shouted over one another. Some proposed battle, but the Archbishop of Canterbury, John Stratford, argued against it. He was cautious and warned the King that the French force was too large to be defeated.

Despite reservations from his Council, the King set about mustering the greatest English fleet to ever sail across the Channel. Coastal towns and ports throughout England were to be stripped of all ships and provisions, to be sent to Orwell in Suffolk where ships prepared to set sail.

At dawn on 22 June 1340, Edward III was on board his cog ship – a merchant vessel with one sail – as it passed Harwich on the southeast coast of England, leading a fleet of around 150 vessels. The naval force was cobbled together from warships, merchant ships and even large fishing boats. They were blown forwards by a north-westerly breeze, towards the superior fleet of French ships, and finally came in sight of the enemy at the mouth of the river Zwin two days later. The sheer scale of the French force was overwhelming – described by the chronicler Jean Froissart as a water fortress. A mass of wooden breastworks, barriers and masts bound together by chains: 'like a row of castles'.

The English fleet, though unprecedented in size, should have been no match for the French. Many of the English vessels were ill-equipped for battle and they were faced by an impenetrable stockade. Alongside six Genoese galleys, the French component of the fleet was led by a Breton knight, Hugues Quiéret, Admiral of France, and Nicolas Béhuchet, its Constable – the commander in chief of the French army.

At around 3pm, Edward III gave the order to advance on the French ships lingering on the horizon. However, at the sight of armoured prows and piercing masts, the morale of the English dwindled. As he paced the deck of his ship, the King delivered an inspiring oration to boost his men. He expounded that their fight was in the pursuit of a 'just cause, and would have the blessing of God Almighty'. He also permitted his men to keep whatever booty they could obtain from the enemy vessels.[1] The incentive of plunder appears to have lifted the mood, for his army soon became 'eager' to face the imposing force ahead and battle drums echoed across the water.

The French ships were bound together to create a single juggernaut that could crush lone vessels in the water ahead. The English would have to break their defence in order to engage. According to the French Chronicle of London, Edward ordered his men to flee – as the French watched. The English drew their sails to half-mast and raised anchor, as if to turn back. As Edward anticipated, the French immediately played into his hands; they 'unfastened their great chains' and pursued the English in anticipated triumph. The French ships, detached from their intimidating unit, were now vulnerable, and proved easy pickings as the English vessels turned back and attacked. To the sound of drums and trumpets, signalling battle, heaving ships crashed into one another, throwing men off their feet with the force of the collision. Both sides boarded each other's vessels and so began close and bloody combat. 'Our archers and crossbowmen began to fire so thickly, like hail falling in winter, and our artillerymen shot so fiercely, that the French were unable to look out or to hold their heads up. And while this flight lasted, our English men entered their galleys with great force and fought hand to hand with the French, and cast them out of their ships and galleys'.[2] In tricking the French into breaking up their fortress of ships, the English were able to beat the odds and trap the French. The result was a rout, described by Jean Froissart as 'a bloody and murderous battle'. Edward III was wounded in the leg, but his injury was minor in comparison to the fate of the French commanders. Hugues Quiéret died fighting and the Constable of France, Nicolas Béhuchet, was strung up from the mast of his own ship.

The Battle of Sluys was a triumph for Edward III, for he had prevailed in one of the largest and most crucial naval battles of the Hundred Years War, winning him what became known as the *English* Channel. This victory was so deeply etched into Edward III's self-image, it was commemorated on a valuable gold noble, depicting Edward ensconced in a ship, gallantly clutching his great sword and shield, branded with the quartered arms of England and France.[3]

As the King of England celebrated his great victory into the night, his Queen, Philippa of Hainault, was still in recovery from her own bloody and highly dangerous experience: childbirth. Childbirth in the fourteenth century was an agonising and fraught event, accompanied by ritual, prayer and carefully considered practicalities. Managed exclusively by women, those in charge of the safe delivery of a royal baby – and the survival of a Queen – were highly skilled midwives. Two months before the Battle of Sluys, in a dark, hot room in the Abbey of Saint Bavon, in the small town of Ghent, the Queen of England delivered a 'lovely and lively' baby boy, named John Plantagenet.[4] After the battle, Edward III made his way to Ghent, but en route he diverted his men to the Shrine of the Lady of d'Ardenburgh, where they abandoned their horses and walked on foot to the shrine. On his knees, the

King of England gave thanks for the great victory at Sluys and for the safe delivery of another healthy Plantagenet prince.[5]

Thirteen years before the birth of John Plantagenet, in the cold winter of 1327, his grandfather King Edward II was murdered. Unceremoniously ousted from his throne and imprisoned at Berkeley Castle, the King of England was then dispatched: the names of his murderers and their method remain a mystery. The popular myth that surrounds his death whispers that he was impaled through the rectum with a red-hot poker; a cruel and brutal death for an accused sodomite. Edward II had been overthrown in favour of his young son, Edward – later Edward III – in a rebellion led by his wife, Queen Isabella, and her lover, Roger Mortimer. They believed that the impressionable new King would be a malleable puppet in their schemes, and that they would be well placed to control the realm as regents (in all but name) for the young Plantagenet heir.

Edward III was crowned aged fourteen on 1 February 1327, and began his kingship under the watchful eye of his mother and the seemingly unstoppable Roger Mortimer. The young King tolerated Mortimer for three years, until 1330, when Edward conspired with his closest friends at court to overthrow the man who really controlled the country. On 19 October, in a coup against his effective stepfather, Edward captured Mortimer at Nottingham Castle and dragged him outside, to the sound of his mother's screams: 'Fair son, have pity on the gentle Mortimer'. Without mercy, he ordered that Mortimer be imprisoned and tried. With Edward's agreement, Mortimer was sentenced to be hanged, drawn and quartered.

On 29 November, Roger Mortimer was dragged to the scaffold at Tyburn on a hurdle and tied to a ladder before the crowd. His genitals were then severed and his stomach was slit, with his entrails yanked free from his open belly before being cast into a fire. Finally, Mortimer's head was cut off and he was hung by his ankles.[6] The bloody, headless corpse of the old power in England demonstrated the birth of a new era: the age of Edward III. Very few shed tears for the man who saw himself as King, or for the Dowager Queen. Isabella was left bereft, mourning quietly in confinement and visited by her son only once or twice a year.[7]

Shortly after the Nottingham coup, Edward III released a proclamation which he commanded be read by sheriffs aloud and in public throughout the realm. '[Edward] wills that all men shall know that he will henceforth govern his people according to the right and reason, as befits his royal dignity, and that the affairs that concern him and the estate of his realm shall be directed by the common counsel of the magnates of his realm and in no other wise . . .'[8] The King's statement made clear that 'royal dignity' went hand in hand with royal authority: he believed in providential kingship.

As he took control of the country in his own right, Edward first had to tackle domestic affairs. When Edward inherited the throne, he also inherited a country in a sorry state. Scotland presented the principal threat, with its King, Robert the Bruce, frequently attacking England's northern border. Wales had been colonised by Edward I and overrun by the English, with a legacy of lingering resentment amongst the Welsh, while Ireland was largely left to its own devices. In 1332, the House of Commons formed after sitting together for the first time in a separate chamber to the lords and clergy. The Commons were made up of country representatives – knights of the shire from the countryside and burgesses from the towns and cities. They were elected locally, whereas lords received direct summons from the King for Parliament. By 1341, the Commons were independent of the clergy or the lords for the first time, which enhanced their position and power as spokesmen for the people. Magnates were appointed to defend the realm, and allocated the responsibility of mustering troops from their county. Edward of Woodstock – the Black Prince – was installed as Prince of Wales, and successfully recruited Welsh soldiers when the time came for war. Edward III strengthened the northern borders against the Scots and later placed his son Lionel in the position of Lieutenant in Ireland.

Despite domestic affairs being of supreme importance, war with France was inevitable. This was in part due to Edward's forceful and ambitious nature, but also down to an old dispute over territory. Edward III had not only inherited the English crown, but the constant monarchal belief that the lands in France that had once been Plantagenet territory were still by right English. The largest and most significant instigator of the Hundred Years War was the disagreement over Gascony.

Gascony was a treasured fraction of what had once been a Plantagenet domain in France. It was also incredibly lucrative and produced the most popular wine in England. Gascony was, above all, a fiscal asset to the Crown. In 1259 Henry III made peace with Louis IX with the Treaty of Paris, and in doing so renounced Plantagenet claim over lands lost in France. It was agreed that Gascony could be kept, but only in fief – held in return for allegiance or service – to the French crown. Edward I, II and now Edward III refused to acknowledge this agreement, causing an enduring friction between England and France.

This tension came to a head when, in 1337, Philip VI confiscated the Duchy of Aquitaine, a region in the south-west of France, bordering the Kingdom of Navarre, and the county of Ponthieu, an original Norman vassal state at the mouth of the Somme – accusing Edward of breaking his feudal bond. Edward responded with an outright claim of what he considered to be his birthright: the French throne. He was, he asserted, the closest male heir of the late Charles IV of France, through his mother Isabella.

As war with France grew imminent, England began to prepare for combat, mustering troops from around the country. In order to defeat the French, Edward was aware he needed international allies and sought the support of Flanders, basing himself and his pregnant Queen in Antwerp. With Louis I, Count of Flanders, in strong support of the French, this was an optimistic move. However, the municipal governments of Ghent, Ypres and Bruges relied heavily on the wool trade with the English, in order to keep Flemish mills running. Finally – through the support of the influential Flemish merchant leader, Jacob van

Artevelde – Edward negotiated a loan and the services of 2,000 men at arms. The Flemish were in a difficult position regarding their allegiance, being financially obligated to remain loyal to the King of France through funds held by the Papal treasury. The only way they could see around the situation suited the ambitious Edward perfectly.

At a Great Council held in Flanders, it was agreed that the only way to avoid forfeiting the money held by the Papal treasury would be for Edward III to style himself King of France. 'They would hold him for King and obey him as their sovereign Lord, from who the county of Flanders ought to be held, and would help him gain sovereign power in his realm'.[9]

On a bitterly cold day in January 1340, the townspeople of Ghent circled around the the market square. Before an audience, Edward III was publicly proclaimed King of France in order to secure support from the Flemish towns.[10] Back at home, however, Parliament was at a deadlock, refusing to budge to support the ambitious alliance, as Edward was attempting to subordinate England's needs to those of his new partners. He promised a subsidy of £140,000, free trade and the removal of the Staple – the centre of the wool trade administration, usually the town in which wool was traded – to Bruges. There was no way of following through with his promises without raising tax and plunging England into financial difficulties.

Eventually, Edward was forced to return home, leaving his family in Flanders as collateral for his onerous promises. He sailed for England, determined to convince Parliament and the Church that the war with France was a necessity, and that he should be relieved of his debts in order to fund the campaign. By 1340, the year of John of Gaunt's birth, his father was in serious debt to Flanders. England teetered on the brink of revolt and Edward had begun to dismiss government officials, creating political divisions and making enemies in the Commons and among the clergy by imposing taxes and borrowing substantial sums. His envoys had overspent drastically in forming terms with the Flemish, promising them wealth as though the English Crown could afford to repay the debts without issue. The Crown jewels were pawned, yet Edward still needed to beg Parliament for further funds. If unable to pay his debts, he would be forced to return to Brussels as a prisoner until the debt was settled. Despite mitigating some of the debt by granting the Flemish merchants English wool, Edward III was broke.

Where the first half of 1340 was marked with crippling financial and military pressure, the second brought triumphs. The Battle of Sluys was a remarkable English victory, gaining Edward the admiration and respect of his soldiers – a force made up largely of his own countrymen – and demonstrating the potential of English military and naval power. His kingship was strengthening and, to add to the promising future, a healthy Plantagenet prince had been born.

Prince John spent the first months of his life in Ghent, baptised at his birthplace – the Abbey of Saint Bavon.[11] He had two powerful godparents: John, Duke of Brabant – an influential landowner in Flanders – and Jacob van Artevelde – a powerful textile merchant – who held the baby John at his baptism ceremony.[12] The choice of godparents for the new Prince was tactical. The Duke of Brabant had been Edward's key ally in the war against France. He had supported Edward's claim to the French throne and donated 1,200 men at arms to the war effort against the French. Jacob van Artevelde was an influential figure in Flanders. Having amassed vast power and fortune in the textile industry, he became a spokesman and leader of the commercial classes. However, van Artevelde was also a reputed dictator and bully, supposedly using his men to injure and even murder anybody who disputed his authority. His influence in Flanders and control over the textile trade made him a crucial ally for Edward, but his bullish nature eventually backfired. An angry mob murdered him in 1345 for his overexertion of power and growing familiarity with the English.

In the autumn of 1340, the King and Queen made the decision to return their children to England for safety, due to the increasing threat of a French invasion of Flanders. The King could not risk his children being taken hostage, not least due to the immense financial strain he was already under. By July, Edward could not even pay the expenses of his household and three loyal earls, including Henry of Grosmont (later Duke of Lancaster) were arrested by the Flemish and thrown into a debtors' prison. The King wrote to Parliament pleading for aid, else 'I and my country, my children, the nobility and my whole people will be undone'.[13] With an impending march on Tournai to arrange, the King said goodbye to his children, whom he would not see for four months. In November 1340, John of Gaunt was taken to England with his brother Lionel, who was two years older, and installed at Woodstock Palace in Oxfordshire where he would receive the care and education of a prince.[14]

John of Gaunt was the third surviving son of Edward and Philippa, and aged two was given the title of Earl of Richmond.[15] Before him came Edward of Woodstock, later known as the Black Prince, and Lionel of Antwerp. The Queen gave birth twelve times in total, with nine children surviving infancy. The relationship between Edward and his Queen, Philippa, was loving and the King famously doted on his wife post-partum, lavishing her with gifts of red velvet and robes of cloth of gold lined with miniver. The new Prince, John, was treated with equal adoration, being given a silk robe and colourful bedding of red and green. The newborn John of Gaunt was also appointed his own cradle rocker and no fewer than eleven servants, instructed to attend to his every need: his nurse, Isolda Newman, was paid generously by the King to care for the royal infant.

Despite attentive servants, Queen Philippa was heavily involved in the upbringing of her many children, and occupied herself with the management of the royal nursery.

In 1319, when negotiations were in place for Edward and Philippa's marriage, Bishop Walter de Stapledon, an ambassador for King Edward II, was sent to Hainault to inspect the future Queen of England. In his register, he provides a detailed report of her appearance; she had dark hair, a 'high and broad' forehead, with 'broad' nostrils, but 'no snub nose, full lips and was 'brown of skin all over'.[16] The chronicler John Hardyng predicted Philippa would bear many children. He described her as having 'good hippes', necessary to successfully carry twelve babies to term. With just thirteen months between John of Gaunt and Edmund of Langley, it is questionable whether the relentlessly virile Edward ever left his wife alone. Philippa was a portrait of maternal femininity. She did what all good Queens were expected to do: give birth to heirs. Her children were her absolute priority.

Philippa of Hainault took on the responsibility of other children as well as her own. She adopted orphaned children of the nobility into the nursery, such as Joan of Kent, after her mother died and her father was beheaded for treason. Philippa also cared for the children of those in her service, such as Katherine and Philippa de Roet, whose Flemish father, Pan de Roet, had died on campaign in France. She extended her interests further, into rural industry by opening mines in Tyndale and Derbyshire, providing opportunity and industry for local communities, and even prompting the English to use their wool to manufacture their own garments – where cloth was previously bought in from Flanders. In 1341 she also enhanced the growth of Oxford University by supporting the foundation of The Queen's College, Oxford.[17] The chronicler Jean Froissart worked for the Queen as her secretary from 1361 to her death in 1369, and described her as 'courteous, humble, devout . . . and tall'.

Where Philippa of Hainault was humble, caring, loyal and dutiful, Edward III was confident, ambitious and hot-headed. He was a leader with exemplary military capabilities – a reckless spender, but adept at war. During the war, the King led destructive *chevauchées* through France, destroying the countryside. Yet, through such an aggressive military policy, he managed to expand Plantagenet lands in a manner not achieved since the reign of Henry II and Eleanor of Aquitaine.

Like most Plantagenet Kings before him, a superior military force was the priority of Edward's kingship. He offered paid military service, an idea that had been initiated by his grandfather, Edward I. This resulted in the most powerful English army assembled for two centuries. Rather than calling on an army of farmers and serfs to do their feudal duty, all men were paid for their skills, from the foot soldier at 2d per day – around six pounds by today's standards – to the Black Prince who earned the far greater sum of one pound per day – around £750. As his sons grew older, Edward was keen to involve them in his campaigns, both overseas and through domestic military propaganda and ceremony. The intention was clear: Edward III and his sons would be accepted throughout Europe as a powerful military and political family.

The firstborn son of Edward III and Philippa of Hainault was Edward of Woodstock, later known as the Black Prince – either due to the colour of his armour or his ruthless reputation on the battlefield. The Black Prince became a respected military leader and the most inspirational and revered Plantagenet Prince in England. To John of Gaunt he was a friend, a mentor, a brother in arms, and, for the first part of Gaunt's life, an inspiration.

The Queen chose Woodstock Palace, her favourite countryside retreat, for the royal nursery – a place only formally established after John of Gaunt's birth.[18] Traditionally, medieval childhood lasted from birth until around seven years of age, at which stage the child would leave the nurse and be placed under the care of women in the nursery. The children's household – and the care of John of Gaunt – was overseen by the 'chief maistresce', Isabella de la Mote, who assigned women to each child. John of Gaunt shared Margery de Monceaux with his slightly older brother Lionel, as well as Margery la Laundere who managed the napiery (linen nappies) and the ewery (washing the princes). As they were still both nursing, however, they had separate wet nurses. As Prince John grew older, he was assigned a page, a valet and a tailor. Education began early; he was allocated a tutor and received a pious education, introduced into the religious community through ceremony and prayer. In total, the royal nursery employed sixty-seven people to serve the children. When John of Gaunt was around eight years old, he was placed in the care of the Black Prince.

Childhood being relatively short meant that girls were expected to marry and bear children of their own by the ages of around twelve to fourteen, while boys were expected to begin military service, which is why Gaunt was soon placed under the supervision of his more experienced older brother.

The Black Prince had received the best education available. He was taught by the scholar and astrologer Dr Walter Burghley, and was expected to excel as the future King of England. This served him well for he gleaned a sense of his own majesty from an early age: at seven he was even accoutred with his own suit of armour. Whilst his parents were in Flanders, the year before John of Gaunt's birth, the Prince opened Parliament on behalf of the King.[19] Before he was ten, the Prince led an elite entourage, greeting the envoys of the Pope at the gates of the City of London (in the fourteenth century London was still encased inside a large defensive wall, with around seven gates that allowed access from the north to south of the City). Aged ten, the Prince represented his father as the head of state, and even served as head of the realm whilst Edward III was in Antwerp around the time of John of Gaunt's birth. Thrust onto centre stage, the Black Prince's ability to work the crowd came from ample experience at a young age in the public eye. Alongside his glittering public image, the Black Prince managed extensive land and property in Cheshire and Cornwall, overseeing local administration, and cultivating loyalty from his tenants. When John of Gaunt lived with his brother he was expected to learn the skills required for leadership – military and domestic. This period of fraternal bonding forged an enduring closeness between the two boys, despite the ten-year age difference between them.

The military victories of Prince Edward were legendary. He went on to be the hero of Poitiers, and his reputation was that of a chivalrous prince, albeit an arrogant one. During the Battle of Poitiers, the Black Prince captured the French King, John II. That night, he served his royal captive on bended knee as a page.

Isabella Plantagenet, born two years after the Black Prince and named after the dowager Queen, was equally as indulged by Edward III as her older brother. She ran up vast debts due to her extravagant lifestyle and remained unmarried until she was thirty-three, having jilted her fiancé, the Count of Gascony, moments before she was to board the vessel which would carry her to France. Her would-be husband retired to a monastery and she was allowed to keep her expensive trousseau. She eventually fell in love with, and married, one of the King's hostages from Poitiers, Enguerrand de Coucy, a French aristocrat. During the war, de Coucy sat comfortably on the fence between the conflicting countries and refused to fight for either England or France.

Princess Joan was five years older than John of Gaunt, followed by William of Hatfield who died in infancy, and was subsequently buried in York. His death was followed by the birth of another prince, Lionel, who would grow to be the giant of the Plantagenet family, an improbable seven feet tall according to chronicler John Hardyng.[20] After John, came four younger surviving siblings: Edmund, Mary, Margaret and Thomas, filling the royal nursery.

Aged fourteen, Edward's 'dearest daughter' Joan left England to marry Pedro of Castile, cementing an Anglo-Castilian alliance crucial to Edward's military agenda. As her ship drew into the harbour at Bordeaux, her retinue were unaware of the horror they were about to face: the relentless and devastating Black Death now spreading quickly throughout Europe. The royal party fled to Loremo, a small village in Bordeaux, but the Princess could not outrun the disease. Joan died unwed on 1 July 1348, with no family around her. His sister's death had a lasting impact on John of Gaunt; in 1389 he endowed an obit – an intimate religious service – for her at the Cathedral of St André at Bordeaux, where she was buried.[21]

In the autumn of 1348, the Black Death crept into England from a ship that landed in Southampton. The deadly disease reached London around 1 November 1348, and by 2 February 1349 around 200 people were being buried daily in mass graves outside the City. Henry Knighton, an Augustinian monk, witnessed the devastation of the Black Death in England: 'there was a general mortality throughout the world ... in the same year there was a great murrain of sheep everywhere in the realm . . . in one place more than 5,000 sheep died in a single pasture . . . sheep and oxen strayed through the fields and among the crops and there was none to drive them off or collect them, but they perished in uncounted numbers . . . for lack of shepherds . . . After the Pestilence many buildings fell into total ruin for lack of inhabitants; similarly many small villages and hamlets became desolate and no homes were left in them, for all those who had dwelt in them were dead'. The Black Death – widely considered to have been bubonic plague – caused a painful and often-gruesome end. First came the shivering and fever, along with extreme fatigue and muscle aches. The illness was named for its characteristic formation of 'buboes': blackened and swollen lymph nodes. Appearing on the armpit, groin or neck, these painful swellings could be as large as apples or eggs. Depending on the development of the infection, a person could then go on to have vomiting, bleeding from the mouth, nose and rectum, and even tissue loss in extremities such as the fingers and nose. Death came swiftly, with the disease usually taking only three to five days to kill eighty per cent of its victims.

As the Black Death gripped the western world, Europe was forced to pause conflicting politics and come to terms with an epidemic of an apocalyptic nature. The visitation would drastically change the landscape of society.

Before the Black Death arrived in 1348, the country and the Crown were riding high on military victory, following success at the Battle of Crécy in 1346. Such celebrations incentivised Edward III to keep war as his national priority. He had proved himself on the battlefield, but as a new foreign enemy silently crept into England, he was faced with an invisible force, a challenge of a different magnitude altogether. The 1349 January Parliament was postponed until Easter, for both Lords and Commons feared gathering together. The nobility and Parliamentary officials fled to their homes in the country and Sheriffs refused to conduct their business for fear of their lives. The King's response was rational, following the belief that poor public hygiene was responsible for the epidemic. He opposed the idea of digging a burial pit for the plague victims in East Smithfield, in close proximity to the Tower of London, and ordered the closure of all of the London ports.[22]

In 1349, John of Gaunt was in York with the Black Prince. The brothers likely sought refuge in St Mary's Abbey from the Black Death, which had now reached the North of England, tearing through York at a terrifying rate. For John of Gaunt the Abbey was both a spiritual and physical sanctuary, because the natural and most common response to the horror of the plague was extreme levels of piety, demonstrated across England and throughout Europe. People believed the pestilence raging across the country was divine punishment – they blamed themselves. According to Henry Knighton, the Scots gathered in Selkirk to plan an invasion of England, for they also believed 'God's dreadful judgement to have descended upon the English'. Their invasion never took place; the Black Death soon arrived in Scotland, claiming 'a monstrous death upon the Scots'.[23]

The King requested that the clergy perform rites calling on the grace of God to help protect the realm from the terrors of the Black Death. Around the end of September 1349, 600 Flagellants arrived in England from Flanders. The Flagellants marched and whipped themselves, drawing blood, before they formed into the shape of a cross and continued to beat each other, chanting all the while. According to Thomas Walsingham, they processed through the streets twice daily, barefoot and wearing only a piece of linen from their waist to their feet. On their heads they wore a hood painted with a red cross – front and back. These men were 'noble men of foreign birth, who lashed themselves viciously on their naked bodies until the blood flowed, now weeping, now singing'.[24] Even above military might, territorial power, wealth and posterity, the medieval community firmly believed in God: their maker, and their destroyer.

Around the year 1300 the population of England had stood at roughly five million; by 1377 this had dropped to around two and half million.[25] Plague had claimed half of the population, wiping out entire families, villages and even towns such as Bristol.[26] Rich or poor, man, woman or child, every person felt the effects of the Black Death. The first crushing wave in 1348 was not a one-off: it would return almost yearly thereafter.

The sudden loss of labourers threatened the feudal system – where landholders provided property to tenants in exchange for their services, as labourers or in war – as survivors began to negotiate their wages, suddenly aware of their enhanced value. In 1349 Edward introduced the Ordinance of Labourers, passed with the intention of keeping the working classes in the same pay bracket as they had been before the epidemic. All able-bodied and 'sturdy beggars' were charged with the task of bringing in the harvest, and those who sought to shirk responsibility were publicly humiliated in the town stocks, which were reintroduced for this very reason. Retailers and manufactures were prevented from exploiting the change in the social economy and Church wages were also regulated. Citizens of England, for a time, were banned from leaving the country for war or for pilgrimage. Over the course of the following decade, however, wages continuously rose and the Ordinance proved unsuccessful. The resulting tension between the governing and the labouring classes would grow into a battle over social and economic order that would endure throughout the second half of the fourteenth century.

The decade following John of Gaunt's birth in 1340 was a period of fluctuation between victory and disaster. The early economic strain on the country in pursuit of an expensive war had been followed by the greatest military victories of the age: battles such as Sluys and Crécy. Then, as the country celebrated a golden age of war, the Black Death tore through the continent. The first ten years of John of Gaunt's life were lived in a polarised world of war and chivalry, poverty and plague. He grew up amid the harsh and uncontrollable reality of the medieval world.

TWO

THE GLORY OF WAR

'I should relate to you that which all should hold in esteem – that is, chiv-alry: this was upheld in his person, in whom it held sway thirty years. Nobly he spent his life, for I would dare to say this, that since the time that God was born there was none more valiant than he'.

Chandos Herald, *The Life of the Black Prince*

PHILIPPA OF HAINAULT STOOD UPON THE CLIFF TOPS OF Winchelsea as a bloody naval battle unfolded in the seas below. A decade after the Battle of Sluys, Edward III was deeply embroiled in another skirmish with French allies Castile. This time the King was joined by his sons, the Black Prince and ten-year-old John of Gaunt, eager to cut his teeth at war.

After the Battle of Sluys the English Channel had lived up to its title, dominated by the English with little in the way of resistance. Now England found itself threatened by a new southern power: the Castilians. During the Middle Ages, Castile was a dominant state on the Iberian Peninsula; so large and influential that chroniclers often referred to the Castilians and the Spanish as one. Castilian pirates plundered English vessels off the coast of Flanders, forming an alliance with the French, threatening the peace along the English coast. At the end of July 1350, the prospect of a Castilian invasion was real and the

King's councillors deemed it necessary to release the first official invasion warning in years. Government feared that the Castilians intended
to 'totally destroy all English shipping in their quest for domination'.[1]
Edward III – anticipating an imminent attack – prepared a fleet for
action and publicised the Castilian threat, instigating a national effort
to protect the coast.

Ships gathered from ports around the country at Winchelsea and
some of the most famous knights of the fourteenth century – the Earls
of Lancaster, Warwick, Arundel, Salisbury, Northampton and
Gloucester, all veterans of Sluys – met at Winchelsea in the hope of
another naval victory.[2] With the King came the Black Prince, who
would command his own ship, and John of Gaunt, who refused to be
parted from his brother.

On 29 August 1350, around forty to fifty Spanish warships sailed
towards Winchelsea – 'huge Spanish galleons towered over our own
galleys and ships, like castles above cottages'.[3] To match the Spanish
force – albeit with smaller vessels – the King had prepared fifty ships to
send into the murky waters of the Channel to confront the new enemy.
Despite the disparity in the sheer size of the vessels, the atmosphere of
the camp at Winchelsea seemed jolly. The Queen came with her ladies
and the nobility drank wine, confident that it would be an easy victory.
The King had accoutred himself in a fine new suit of black velvet, which
chronicler Jean Froissart claimed 'suited him nicely'. The Black Prince,
however, carefully drafted his will in preparation for the possibility of
death at the hands of the Castilians, though this did not seem to detract
from the general mood in the camp. The men were merrily entertained
by John Chandos, a close friend of the Black Prince and important
military leader in the Prince's future campaigns. His herald – an official
spokesman – later composed a long poem about the Prince's life.
Chandos led singing and dancing, making the nobility snort with
laughter as he danced about the camp. Although Edward launched a
national alert, the chroniclers suggest the impending battle was treated
with such levity that neither the King nor the nobility seemed aware
that the Castilians were in fact experienced sailors and warriors. If so,

this could explain why ten-year-old John of Gaunt was permitted to attend the battle.

Shortly before 'the hour of vespers' the King's watch sighted ships looming on the horizon. The music juddered and stopped. 'I see two, three, four, and so many that, God help me I cannot count them'.[4] According to Froissart, the Spanish were moving so fast – cutting through the Channel from Flanders – they could have sailed clean past without engaging. 'They were in big ships, well-trimmed, with the wind astern, and need never have tangled with the English unless they wanted to. But such was their pride and confidence that they scorned to slip by without fighting. Instead, they prepared to give battle in earnest with their full strength'. Vast Castilian ships, well equipped with heavy artillery, advanced on the smaller English fleet and the fight ensued amongst the waves. Archers leaned over the sides of the galleys, hailing arrows at the opposing side's crossbowmen, to the sound of 'blood curdling cries [that] ascended to the heavens'.[5] The Spanish catapulted heavy rocks into the English ships, smashing through the timber and crushing masts, which toppled onto the decks; men even 'had their brains knocked out by stones thrown from the masts'. John of Gaunt was stationed aboard the Black Prince's ship, which was rained upon by rocks and 'quivering bolts and arrows'. Geoffrey Baker adds that men had 'never experienced anything more dreadful than this frightening conflict, which grew more and more intense . . .' and John of Gaunt was amidst the action.

The Spanish attempted to take possession of an English warship, the *Salle du Roi*, under the command of Lord Robert de Namur. As the sun set, the English warship was hooked with ropes to a Spanish galley, which intended to pull it away from the battle and sail off. As Robert de Namur attempted to save his ship, he fought a 'large Spaniard' in 'severe' one-to-one combat. Overcoming the English resistance, the Spanish sailors unfurled the sails of the *Salle du Roi* so they could catch the strong wind. As the ship passed the King's cog *Thomas of Winchelsea*, the men on board tried to save the *Salle du Roi* from capture, but their shouts for help were drowned out by the noise of battle. Seeing the ship hooked to the Spanish galley, a young servant of de Namur called Hannekin took it upon himself to save the boat: 'with his sword drawn on his wrist, leaped on board the enemy, ran to the mast and cut the large cable which held the main sail . . . the sails fell on the deck. Lord Robert seeing this, advanced with his men . . . [he] attacked the crew so vigorously, that all were slain or thrown overboard'.

Though the *Salle du Roi* was rescued, the Black Prince was in trouble. His ship was so badly damaged that 'water came in very abundantly'. The Prince was forced to abandon the vessel and board a Spanish ship, the *Bilbao*, and watch 'as his own vessel sunk'. In high drama, Henry of Grosmont swooped on board the Spanish ship, yelling 'Derby to the rescue!' as he hurled Spaniards overboard into the thrashing water, and took the ship. According to Froissart the overall battle lasted 'considerable time', but finally 'victory [was] declared for the English'. The Queen who had inevitably 'suffered that day' was relieved to see her children safely return to shore.[6]

The *Bilbao* was taken by the Black Prince as a trophy, which he dutifully gifted to the King, in honour of the victory, after they disembarked at Rye. The English had won their second naval victory in ten years and those who fought hard and survived were generously rewarded.[7] Fatalities were immense; Geoffrey le Baker insists that Winchelsea was a sea battle 'so massive and so dreadful that a faint heart would not have dared to look upon it'. Although the Castilians lost almost their entire fleet, he exaggerates the death toll at 25,000 killed in battle or drowned. He estimates the English loss of 4,000 men, including four knights.

The Battle of Winchelsea lost the French their most important ally – Castile. Weakened by English success at Crécy in 1346, the French suffered once again in 1349 when Henry of Grosmont inflicted a brutal *chevauchée* – a guerrilla-style raid through the French countryside from the Garonne, marching all the way to the walls of Toulouse. Days before the Battle of Winchelsea, the Valois King, Philip VI, died and was succeeded by his son, John II. With France in a period of readjustment under a new King, an English campaign into France in 1350 was tempting. Although this was an opportune moment to strike, a large-scale invasion of France was problematic: England was still in recovery after the scourge of the plague and could not finance the operation. In order to repair England's economy, Edward III needed to stall engagement with France and turn his attention to the desperate state of his own realm.

As part of John of Gaunt's tutelage under his brother, he observed the requirements that came with being a prince, feudal overlord, warrior and leader. The education received from his brother was a type of apprenticeship in which, alongside military training, he was expected to learn about domestic responsibility, such as the maintenance of land and tenants. From 1352 John of Gaunt spent time with the Black Prince touring his lands in Cornwall and Cheshire, seeing to their management and resolving various local issues.

No expense was spared for the brothers to spend the summer months together. New clothes and saddles were ordered and they spent significant time at the Black Prince's luxurious palace at Byfleet in Surrey, preparing for their progress around the country.[8] The Black Prince was a fair feudal overlord, but had eye-watering spending habits. He decked out his knights in new girdle tips – the tip of a long belt that hung from the waist – and ornate belt buckles. After he married Joan of Kent, she spent an extortionate amount on high fashion, enjoying swathes of silk and ermine gowns, and she often wore pearls in her hair.[9] The King and Queen also had a love of fine things; Philippa's household accounts reveal 'great riches, lavish expenses and debts of ye Queene'.[10] Although Edward III was forced to pause the war effort, he occupied himself with the extensive remodelling of Windsor Castle, at a cost of over £50,000 – the equivalent of around £30 million today. The luxurious new design included a vineyard, managed by a personal vintner who was paid a generous sum of 7s per week.[11]

While in Cornwall, the Black Prince also embarked on building projects: strengthening his castles, intent on creating fortresses that would serve to protect his tenants if needed. He also received local petitions and dealt with them accordingly. In 1351 he helped a widow, Iseult, with the crippling debt left by her deceased husband, who had committed suicide. He also chastised an official of the archdeacon of Cornwall for oppressing his tenants.[12] However, not all of his tenants were happy with his actions as a feudal overlord. In 1353 the people of Cheshire revolted against his authority, attacking his men, murdering a bailiff and causing uproar in the county. Following face-to-face nego-tiations with the Black Prince, the disgruntled citizens of Cheshire agreed to a hefty fine for their actions but also gratefully accepted new liberties he bestowed on them: no more blood was spilled.

It is likely that John of Gaunt – shadowing his older brother – was largely on the sidelines of the administrative war effort, but had ample opportunity to observe how a powerful magnate exercised his author-ity domestically. Gaunt watched how the Prince handled the discon-tent in Cheshire, and dealt with grievances from the people in Cornwall, going to great efforts to protect them. When John of Gaunt inherited an enormous responsibility as Duke of Lancaster, he would demon-strate the same fairness and generosity.

The Black Prince was – without doubt – John of Gaunt's role model and, of all his many siblings, his closest friend. It is possible that the King saw the brothers as a natural duo and, later in his life, Edward III would come to rely heavily on Gaunt. Even from a young age John of Gaunt sought to emulate his brother and after years of local politics and lessons on land management, he was eager to follow the Prince's lead on campaign in France. In 1355, aged fifteen, he was finally given the opportunity.

In the fourteenth century, the Kingdom of Navarre – a territory sandwiched between France and Castile and Aragon – stood as an independent sovereign state. The King of Navarre, Charles d'Evreux, held lands in France, for which he paid homage to the French King. As Navarre was a small state it wielded comparatively little power on the grand political stage of Europe, certainly in comparison to France, England or the Holy Roman Empire. However, during the war between

France and England, Charles of Navarre played a shrewd game of back and forth between the two powers, who both relied on his strategic aid. Navarre, as a border country, was crucial for the movement of large armies through France and Spain during the Hundred Years War. Navarre and England already had a historical tie: Edward III's grandmother, Joan I, had been Queen of Navarre in her own right and was also the great-grandmother of Charles. This made Edward III and Charles second cousins, a precedent for a potential alliance.

In November 1354, the King of France, John II, confiscated the lands of Charles of Navarre that he held throughout the Kingdom of France after Charles had ordered the ambush and murder of the Constable of France, Charles de la Cerda. According to chronicler Jean le Bel, King John of France 'unrelentingly hated the young King of Navarre ... This hate never left his heart, regardless of whatever appearances he might put on for them'. With King John and Charles of Navarre at odds, an opportunity arose for Edward to resume war against the French. In January 1355, a peace conference was held in Avignon, hosted by the Papacy. The English – represented by Henry of Grosmont, now Duke of Lancaster, and the Earl of Arundel – sought to ratify the draft Treaty of Guines from the year before and, as discussions began, pushed the French embassy – led by the Duke of Bourbon – to agree to the terms. The treaty had stipulated that Aquitaine would be held by the English in full sovereignty, rather than in fief to the French crown. The French refused, stating that the King's promise on his coronation was to protect France and keep the country whole. Talks dragged on but neither side was willing to budge and eventually the negotiations collapsed. However, as the conference played out, Charles of Navarre hovered in the background. He accosted the Duke of Lancaster and proposed an alliance with Edward III to oust the Valois King, John. The olive branch was too tempting. Charles of Navarre spent weeks in covert discussion with the Duke of Lancaster and he promised to return to Navarre to raise an army.

Later that year, plans for a major campaign were fully underway. Charles of Navarre – now the promised ally – suggested that Edward himself should invade France by landing in Normandy, where Charles would meet him with a large force, ready to press on with a joint invasion.[13] After the Duke of Lancaster returned from Avignon, he began conscripting for war.

Thirty-eight ships were moored at Rotherhithe with streamers in the Duke's colours – white and blue – and young nobles were selected to join the Duke on the forthcoming expedition. All hopes were pinned on Charles of Navarre's word, at a substantial cost. King Charles consistently shirked on agreements and promises to both the English and the French throughout his involvement in the Hundred Years War, and conspired with opposing powers to extract advantage and opportunity from every situation. His double handed politics, lies and deceit earned him the nickname Charles the Bad and, unsurprisingly, his pledge to the Duke of Lancaster proved false.

With war on the horizon, John of Gaunt was hurled into preparations, in the expectation that he would join the King on campaign. At only fifteen, he was placed under the supervision of his father's closest friend and ally, the Duke of Lancaster. The Duke was good at war. A diplomat and soldier, he had fought alongside Edward III for the duration of the war and achieved victory over the French in 1345 after leading a raid through Bergerac and northern Aquitaine. His loot and the ransom of various noble prisoners made him rich on the back of war. The notoriety and wealth he gained during the 1340s – as a soldier and as a diplomat – made him a powerful lord and he became an influential figure in Gaunt's life. Though Gaunt was royalty and Grosmont was not, to be included in his army for a first taste of war in France represented a great honour.

Gaining land and the titles of Bergerac and Beaufort, Henry, Duke of Lancaster, was able to pay for extensive building works on the Savoy Palace, the formidable powerhouse of Lancastrian administration situated on the banks of the Thames between the City and Westminster. Further to his accumulated wealth, the new Dukedom of Lancaster came with its own palatinate: a county distinct from the rest of the country, ruled by a lord who enjoyed special rights and privileges. His position and prestige in England sat close to that of royalty.

In 1355, it was intended that Henry, Duke of Lancaster – with John of Gaunt alongside him – would join forces with Charles of Navarre and conduct the proposed invasion of Normandy with a force of 9,000 soldiers. The intention was a double-pronged attack. As the Duke of Lancaster landed in Normandy, the King – with the Earls of March, Northampton and Stafford – intended to land secretly at Calais, further east along the French coastline. The complicated strategy was perhaps – as chronicler Geoffrey Baker believed – because Edward planned to confuse the French by appearing to give the command to the Duke of Lancaster, before landing at Calais to launch a surprise attack.[14] The Black Prince also mustered a separate force, accompanied by the Earls of Warwick, Suffolk, Salisbury and Oxford. The Prince intended to sail for Aquitaine where he planned to confront the Valois force head-on as they mustered in the south-west.

With three separate fleets, the Duke of Lancaster, Edward III and the Black Prince left England in July bound for Normandy, Calais and Gascony. Within days, strong winds pushed the ships back to the English coast where they were forced to wait until September for optimum weather. The first of the fleets to sail successfully was that led by the Black Prince, still intending to disembark and advance on Aquitaine. As the Prince sailed across the Channel, hopeful for victory, Charles the Bad reneged on his promise to the English and made amends with John II, scuppering plans for a joint invasion of Normandy with Lancaster.

After three months of waiting – and an abrupt change of plan – the King and the Duke joined forces and landed at Calais on 2 November 1355. Edward III was accompanied by his sons Lionel of Antwerp and John of Gaunt. The army that landed at Calais was largely English, augmented by 1,000 mercenary soldiers from the Netherlands and Germany. Calais was a town of war: equipped with greater military resources than any other town in England or France, it now billetted around 10,000 warriors in its garrison.[15] [16] It was an arena for the practice of and the preparations for war, in all its physical and administrative manifestations, and was the jumping-off point for the largest invasions of France that took place throughout the late Middle Ages. Strategically, Calais was crucial to the English. Only twenty miles from the coast of Kent, Calais also served as the Staple, the gateway for the wool export between London and Flanders. It was surrounded by a walled circuit, including five castles, plus another ten miles of external fortification. The garrison permanently housed around 1,000 soldiers with another few hundred armed citizens.

In 1355, as the English army settled into the garrison, bustling with the promise of battle, John of Gaunt prepared himself for the most sacred, honoured and formal moment of his apprenticeship at arms: knighthood.

Knighthood, in the Middle Ages, was an elevation of status and a celebration of ideological and behavioural values unlike any other military or social ceremony of the time. To be knighted, was to be invited into a fraternity that was bound by military and chivalric ethos for the remainder of one's life. The ceremony itself was a deeply pious and meaningful event. As was traditional, John of Gaunt was bathed, expected to pray and confess before reciting the Oath of Knighthood; this was then sealed by the King dubbing the flat of a sword on his shoulders. This tradition was part of the pomp of chivalry, but its ceremony was essential to formalise knighthood as a lifelong dedication. For Gaunt himself, this was no empty ceremony: the knightly code sat at the very heart of his being. Gaunt remained dedicated to the duty and honour expected of a knight of the realm throughout his life.

Departing Calais, the English moved south, raiding and burning, before settling at Ardes, where the new French Constable, James I, Duke of Bourbon and Count of La Marche, arrived to confront Edward III. He offered battle, to take place the coming Tuesday – proposing a formal time of engagement in a manner dictated by chivalric protocol. Edward III, antagonising the Constable, suggested that instead of taking their armies into battle, 'to avoid the effusion of Christian blood', the two Kings should fight it out themselves, in one-to-one combat, so that 'all the rights which each of them held in the realm of France should be staked on the fight'.[17] The French ignored the bait. The offer of single combat was used to provoke and shame the opposition into action. If a King rejected the terms of a battle, or even single combat, that could damage the morale of his men and jeopardise his reputation. Although single combat between Kings never took place in the Hundred Years War, it remained a useful device to prod the enemy into a decisive battle. Edward III had perhaps anticipated John II's next move, and his offer of combat was an attempt to outflank him.

The French King changed his course of action – which was perhaps his plan all along. He stalled and deliberately avoided battle. Edward threatened that if John II did not appear for battle in three days, he would leave. His intention was to shame the French King into fighting – not to appear for battle demonstrated cowardice. All to no avail: the ultimatum did not lure the French onto the field. Instead, John II implemented scorched earth tactics: all bridges in the path of the English invasion should be broken down, and citizens and supplies be hidden inside the walls of nearby garrisons for protection.[18] A furious Edward III was forced to turn back towards Calais from Ardes, further torching and ravaging the country as he went. On his return to Calais he received inflammatory news – the Scots had invaded and taken the English garrison at Berwick-upon-Tweed.[19]

While Edward had been trying to coerce John II into battle in France, a Scottish force, led by the Earl of March and William, Lord of Douglas, 'laid waste' to land south of Scotland, as far as Durham, in a four-day rampage. In a surprise attack they scaled the walls of Berwick-upon-Tweed Castle and butchered all opposition, claiming the castle as Scottish property. Edward now returned to England, cutting short his French expedition. He landed on 12 November and hurried north, taking his sons John and Lionel with him to deal with Scottish lords who had attacked the pivotal border stronghold of Berwick-upon-Tweed. They had Christmas at Newcastle where Gaunt and Lionel celebrated the festivities and their initiation into the army, indulging with their retinues in the King's personal stock of wine. After the

Christmas period was over, the English force advanced further north, intending to punish the Scots for their opportunistic attack.

In January, Edward III arrived at Berwick-upon-Tweed and wasted no time in laying siege to the town, which quickly surrendered.[20]

By the end of January 1356, the King met with Edward Balliol at Roxburgh. Edward Balliol was the King of the Scots, having replaced David II – the son of Robert the Bruce – during the Second War of Independence in Scotland, with the support of Edward III. David II had been taken prisoner and held in England whilst Edward III tried to control Scotland through Edward Balliol. However, the attack on Berwick-upon-Tweed proved that neither Edward III nor Edward Balliol had control over the unruly Scottish nobility. Furious that Balliol was unable to prevent his lords from harrying the Borders, Edward III forced him to abdicate. At their meeting in Roxburgh, Balliol removed his crown, lifted a handful of Scottish earth and handed both to Edward III.

Intent on pacifying the rebel Scots, Edward marched his army to Edinburgh and on the way launched a guerrilla-style raid across the Lothians, burning, pillaging and murdering. This destructive exercise eventually became known as 'Burnt Candlemas'; the land was scourged and blackened, and the Scottish people were left homeless, starving and desolate. According to Jean le Bel, the English force remained at Berwick-upon-Tweed 'until after Candlemas [2 February], and burned and laid waste to all the land of Scotland, that had rebelled against him'.

The fast march north had given the King little time to prepare supplies for the army and, as the Lothian burned, his own men also went hungry. They survived off rainwater and short rations for a fortnight – eventually Edward III was forced to abandon the attack on Scotland and return south.[21]

John of Gaunt was witness to his father's severe handling of the Scots. They had been fighting the authority of the English for generations and in 1356 were once again forced to yield. The discord between England and Scotland had continued throughout the reigns of Gaunt's grandfather and great-grandfather and, by now, was a near-constant issue in domestic politics – one that would heavily occupy Gaunt throughout his life. It is likely that John of Gaunt's harsh first experience of Scotland stayed with him in the coming years. In 1357 – after the Treaty of Berwick-upon-Tweed in which the captive David II was restored – John of Gaunt was awarded the Lordship of Liddell in Cumberland, and in 1363 he was proposed as the ideal candidate to succeed David II on the throne. Gaunt was always popular in Scotland and managed uncomfortable political matters well, becoming a regular crown representative over the border. The Plantagenet and Bruce families were also united by marriage – Edward III's sister Joan was married to David II. The prospect of a Scottish crown possibly sparked a craving for kingship that later resulted in Gaunt's relentless twenty-year pursuit of Castile.[22]

The streets of London were filled within the hour, men, women and children clamouring to witness the spectacle about to take place: the Black Prince had returned from France and was due to process through the City with a royal French captive. After King Edward had been forced to return to England following his abortive expedition of 1355, the Black Prince had remained in France and continued his march into Aquitaine. He prosecuted a vast *chevauchée*, tearing through the countryside from Bordeaux to Narbonne, in an attempt to destroy the French economy and undermine the country's morale. Towns were destroyed, crops burned, innocent people injured or killed and women raped. It was the most destructive raid of the Hundred Years War, and over 500 towns and villages fell victim. Eventually, on 19 September 1356, the Prince engaged in pitched battle with the Valois army at Poitiers and won a crushing victory.

In May 1357 the triumphant Black Prince disembarked at Plymouth after an eleven-day voyage from France, and made a leisurely progress towards London. The City treated his return like a pageant. Merchants, labourers, vintners and butchers all crowded onto the streets to welcome the Prince home. As he proudly rode into London, the crowd erupted on finding that he brought with him the greatest prisoner of war he could possibly have won – the King of France himself.

As chivalry dictated, the Prince showed the French King courtesy. John II took precedence, riding an impressive white charger, coming before the Prince as he progressed through the packed streets. The Prince's mount was, deliberately, an inferior, smaller black horse, allowing his captive the spotlight, welcoming and celebrating him as an honoured guest. The crowds loved him for it. The procession made its way across the Strand, and the grand entourage passed through the gleaming gates of the 'fairest manor in the Kingdom', where the captured French King would reside in a luxurious prison, inside the golden walls of the Savoy Palace.[23] According to Froissart, the French King's captivity proved an opulent affair. He spent 'the winter very gaily with his countrymen. The King of England visited him very often, as did his children, Lionel, Duke of Clarence, and the Lord John, Earl of Richmond, and the Lord Edmund. There were several times great feasting between them in dinners, suppers and other entertainments at this palace of the Savoy and at the palace of Westminster which is not far off, and whither King Jean went in a private manner whenever he chose it, by means of the river Thames'.[24] Froissart also writes that the French King was 'lavishly entertained by his captors, in a manner of chivalry which Edward III vigorously upheld'.

Chivalry – traditionally – promoted clemency between opposing sides. Taken up by the church, the ethos was represented by St George – the patriotic hero of English culture – and in literature through the legend of King Arthur: 'men say that he shall come again, and he shall win the holy cross'. The concept of chivalry and the chivalric code was not only upheld by Edward III but repurposed to suit the agenda of his entire campaign in France: he used it as a unifying force. The chivalric code encapsulated courtly love, piety, military ethos and honour, and was intended to create the perfect knight. In his bid for kingship of France, Edward III reinvigorated the chivalric ethos in a manner that would exhume the legend of King Arthur and refashion Edward as his descendent. In the first year of his reign, Edward toured Glastonbury with the Queen, visiting the abbey where the supposed remains of Arthur and Guinevere had been interred above the altar by Edward I. In 1345, Edward III went as far as to search for the tomb of Joseph of Arimathea at Glastonbury – another figure of legend.

During the early years of the Hundred Years War, the financial strain imposed on England was significant and Edward was struggling to convince Parliament to fund his war effort in France. War required money to equip and maintain an army, which was accumulated at the nation's expense through tax and proceeds from customs. The only other option was extensive loans from allies and foreign bankers, plunging the country into debt. If Parliament were to agree to back the war, Edward III would need to offer a very convincing argument. In addition, he needed public support. His army was recruited mostly from Englishmen and another tax on the people was needed to support it. The only incentive that would entice both parties was the promotion of his war as being in the national interest. By repurposing the cult around King Arthur, Edward was able to propagandise his campaign, which in turn gained him massive popular support.

Chronicler Jean Le Bel suggests that Windsor Castle was originally built by King Arthur and even housed the iconic Round Table. Windsor was Edward III's main residence – it was also where he was born. Over a twenty-five-year period he refashioned himself as an avatar of Arthur and Windsor Castle as his would-be Camelot. An impressive edifice, surrounded by an impenetrable curtain wall, Windsor was the most formidable castle on the periphery of London. During the renovations, Edward took particular care over the rebuilding of St George's Chapel, which was intended to serve as the spiritual home of his new chivalric order. In 1348 Edward III formed an elite fraternity whose members embodied the ethos of chivalry – the Order of the Garter. In a formal celebration, twelve knights were dressed in robes emblazoned with garters. The traditional French blue was chosen for the colour of the garters and an inscription in gold read '*Honi Soit Qui Mal y Pense*' – 'Shame on him who thinks badly of it'. During the festivities the King and twelve knights wore a garter around their left knee and tilted in a mock battle, honouring the military prowess of Edward and his army. The use of the French colours, blue and gold, in addition to the French vernacular for the motto, was a blatant nod towards Edward's dynastic right: rulership of France. The inception of the Order of the Garter was clearly an integral part of the propaganda campaign. However, it was not the glorification of Edward's dynastic ambition that made the Order so successful, but the fact it represented an irresistible honour to the military elite.

The Order of the Garter was a mark of chivalric hierarchy that was not only elitist, but politically strategic. In creating a brotherhood, Edward III forged a bond of loyalty in his knights, connecting them to St George and the resurrected national hero, Arthur. The loyalty to both saint and legendary King also cultivated a loyalty from the people of England, who bought into Edward's military ambition. The quest for kingship in France grew into a national priority. As English national identity blossomed, membership of the Order of the Garter became highly sought-after, for it encapsulated military and chivalric prestige. The Knights of the Garter enjoyed celebrity status, re-enacting battles during tournaments before an enraptured audience. The display was a spectacle, an excuse for celebration, pomp and massive opulence, all neatly tied up as chivalry, yet it also served as practice for war. Like the Black Prince and Lionel, Duke of Clarence, John of Gaunt was fast-tracked into the Order of the Garter and spent his early adulthood enjoying the limelight. But chivalry was a luxury enjoyed by the nobility. In the real world of war, ordinary people were shown little clemency, as amply demonstrated by King Edward and the Black Prince on those destructive and bloody *chevauchées* through France. As the Black Prince chivalrously processed through the streets of London, celebrating his royal prisoner, the French landscape he had left behind lay scorched and fragile, and the people equally so. In England too, men, women and children who lived on the coastline were subject to brutal harassment from the French, with pirates pillaging what they could, leaving towns and villages ablaze.

After the apocalyptic devastation of the plague, the country was in sore need of a boost to morale and a unifying force. It was after the formation of the Order of the Garter that a sense of national identity came to the fore. War against France became celebrated rather than dreaded.

During the 1350s, the English vernacular became fashionable. Following the Norman Conquest in 1066, Anglo-Norman – a variation of old French – became the language of the nobility and endured until the mid-fourteenth century. The nobility were bi-, even tri-lingual, with Latin also part of regular vocabulary, and with French as the language most commonly used and read at court.

The royal court stood as the political and cultural hub of the realm, in many of its aspects, even superseding the Church. An extension of a household – the monarch's immediate body of family and servants – the court included members of the nobility, their families and servants and visiting emissaries or those who had been specifically invited to court for a political purpose. The focus was the monarch and being *at* court offered the opportunity to gain favour and prestige, resulting in a continuous cycle of competition, even corruption. Court was, however, a glittering experience. Elaborate banquets, ceremonies and tournaments were a regular part of court life, as well as hunting or hawking and music performed by minstrels and comedy from the court fool. Developments in fashion, art and literature emerged from within the elite coterie, and artists flocked to the royal courts of Europe for patronage. As a result, some of the most striking and avant-garde art, literature and music of the Middle Ages emerged from the royal court.

Moving towards a national identity, court circles also adopted English, leading to a surge of interest in poetry and literature in the vernacular. The most famous writer of English verse was the diplomat, courtier, loyal servant and friend of John of Gaunt – Geoffrey Chaucer.

THREE

FIRE AND WATER

'Whiles that his mountain sire, on mountain standing,
Up in the air, crown'd with the golden sun,
Saw his heroical seed, and smiled to see him,
Mangle the work of nature and deface
The patterns that by God and by French fathers
Had twenty years been made. This is a stem
Of that victorious stock; and let us fear
The native mightiness and fate of him'.

William Shakespeare, Henry V, Act II, Scene IV

JOHN OF GAUNT AND GEOFFREY CHAUCER ALMOST CERTAINLY first met in 1358 at Christmas. At eighteen, John of Gaunt was invited to share in the festivities at Hatfield House by his sister-in-law, Elizabeth de Burgh, the Countess of Ulster. Elizabeth was a rich heiress. Her father was the greatest landowner in Ireland, she was the niece of Henry, Duke of Lancaster, and had recently married Gaunt's older brother, Lionel. The fashionable young couple lived in luxury and their household – filled with young hopeful courtiers – was a hedonistic, vibrant and convivial environment. Chaucer, around the same age as John of Gaunt, was employed by Elizabeth as a page. He first appears in the records as the fashion model for a paltok. Worn by men, paltoks were a type of tunic, and were to cause quite the scandal. They were criticised as 'extremely short garments . . . which failed to conceal their arses or their private parts'.[1] The paltok became so popular that in 1361 Edward III ordered one custom-made to wear at Christmas. It is possible that the trend began amongst the young members of the royal household who congregated at Hatfield that Christmas, including John of Gaunt. From this point on, Chaucer and Gaunt continued to connect and collaborate, living in tandem, moving on and off the pages of each other's life stories.

It is possible that Elizabeth de Burgh had invited John of Gaunt for Christmas following the announcement of his forthcoming marriage to her cousin, Blanche of Lancaster. Marriages amongst the elite in the fourteenth century were rarely love matches. Politics, territory and wealth determined the course of matrimony for young noblemen and women. The marriage between Gaunt and Blanche was another link in the political union between two powerful houses – Plantagenet and Lancaster.

Shortly before his marriage to Blanche, John of Gaunt had an affair with a young Flemish woman called Marie de Saint-Hilaire, one of the Queen's ladies. Marie fell pregnant, and before her baby was born she was removed from court and granted a yearly allowance, for her 'sustenance'.[2] The same year that Gaunt and Blanche married at Reading Abbey, Marie gave birth to a baby girl, whom she called Blanche, probably in reference to John of Gaunt's wife. The baby was acknowledged by Gaunt throughout his life and, when Blanche was around twenty-one, he arranged a good marriage for her, one that promised security and prosperity. Her chosen husband was Thomas Morieux, Constable of the Tower of London, who loyally served John of Gaunt for the rest of his life.

As Gaunt and Blanche were distant cousins, their marriage required a Papal dispensation, as interfamilial marriage was in breach of Canon law. In the New Year of 1359, at the Papal court at Avignon, Pope Innocent VI was duly presented with a request from the King of England: that he 'enable his son John, the Earl of Richmond and the

Lady Blanche, daughter of Henry, Duke of Lancaster, to intermarry, they being related in the third and fourth degrees of kindred'. The Pope sanctioned the marriage and, soon after the dispensation reached England, the date for the wedding was set for May.[3] The ceremony would be held at Reading Abbey, one of the largest royal monasteries in Europe.

The abbey was founded by the youngest son of William the Conqueror, Henry I, who invested heavily in it, supporting learning as well as prayer by funding an extensive library. Support of the abbey remained in royal consciousness following Henry's death, for Empress Matilda – his daughter – donated a sacred relic: the hand of Saint James of Santiago. Over the next three centuries Reading Abbey grew to become a popular place of worship and burial for the elite, as well as a suitable location for Parliament to convene outside of London.

In May 1359, members of the nobility gathered to witness the marriage of John of Gaunt to Blanche of Lancaster. It was a union of cousins as well as great allies, heavy with the promise of peace between historic rivals, Lancaster and the Crown. The union made sense. Blanche's elder sister, Maude, was married to William III, Count of Holland, Zeeland and Hainault, and the match between John and Blanche would strengthen domestic relations. On a personal level, it was also a nod to the friendship between Edward and Henry, and the loyalty the Duke had shown throughout the highs and lows of the war in France. Seventeen-year-old Blanche was an attractive choice of bride for the nineteen-year-old John of Gaunt. She was beautiful, pious, young and, shared with her sister Maude, she stood to inherit her father's enormous fortune, which through marriage would be controlled by Gaunt. As medieval tradition dictated, when a woman married a man, she relinquished to him her 'chattels', meaning land, property and money.

'In the presence of a priest and of three or four respectable persons summoned for the purpose', John of Gaunt and Blanche of Lancaster exchanged rings and were married in the eyes of God and witnesses, overseen by the clerk of the Queen's chapel.[4] Blanche was showered with generous gifts: silver buckles from the King and two rings of ruby and pearl and diamond from John of Gaunt. The wedding was an elaborate celebration and the subsequent banquet was particularly extravagant: guests were served richly spiced food and wine on tables covered in linen, silk and cloth of gold, and minstrels played for the duration of the feasting.[5] The celebrations continued for days, with jousts held locally to mark the occasion. The wedding party then cheerfully made its way to London, where preparations were underway for an even larger and more spectacular event.

On the periphery of the City of London lay Smithfield, a flat, open, grassy area highly suitable for tournaments. One week after the wedding, Smithfield was transformed into a colourful scene. Wooden viewing platforms, hastily knocked together, were draped with heavy canopies, bright flags and all the insignia of heraldry. On the day of the tournament, colourful tents peppered the field, the stands were filled to bursting and chargers dressed in full expensive regalia prepared for the tilt.[6]

The tournament at Smithfield became known as the Merchants Fair, alluding to the wealthy merchants who occupied the City of London. The City was controlled by these various merchant oligarchs, who made their money through an international trade network that saw the import and export of various luxury items. Spices (particularly pepper), cloth, wine and wool were all consumed in such quantities that mercantile wealth in London flourished. The tournament included the organised fight known as a mêlée; the London mercantile elite were represented by the mayor, Simon Dolseley – a grocer from Cornhill – and twenty-four aldermen. They were expected, as a team, to defend the City in the tilt against all challengers. The fight was rough and chaotic and such combat – supposedly regulated as it was – nevertheless frequently left men bruised and bloodied. It was also an incredibly popular sport. In the end, the merchants went unbeaten, but being armoured throughout it had been impossible to distinguish their true identities. Eventually, the jubilant winners were stripped of their armour and they revealed themselves: not as merchants, but the King and his sons, the Black Prince, Lionel, the young Edmund and the newly-wed John of Gaunt. King and crowd both adored spectacle and surprise, and disguise was a popular part of court culture, drawing on the tropes of romantic literature and ballads. By circumventing social barriers, the incognito Edward III was able to demonstrate both his cunning and his superior military ability in the fight. By drawing on Arthurian medieval romance – through disguise and revelation – the appearance of the King and his sons at the Merchants Fair was another demonstration of chivalry and war as a national identity.

The bourgeois merchant class in London was an important source of funding for the King during the first part of the Hundred Years War, loaning the gold needed for the war in France.[7] In 1359, Edward launched a new campaign, which he characterised as a *defence* of the realm against French attack. He was eager not to resort to a heavy tax on the people and managed to fund the entire venture through customs charges on the wool trade – charges paid by merchants.

In the summer of 1359, muster rolls – official lists of fighting men – were prepared in order to assemble a vast army. Edward proposed raising a force of 12,000 men, including his sons the Black Prince, Lionel of Antwerp, John of Gaunt and Edmund of Langley as military leaders, all aged between twenty-nine and eighteen. Other preparations were made. The hostage French King, John II, was moved inside the Tower of London in order to hinder any possible rescue mission whilst the English army were occupied in France, and Queen Philippa and her youngest son, Thomas of Woodstock, were to rule the country in the absence of the King and his other sons. John of Gaunt left Blanche in the household of the Queen; she was now pregnant with their first child.

This was Edward's most ambitious campaign yet, marking twenty years since he had formally declared himself the King of France. His first objective, though, was not a wholly military one. Edward intended to force his way straight to Reims, the sacred city where French kings had been officially anointed in a tradition going back to Louis the Pious in 816 CE.

* * *

The garrison at Calais was bustling with mercenary soldiers; paid warriors in the employment of Edward III, waiting for the campaign to begin. The mercenaries – mostly from Germany – were bored, hungry and impatient for the arrival of the English army. After weeks of no pay, they began to cause anarchy at Calais, using up precious supplies and fighting amongst themselves, as well as attacking English soldiers reluctantly sharing the garrison with their German counterparts.[8] Henry, Duke of Lancaster, was the first of the invasion force to land, and he was appalled to find Calais in complete disorder. The mercenary force could not be controlled directly, and was best utilised raiding, which would at least distract the men from their late payments. Henry quickly led the force outside the confines of Calais and into the countryside, where they could relieve their frustrations by looting, burning and pillaging. The force tore through Picardy, destroying Cambrai and St Quentin, but despite ongoing attempts at plunder, the area provided little loot. This land, where people would ordinarily be seen farming, selling goods or travelling, now lay empty and eerily still. The raiding party marched through ghost towns, getting a regular drenching as heavy black clouds loomed over it with dreary persistence. For soldiers, the attraction of war came in the promise of plunder; for mercenaries even more so. When they set about pillaging the French towns and villages, the soldiers were invariably disappointed to find that the local people had left nothing to be stolen. Towns as far as Arras – around one full day's march from Calais – had been emptied: raiding turned out to be a fruitless exercise.

Whilst Henry, Duke of Lancaster, was occupied trying to corral the fractious mercenary element, Edward and his sons prepared to depart from England. The sheer scale of the operation had unsurprisingly delayed plans to set sail in the summer. Finally, in October 1359 – after the King had wrapped up his remaining affairs at home – the royal party boarded the ship *Philip of Dartmouth* in Sandwich and set sail for Calais.[9]

When the King arrived with his sons, they met with the Duke of Lancaster outside Calais. The delay had been far from ideal. Edward's tardiness set the tone for what would be a long, cold and exhausting campaign, tramping through the French countryside in the middle of winter. But now the grand eastern march inland to Reims could begin, and it was agreed to split the army into three formations in order to preserve supplies, led by the Duke of Lancaster, the Black Prince and the King.[10] John of Gaunt accompanied his brother and they planned to rejoin Lancaster and Edward outside Reims. As part of Lionel of Antwerp's household, Geoffrey Chaucer went on this campaign too. It is likely that Lionel also marched with the Black Prince, putting Chaucer in the same division as Gaunt.[11]

According to Jean le Bel, the King left Calais almost immediately, 'with the finest supply train ever seen'. Around 6,000 wagons, stretching four miles, were dragged 200 miles through the mud towards Reims, carrying everything from grain for bread to the ovens to bake it. Edward was doggedly determined not to be forced back by the French due to lack of nourishment for his army. Even so, it was now a winter campaign, which instantly placed more pressure on the supplies brought over from England. Hungry troops searched the area for food, but, as they moved through the country, they faced the same situation as the German mercenaries at Calais: little sustenance and few people. The French had anticipated attack and those who could sought shelter in garrisoned castles and churches. Others fled.

The Black Prince and John of Gaunt – en route to Reims – searched for opportunities for easy plunder among the poorly protected small castles that littered France. Plunder of civilian property was ever a consequence of war: unfortunate and utterly predictable. To hungry soldiers, everything was fair game. All forms of property were stolen: plate (household objects made of gold or silver), food, wine, cloth, weapons and livestock. The impact of the English invasion can be seen in the petitions to the King of France from his desperate subjects: they escalated, begging for better protection against the armed raids. It was the local people – labourers, clerics, peasants, women and children – forced to live in occupied territory, who suffered the worst consequences of the war.

After a slow and cumbersome march, the English finally reached the holy city of Reims in early December. Exhausted by the journey, the Black Prince established a base for his men at the monastery of Saint-Thierry, where they rested, anticipating that the gates of Reims would soon be flung open. The King himself was camped at the Abbey of St Basle, in nearby Verzy, a wine-making village, which in the summer was rich with thick vines and red grapes.

12,000 soldiers stood beneath the high walls of Reims as the King dispatched envoys to the French Archbishop within, Jean de Craon. Edward was determined not to take Reims by force, but rather be welcomed by its citizens. To avoid destroying his chances of such a welcome, he gave an unpopular order: no looting or violence was to take place in the city. Edward waited and hoped that the Archbishop would permit him entry. The tactic did not work, so Edward resorted to bribery and coercion. The Archbishop – prepared for an English siege – remained loyal to the French Crown, and employed the same tactical patience used by the heir to the French throne, the Dauphin, in the wider campaign.

Reims was prepared to ride out any siege. Food supplies, grain, live-stock and personal property had been brought within the walls, and the citizens armed themselves in preparation for an English attack. By the time the English army arrived at its gates, nothing in the environs was available for plunder; and nor, so it seemed, was Reims itself.

A siege would traditionally begin when the first shot was fired against a town or city. It would be won through outright assault, or stealth, or capitulation, and common tactics were bombardment, mining, blockade of supplies, and of course the storming of the walls with siege engines and ladders. When the defenders surrendered, it was either by waving a white flag or symbolically handing over the keys. During a *chevauchée* civilians were victims of war; during a siege, civilians were targets of war, forced to suffer starvation, thirst, sickness and the destruction of the local economy without the ability to work or manage land and livestock. Fortunately for the people of Reims, Edward III remained adamant that he would not lay siege to the holy city – doing so would threaten his legitimacy as its King. Edward could only hope the city would capitulate under pressure from his army, and open its gates.

By Christmas, the English were still waiting outside the walls, increasingly bored, hungry and agitated. Around Christmas Day, a French freebooter called Eustace d'Auberchicourt arrived at the English camp bringing a generous gift for the army to boost its morale: 3,000 barrels of wine. Eustace d'Auberchicourt was a lawless plunderer, who filled his pockets on the back of war by leading bands of mercenaries across France, seizing towns, taking prisoners. He was on the side of nobody and, like many freebooters, he was an opportunist who turned outlaw, fighting only for himself when disappointed with the fortunes of war.

As the English army was made up of fighting men on short-term contracts, the King was anxious to distract them from seeking plunder against his orders, and to dissuade them from joining vagrant free-booter armies like that of Eustace d'Auberchicourt. To keep his men occupied, Edward ordered a series of raiding parties around the local-ity. Henry Knighton describes one particular raid, on a cold night at the end of December. John of Gaunt and his father-in-law the Duke of Lancaster led a mission under cover of darkness to attack the fortified town of Cernay. The town was well defended: a double ditch, walls and turrets. With such strong defensive infrastructure, the English would not be able to overcome the town before daylight and the men were forced to wait. As dawn broke and light crept over the walls of Cernay, the English were spotted by the town's watch as they crept over the ditches, led by Lancaster. As the watch raised the alarm, the Duke ordered the attack. He, Gaunt, and their raiding party scaled the walls of Cernay and slaughtered the town's defenders. Survivors were forced to surrender to the English and watch as their town was 'destroyed . . . with fire and flame'. As some defenders fled, many were sucked down into the marshland surrounding their town and drowned. Eventually Henry and John of Gaunt 'returned with their army to King Edward, safe and with all their men unharmed, praise be to God'.[12]

English raiding was notorious in France. Fear, murder and rape were weapons of war, and although the King issued orders against violence towards non-combatants, atrocities still occurred. A scorched-earth policy had benefits for the English far beyond loot: the French nobility were exposed to the anger of the people for failing in their feudal duty to protect people and property. The devastation inflicted by the King, the Black Prince, John of Gaunt and Henry of Lancaster was calculated. When it came to individual human lives, they generally adhered to the code of chivalry; unless people were armed and combatants, they would not be harmed. Following the attack on Cernay, Lancaster and Gaunt rode around the area for a few more days, seeking towns and villages with ample supplies, yet due to the smoke and embers left at Cernay, their presence and intent were well known. In a panic, towns and villages were hastily abandoned and as much food and property possible was gathered up and taken before the English descended. Hoping for the same plunder as at Cernay, Gaunt and Lancaster were disappointed to find most towns and communes in the area now empty. Finally, they moved on to Manre in Champagne but, seemingly like everywhere else around, it lay desolate. Frustrated with their lot, they burnt the town anyway before returning to the encampment outside Reims.

After a bleak and boring six weeks of waiting and hunting, Edward had still not set foot inside Reims: the town was better prepared to endure a blockade than the English were to wait it out under the elements. The people inside Reims had ample provisions, were warm and relatively comfortable, whereas the English army was hungry, cold and suffering under the icy rain. Rations were exhausted and the raiding parties the King dispatched to collect supplies consistently returned empty-handed. It became plain that it was time to move on, and so the King was forced to give up on his dream of Reims. In the middle of the night, on 11 January 1360, the English army vacated the camp and by morning were nowhere to be seen.

Fatigued and hungry and roaming around in the middle of winter, by January 1360 the English army was highly frustrated. Edward III's chief priority was to feed his men. New supplies were arranged: some shipped over from England, with the rest coming from raiding and foraging around Honfleur. A new baggage train was to be prepared and dispatched from Normandy. With the army expecting new provisions to catch them up, they now turned their sights on Paris; if the Dauphin would not come out to fight, the English army would go to him. The King won a few small victories on the march, including extracting a lucrative ransom from the county of Bar in exchange for an undertaking to leave the region in peace.[13]

As the army marched they did not encounter any organised resistance from the French. Straggling English soldiers were harassed or picked off by French locals, and small guerrilla attacks took place, often under cover of darkness. The *Scalacronica*, written in Anglo-Norman French by Sir Thomas Gray of Heaton of Northumberland, gives an example of one such ambush as the army moved on from Reims. As the English marched towards Paris, the Black Prince and Gaunt's division separated and headed towards Auxerre, taking a detour to find 'forage for the horses'. They stopped to rest for the night at Ligny-le-Chatel outside Auxerre. In the dead of night, as the men lay sleeping, they were attacked by a force of freebooters, who unlike Eustace d'Auberchicourt were not on their side. The freebooters stabbed some of the Prince's men, nobles and squires whilst they slept. Others they took as prisoners. The Black Prince was left demoralised; used to claiming grand victories, he was not accustomed to being beaten by thieves and outlaws. While men were slaughtered in their sleep on this occasion, Gray did have a more rousing tale to tell. Near Les Régniers, an English-held fortress near Auxerre, five of the Prince's men were grinding corn in a mill when they were ambushed by French soldiers. They fought back and, despite being outnumbered, the English defeated their attackers and took eleven prisoners.

The constant ambushes, raids and small skirmishes that occurred throughout the war resulted in the taking of prisoners from both sides. Around the time the Prince's men were attacked at Auxerre, Geoffrey Chaucer was taken captive. In *The Knight's Tale*, Chaucer wrote about captivity and war, drawing on his own experiences, some of which were shared with John of Gaunt. Chaucer describes a world turned on its head – where there should be safety, there is danger. It is a world in which war affects everybody, including the innocent. Chaucer describes Mars, the God of War, standing proud and gallant beside a wolf; a wolf that is hungry for blood, devouring a man. Through this vision, Chaucer opposes Edward III's romanticised notion of chivalry and glory in war, portraying it as bloody and ignoble.

Like many prisoners of war, Chaucer was ransomed. Ransom culture was one of the most lucrative aspects of war and, coupled with the promise of booty, incentivised men into battle. According to the conduct of war, a prisoner should surrender by delivering a sign – a hand up, or a word – and then give his captor a material item, such as his gauntlet.[14] Commonly, the prisoner was freed only after the ransom was paid. In Chaucer's case, after around two months in captivity, a ransom of sixteen pounds was paid by the King and he was free to return home.[15]

The King's army moved through the barren countryside, from Troyes to Burgundy. Soon after the English had passed through the region, the Italian poet Petrarch travelled the same route. He wrote of the appalling state of the landscape: 'everywhere was grief destruction and desolation, uncultivated fields filled with weeds, ruined and abandoned houses'. All property surrounding Paris was abandoned and people fled inside local fortifications, though the poor were often left at the mercy of the raiding army. As the campaign dragged on through winter, discipline slipped, soldiers were not so easily controlled and showed less clemency and patience to the local people. However, the most dangerous consequence of war for the local population came from deserting troops, and desertion was an inevitability on these campaigns. Those who abandoned service would usually form small armies that answered to no one, roaming the country looking for plunder.

Some people tried to live quietly, away from the main raiding areas and roads. The chronicler Jean de Venette was a Carmelite prior based in Paris during the war. He recounts the traumatic experience of Hugh de Montgeron, a prior from Breuillet – a commune in northern France between Orléans and Paris. In 1358, Hugh de Montgeron lived deep in the woods, but was forced to flee when English soldiers came upon his home. Taken by surprise, he ran for his life, wearing only his monk's habit. From a safe hiding place in the thicket he watched his property devastated by lawless soldiers. The prior wrote an account of his trauma in the inside cover of his prayer book – 'do you, who live in cities and castle ever see equal to my trouble?' The prior of Breuillet experienced the harsh reality of war, as inflicted on local people throughout France. The most devastating raids were enacted by the same freebooter parties that the Black Prince encountered at Auxerre: outlaws who roamed the countryside in pursuit of shelter, food and women. These freebooter armies were so effective that, in 1362, they annihilated a French army near Lyons. They continued to cause major problems in France, even at times of ostensible peace.

War was cruel on both sides of the Channel. As the English army tore their way through France, the French responded by launching a guerilla raid-cum-rescue-mission. They intended to attack the English coastline and liberate John II from captivity. Led by the Constable of France, Jean de Neuville, the French mustered a fleet at Crotoy, a harbour at the mouth of the Somme river, and set sail for England. It was a small-scale invasion, but with the English army occupied in France they anticipated a smooth operation. However, news of the plot had already reached Westminster. Before Edward III left for France, he first and foremost saw to the protection of all English, Welsh and Irish coastlines and borders. He organised a force of fighting men to guard the coastline, anticipating possible French counter-attack. Archers were employed to protect the beaches and even members of the clergy were armed; the King requested the Archbishop of Canterbury 'array his men and send them to the coast'. The French force inflicted some damage as they landed at Winchelsea, killing those defenders who resisted, plundering and raping local women, but they gave up when they learnt that John II had been moved to Wales. As the French army withdrew, the defensive English force arrived in Winchelsea, closing in on the French on the beach as they tried to make it back to their ships. In a moment of decisive combat, the French gathered into a defensive formation as the English cavalry charged the invaders. French soldiers were cut down and others drowned as they tried to swim towards their ships. Most escaped across the Channel, but two ships were beached, unable to catch the tide, and were promptly captured by the English. The invasion was repulsed, and three hundred French soldiers were killed.[16,17] The national effort to protect the coastline against French invasion had paid off.

As the driving rain and sleet subsided at the end of March, the English army reunited south of the walls of Paris and pitched their camp across the Seine. The army lines stretched out for miles as they occupied communes all along the left side of the river, taking over churches and looting any building they could find. Edward III intended to wait outside Paris, in the hope or expectation that the Dauphin would ride out and meet him in pitched battle. Jean de Venette states that, by early Spring 1360, 'not a man nor woman was left in any of the villages near Paris, from the Seine to Etampes'. Whilst some local people fled their homes outside the city and travelled deep into the countryside, others sought sanctuary behind the high walls of Paris. The English army was arrayed in three battalions, with the Black Prince commanding the vanguard – the front line and usually the first to advance into combat – possibly with John of Gaunt at his side.

The English were prepared for pitched battle, but the French had no intention of offering it. The English army had won two major victories in the previous fifteen years of campaigning; another such could lose the French the entire war. One of those victories, Poitiers, had resulted in the capture of the French King. For his son the Dauphin, pitched battle against Edward III's eager army represented too much of a risk. Throughout the campaigns in this phase of the Hundred Years War, the French relied heavily on evasion rather than attack. Their methods worked: the English army was left bored and demoralised, with waning enthusiasm for the task.

March gave way to April, and the English had not moved from their camp. On Wednesday 8 April, from sunrise to midday, the Black Prince's division waited on the plains outside Paris, before setting the land on fire. Despite the thick black smoke snaking up the walls of the city, the Dauphin still did not respond. Watching the land smoulder, the Prince's division moved off, leaving some soldiers in hiding, waiting for a possible response. A few French soldiers rode out of the city, possibly to assess the English position, having seen the Prince move out. Spotting the lingering soldiers, the French 'spurred forth and charged at them' before returning inside.[18] But with no sign of the full French army, Edward took his army to 'make a very long march toward Beauce, by reason of want of fodder for the horses'. Furiously, the King ordered that the landscape be set alight as they rode for three days, 'burning, slaying and laying waste', leaving a trail of ashes 150 miles long.[19]

On Monday 13 April, as the army marched north to Beauce, the heavens opened and released 'a terrible tempest' as rain poured over the scorched land. The discouraged army now learnt the full measure of suffering at the hands of the elements. Trudging through mud and sleet, the English encountered a storm so intense it was memorialised in the chronicles as 'Black Monday'. According to Froissart, 'thunder and hail . . . fell on the English army, that it seemed as if the world was come to an end. The hailstones were so large as to kill men and beasts, and the boldest were frightened'.[20]

Thick mud clung to the hooves of war horses – equine juggernauts, chosen for their strength, size and stamina. They were able to bear the weight of an armoured knight, as well as carrying their own heavy plated armour, and were trained for battle . . . but they were not able navigate a mud bath. They collapsed in the same quagmire that would later claim the French horses at Agincourt. Mud clogged the heavy wooden wheels of the baggage train and miserable soldiers desperately clamoured to salvage the supplies as the carts were swallowed by the boggy earth. Those huge hailstones hammered the English, compelling the King to steer his horse towards the church of Our Lady at Chartres where, on his knees, he beseeched the heavens for mercy. Edward III's dream of French kingship floundered in the sodden earth outside Paris.

King Edward was forced to consider peace, and there were other powers involved in the conflict also pressing for an end to hostilities. In the final weeks of April, as Edward marched away from Paris with a dispirited army, Pope Innocent IV pleaded with both Kings to give up the war and sign a peace treaty. Anticipating Edward's reluctance, Innocent IV also wrote to the Black Prince, 'desiring him to use his influence with the King in fostering peace'.[21] From his comfortable captivity, King John II also wrote to Edward III, expressing a wish to end the war and its constant 'anguishes and sorrows'.[22]

On 1 May 'in a small village, near Chartres, called Brétigny' a peace conference took place attended by sixteen French delegates, twenty-two English and three papal legates. It was agreed that in exchange for renouncing his claim to the French throne, Edward III would be granted territories in France that included Poitou, Saintonge, Montreuil, Guînes, Gascony, Agenais and Limousin.[23] It was also agreed that the French King would not stoke an old alliance with the Scots against the English, in return for Edward not supporting the Flemish in any alliance against the French.[24] A ransom was finally accepted for the safe return of John II: 3,000,000 gold écus to be paid over six years. After Edward III happily accepted the extortionate ransom, John II was released from his captivity and told that he would return to France in the summer; he then dined lavishly with Queen Philippa at Westminster.

In late spring, Edward III embarked on his ship at Honfleur and prepared to cross the Channel to Rye, after seven long months of arduous marching, raiding and waiting. By Autumn 1360, peace in France had been formalised in a further treaty signed at Calais and ratified by the 1361 Parliament. Despite the sodden end to the campaign, Edward III had regained more land from the old Angevin Empire – lost by King John – than any of his predecessors.[25]

In celebration of the peace agreement, and of John II's imminent return to France, both Kings dined together in a lavish banquet held at the Tower of London. In a display of peace and friendship, they gave each other gifts: ornate drinking cups. Edward also gifted the French King a sword belt and a live eagle. John II had enjoyed his period of captivity; in accordance with chivalric custom he had been showered with all the comforts England could provide. He returned home to find his kingdom destroyed by war and financially crippled by his enormous ransom. Four years later, demoralised by the bleak state of his country, and determined to honour the terms of his – still largely unfulfilled – ransom agreement, John II voluntarily returned to England, where he would eventually die. On his ascension in 1364, Charles V inherited a nation that was burnt and broken while England revelled in the power, glory and wealth accrued by the Plantagenet King and his sons. John of Gaunt had loyally supported his father throughout this campaign, from Calais to Brétigny. Grateful for his son's steadfast obedience, Edward III granted him Hertford Castle as soon as they returned to England.[26] Gaunt returned home to a new baby as well as new lands. On 31 March, whilst her husband marched on Paris, Blanche gave birth to their first daughter, named Philippa after the Queen.

The campaign in France was sandwiched between two royal marriages: the first, John of Gaunt's and the second, the Black Prince's. As a future King and esteemed warrior, Prince Edward was one of the most eligible bachelors in Europe, and the King spent perhaps too long carefully considering the choice of bride. The right wife would bring with her a formidable international alliance, expansion of trade networks and territories, and the strengthening of the Plantagenet dynasty at a continental level. However, all such hopes were thwarted when the Black Prince fell in love with the twice-married Joan of Kent.

Joan of Kent, sarcastically nicknamed 'the virgin of Kent', or more generously 'the fair maid', was a famous beauty within the inner court circle. She had grown up in the royal nursery, alongside the Black Prince and his siblings as a ward of the King and Queen. By the time of her marriage to the Black Prince, Joan was nearing thirty with at least five children. Joan's clandestine union with the Prince of Wales was not the first time her romantic liaisons attracted attention. In 1340 – when she was only twelve – Joan of Kent had embarked on a secret marriage to Thomas Holland, later titled the first Earl of Kent, shortly before he left on campaign to France. Joan kept silent – probably out of fear and naivety – as she was subsequently wed to William Montagu, the future Earl of Salisbury. On his return from France, Thomas Holland was aghast to find his wife married, and appealed to the King for her return. Pope Clement VI was involved in the scandal and finally sanctioned as lawful the first marriage between Joan and Thomas, to the distress of the now jilted William Montagu. Joan of Kent's marriages were already notorious. To embark on another secret affair shortly after Holland's death in 1360 was a brazen move, let alone with the heir to the throne.

Joan of Kent attracted gossip. In the sixteenth century, the Italian scholar and historian Polydore Vergil attributes to Joan the motto of the Order of the Garter. As Joan was dancing with the King, her garter slipped down her leg. To save her from embarrassment, he slipped it onto his own leg declaring, '*Honi soit qui mal y pense*' ('Shame on him who thinks badly of it'). This is most likely a myth, but has nonetheless projected Joan as a flirtatious court beauty who eventually captured the heart of the Black Prince. After their marriage was revealed, the couple were forced to appeal to the Pope for a dispensation; if the Papacy refused to accept the match, they were in danger of being branded 'fornicators' and made to do penance with all future offspring considered illegitimate. Their marriage was approved and eventually formalised in a ceremony at Windsor in October 1361. The following year, the Black Prince and Joan of Kent left England to govern Aquitaine in southwest France.

Lionel of Antwerp moved to Ireland in the summer of 1361, where he was to become lieutenant, representing the King. Through his marriage to Elizabeth de Burgh he was due to inherit the Earldom of Ulster. With his elder brothers absent, John of Gaunt seized the opportunity to demonstrate his political acumen, prompting the King to send him on a series of diplomatic missions to secure a crucial marital alliance between his younger brother, Edmund of Langley, and Margaret of Flanders.

With the Black Prince in Aquitaine and Lionel in Ireland, John of Gaunt took on a large part of the crown's administration, rapidly gaining approval from his father, to whom Gaunt displayed unbending loyalty and respect. Gaunt sought to establish himself as a prince, politician and nobleman, as well as a soldier. In early 1361, tragedy provided the opportunity to advance into the highest echelons of nobility, a position of almost incomparable wealth and power. A second plague swept the country and took with it the most formidable knight, diplomat and nobleman in the county: John of Gaunt's own father-in-law, Henry, Duke of Lancaster.

FOUR

THE BLEEDING TOMB: A LANCASTRIAN INHERITANCE

'Many miracles were reported to have occurred at the tomb of Thomas
Earl of Lancaster. Blood was said to have flowed from it'.

Collectio Rerum Ecclesiasticarum de Diœcesi Eboracensi

IN 1361, THIRTEEN YEARS AFTER THE BLACK DEATH PURGED
almost half of the population of England, another epidemic broke out.
Although less severe, this second outbreak threatened, once again, to
destabilise the social and economic infrastructure of England, claiming lives regardless of age, sex or status.

In the wake of the 1348 epidemic, labour was in high demand. The
labouring classes had suffered the highest mortality rate; those who
survived demanded higher wages, whilst some sought to rise up the
ranks of an acutely hierarchical society. William Langland, author of
the allegorical poem *Piers Plowman*, describes a situation where a man
wanted to be hired 'at a high rate, else he will chide and wail', and that
'no penny ale please them, nor no piece of bacon. Only fresh fish or fish
fried, roast or baked'. This was a problem for landowners and merchants,
for they could not – or would not – pay what the labourers now asked.
In some parts of the country, landowners were forced to pay fifty
percent more than before the plague hit. In response to the economic

shock, the King promulgated the 1349 Ordinance of Labourers which stipulated that all healthy labourers should be forcibly put to work. Over ten years later and facing another deadly wave of plague, the issue of labour regulation and the enforcement of class status was still a high priority. The Commons pushed hard for further labour regulation and the Crown authorised a wage cap. It was agreed that those who flouted the law and left employment to seek better pay elsewhere would face imprisonment, or even branding on the forehead with the letter F denoting 'falsity'.[1] A sumptuary law restricting personal expenditure was also introduced. Certain ranks of society were ordered to dress only according to their class. Labourers were forced to wear clothes provided for them by their employers, and the lower and middle classes were prohibited from buying cloth in certain colours – such as purple. Expensive fur was reserved for the nobility. It was agreed by the government that dressing above one's station presented a danger to the prevailing social order in the wake of the Black Death. By the time the second plague arrived, it was clear that the government was in fact unable to enforce a countrywide cap on wages – they showed a gradual increase in defiance of the law. The attempt to create what was effectively a second level of serfdom on free labourers prompted anger and mistrust of government officials – it was a key causal factor in the Peasants' Revolt twenty years later.

Henry, Duke of Lancaster, was present with John of Gaunt at the January 1361 Parliament as the societal problems thrown up by the plague were batted from Lords to Commons. Two months later he lay incapacitated at his castle, Leicester, anticipating imminent death as his body battled the violent effects of the plague itself. By the end of March, the Duke of Lancaster, the greatest magnate in the realm, was dead.[2]

The Duke made a detailed will dividing the vast Lancastrian inheritance between his two surviving daughters, Maude and Blanche. Maude was given most of the lands in France and in the south of England, and Blanche was granted lands north of the River Trent – including Lancaster – and in Yorkshire and Northumberland. Perhaps the knowledge that John of Gaunt was familiar with Anglo-Scottish issues influenced these decisions.

Henry, Duke of Lancaster, had been a pious man, and he planned his funeral in meticulous detail. It was modest, but elegant enough to reflect his wealth and position. A cortège dressed in blue and white, holding flaming torches, carried the coffin to Newarke, the perpendicular collegiate church he had erected in Leicester, where he wished to be buried.[3] The King and his family attended the funeral and mourned the loss of their cousin and much-loved friend. The Black Prince ceremoniously draped the coffin with two cloths of gold before it was interred, and Lancaster the man was written into the chronicles as a 'noble Duke . . . worthy of everlasting remembrance'.[4]

In January 1362 a violent tempest whipped through England. The chronicler Henry Knighton watched it blow from the confines of the Abbey of St Mary of the Meadows in Leicester, where he was based as a canon. He describes the storm having 'flattened woods, orchards and all kinds of trees . . . and destroyed churches, mills, bell towers and houses'. It struck across the whole country, but in London 'did incalculable damage'. As the 'fearsome wind' tore down churches and houses in the capital, the royal family were plunged into mourning. Mary, Duchess of Brittany and Margaret, Countess of Pembroke – both younger sisters of John of Gaunt – died of the plague. This second wave was spoken of as another 'great mortality' that raged through England, this time killing mostly young people. In April 1362, Blanche's sister Maude of Lancaster also suddenly died, possibly from the same epidemic. Maude had suffered a miserable marriage to William, Count of Holland, Zeeland and Hainault. In 1357 he had begun to show signs of insanity; his illness grew so unmanageable that the following year he was incarcerated at Quesnoy Castle in Northern France. When Maude died with no surviving children, her portion of the Lancastrian estates went to her sister. John of Gaunt and Blanche of Lancaster found themselves extraordinarily rich.

The level of wealth they inherited was enviable, yet such extensive lands and titles came with an overwhelming feudal responsibility, which John of Gaunt – still relatively inexperienced – would now have to shoulder. Shortly after the death of Maude, Gaunt was given a sword, a fur cap and a gold and pearl circlet, and was by royal charter declared Duke of Lancaster. On St George's Day, he was admitted into the Order of the Garter. The wealth and territorial power that came with his new title attracted suspicion, and a rumour circulated that John of Gaunt had orchestrated the murder of his sister-in-law. Henry Knighton suggests that by 'vulgar repute' this was to 're-unite the inheritance' so it would fall entirely to him.[5] This was almost certainly wild speculation; however, this stain on Gaunt's reputation as early as 1362 set a precedent for years of near-continuous scandal, gossip and scorn.

The Lancastrian inheritance was second only to the crown's, and the governing of its extensive lands presented a difficult and complex job. John of Gaunt had been educated in feudal responsibility, observing at first hand the Black Prince's administration in Cheshire and Cornwall. He had also been prepared for political responsibility, witnessing peace talks, diplomatic negotiations and treaties. With his elder sons still abroad, Edward III had high expectations of John of Gaunt, even fostering a scheme to place him on the throne of Scotland. The King was confident of his son's loyalty and capability, and hoped that a dynastic settlement that brought the two crowns so close would avoid further war between England and Scotland. Although the plan never came to fruition, it precipitated a diplomatic and seemingly amicable relationship between John of Gaunt and the Scots thereafter. With royalty, wealth, territorial power and the potential for kingship, the House of Lancaster was amassing yet more prominence and prestige.

The Houses of Plantagenet and Lancaster had not always been so united. The Duchy of Lancaster – as it was later called – had emerged in the thirteenth century at the end of the Second Barons' War and the death of the rebel Lord Simon de Montfort at Evesham. The youngest son of Henry III, Edmund Crouchback, inherited de Montfort's Earldom of Leicester and, later, Lancaster. By 1269, Edmund was on track to become an incredibly wealthy territorial magnate, like all who would succeed him. Edmund, Earl of Lancaster, was a popular prince:

a capable and pious soldier – nicknamed 'Crouchback' due to the motif of a cross he bore on his shield and wore on his back whilst on crusade. He was fiercely loyal to his brother King Edward I ('Longshanks'), fighting in his various wars across Scotland and France and overseeing extensive Plantagenet castle-building projects in Wales. Over time Edmund accumulated a series of dignities, land and property. By the end of his life he was extremely powerful, with land dotted throughout the realm.[6]

After Edmund's death in Bayonne in 1296, he was interred at Westminster Abbey and his wealth distributed among his children: Thomas, Henry and John. Thomas inherited the title Earl of Lancaster. At the end of the thirteenth century, the relationship between the house of Lancaster and the Plantagenets was positive.

After Edward II ascended the throne, he immediately bestowed a royal title – Earl of Cornwall – on his favourite (and suspected lover) Piers Gaveston. This instantly sparked massive opposition from the nobility, and Thomas of Lancaster became a leading player in an uprising against the King and his favourite. In an unforgiving dispute, Gaveston was eventually caught and executed on Lancaster's lands near Kenilworth, infuriating the King and leading him to call Thomas of Lancaster a rebel and a traitor. After Gaveston's death, domestic politics was turned on its head: Thomas of Lancaster exercised his authority and undermined the King. He refused to serve in the war against the Scots, and went so far as to agree to a personal truce with the Scottish lords, working under the pseudonym 'King Arthur'. After years of growing animosity between the cousins, an influential noble family – the Despensers – rose to prominence at court and helped Edward II seek retribution. Edward II had never forgiven his cousin for Gaveston's murder and, in 1322, finally took his revenge. Thomas of Lancaster was arrested after the Battle of Boroughbridge and tried for treason – with the Despensers and the King as members of the tribunal. A week after his arrest, Thomas of Lancaster, dressed in an old surcoat, was carried on a donkey a mile from Pontefract Castle, where he was executed. The only mercy extended was that he was at least spared the prescribed fate of a convicted traitor, that of being hung, drawn and quartered. As he was of royal blood, he was granted death by beheading. After Thomas's conviction and execution as a traitor, Lancastrian loyalty was called into question: that historical mistrust of the name of Lancaster would haunt John of Gaunt throughout his political and personal life. When Gaunt inherited the Lancastrian lands nearly forty years later, it was claimed that blood trickled from Thomas of Lancaster's tomb – a grim omen of an uncertain dynastic future.

Thomas became a posthumous icon, which perhaps made the Lancastrian position all the more dangerous. Shortly after his death a cult began to emerge around his effigy, said to induce miracles – even his hat was believed to cure headaches. By the time Henry – his younger brother and heir to the Lancastrian lands – installed a memorial cross for the murdered Thomas, the dead Earl had achieved a significant following, with three attempts to have him canonised.

With Edward II pitted against his Queen, Isabella, and her lover Roger Mortimer, the dynastic future of England was precarious. The Lancastrian administration, however, remained constant. Whilst the royal family were embroiled in a bitter feud, Henry, Earl of Lancaster, invested in Leicester as the heart of Lancastrian affairs. He renovated Leicester Castle but his greatest project was in the south-west of the town, the Newarke – a hospital and church – that employed generations of local labourers. From 1330, Henry of Lancaster created a home for the Lancastrian dynasty in Leicestershire and brought the previously quiet town of Leicester to the forefront of English consciousness.

Henry was popular in Leicester; the citizens of the town respected him and he carefully considered their needs, even endowing funds for a public latrine, 'for the ease of all the said community'.[7] Yet it was his large building projects in Leicester that benefitted local people most significantly. This positive relationship with the town continued with his son, Henry of Grosmont, the future Earl of Derby, Duke of Lancaster and father-in-law of John of Gaunt. Over the course of his flowering career, and even after being raised to his Dukedom, Henry of Grosmont never shirked his feudal responsibility in Leicester, and the relationship between people and magnate remained steadfast. By the time Gaunt inherited the town, Leicester was unbendingly loyal to Lancaster.

In the summer of 1362, after John of Gaunt and Blanche took charge of the Duchy of Lancaster, they toured the extensive lands now in their possession. Leicester was part of their tour and welcomed the new Duke and Duchess with open arms, offering gifts on their arrival. Gaunt continued the commitment of his forefathers-in-law and treated the people of Leicester with respect and kindness. The goodwill between citizens and Lord endured, and during the Peasants' Revolt in 1381 the people of Leicester flocked to defend Gaunt's property in the town.

With extensive territory to manage, John of Gaunt spent time over its redistribution. He granted Bergerac and Champagne – which had been acquired by Henry during the war – to the Black Prince, who now lived in Bordeaux, in Aquitaine. The lands in France were a generous gift, but also allowed John to consolidate Lancastrian territory within England, thereby creating a more manageable, localised administration. The Duchy of Lancaster was a palatinate, meaning it was ruled by Gaunt to a large extent independently from the Crown. With lands in Yorkshire, Cheshire, Hertfordshire, Leicestershire, Cambridgeshire and Sussex, he ruled a larger portion of the country than any other magnate and needed an administrative body that ran like clockwork: a Lancastrian affinity.

John of Gaunt's retinue was abnormally large. The men and women surrounding Gaunt formed a well-oiled hierarchical machine, and they divided into three principal categories. The closest among Gaunt's retinue were his household attendants, who served his daily needs. They were followed by indentured retainers, who would be called to serve under him on campaign, and his estate officials, who managed his lands.[8] All of these members wore his collar of linked esses. It is unclear exactly when the linked esses were adopted as the Lancastrian livery collar, or exactly what they represent. In Gaunt's will he refers to a collar of gold given to him by his mother Queen Philippa; perhaps he adopted the design of this treasured gift for his own purpose. Another interpretation suggests the letters allude to the Sanctus – a prayer from the Christian liturgy.[9] It is also possible that it refers to a Lancastrian motto: *souveignez vous de moi*, meaning 'remember me'.[10] There's no clear indication *who* exactly the Lancastrians are meant to remember, but as Gaunt's son Henry IV adopted the collar throughout his life and reign, it is possible that this nods to his mother, the Duchess Blanche.

John of Gaunt treated his retainers well and in return they were faithful to him; and so, by proxy, to the Crown. The King needed the loyalty of the magnates and the county commonwealths they represented. With John of Gaunt owning land in almost every county in England, which generated an income of around £10,000 per annum – an unprecedented sum in medieval England for anybody other than a King – Lancastrian support was crucial to the Crown in cultivating and maintaining a strong and wealthy political nation.[11] Throughout John of Gaunt's life, he interwove Crown politics with the Duchy of Lancaster. He mustered an army from his retainers at times of war – in 1367 he took 100 of his men to aid the Black Prince in Aquitaine – and members of his retinue enjoyed prominent positions at court; Lord Scrope, the future Chancellor of Richard II, was a loyal Lancastrian retainer.

Conventional practice for wealthy young knights in the fourteenth century – if the country was at peace – was to go on crusade. By travelling and fighting for a holy cause a young man was expected to embody knightly decorum, experience battle and practise piety. With the responsibility of the Lancastrian inheritance and his role at court, John of Gaunt bypassed this rite of passage and was plunged into the political power-play of European politics. In autumn 1364 Gaunt led an embassy to Bruges to broker a marriage agreement between his younger brother, Edmund of Langley, and Margaret, the daughter of the wealthy Count of Flanders. Margaret was set to inherit her father's wealth and the counties of Artois and Brabant in the Low Countries.

Gaunt's mission was important; through a Flanders marriage, Edward III hoped to extend English power in the Low Countries – contravening the terms stipulated at Brétigny and forging an alliance with a powerful principality in Europe. The initial negotiation was successful and an alliance was agreed. However, a formidable accord between England and Flanders threatened the position of the county of Burgundy, held by the French King's brother, Philip, an adversary of the Count of Flanders. Resolutely set against the alliance, Charles V of France petitioned Pope Urban V to refuse the match. In a desperate attempt to finalise the agreement, John of Gaunt offered his retinue's assistance against the Burgundians, to 'aid in fulfilment of his father's obligations'.[12] Despite Gaunt's dutiful efforts to please his father and provide a good match for his brother, the marriage never materialised: French pressure and Pope Urban's refusal to allow the union won out in the end. The broken alliance inflamed the rivalry between England and France and, with hopes of support from the Low Countries dashed, Edward III turned next to Spain, with his eldest son making the first move.

After the Black Prince arrived in Aquitaine in 1362, he inaugurated a glamorous court in the city of Bordeaux with his wife Joan and a close circle of knights. The couple's extravagant lifestyle was funded by the King's wealth, which was abundant thanks to John II's (partial) ransom and the profits from the wool trade. The Black Prince was popular in Bordeaux. According to Chandos Herald, the nobility were 'joyful and happy, generous and noble' and 'all his subjects loved him well, because he did so much good for them'.[13] The Prince held jousts and elaborate feasts and hung vast, expensive, colourful tapestries from the walls of his banqueting hall: his favourite tapestry was black with silver ostrich plumes and many swans, depicted with women's heads.[14] The success of Crécy and Poitiers meant the Black Prince was known around Europe as a powerful, capable prince and warrior, 'a worthy man, bold, and with such a force of men at arms no living man could do him wrong'.

While the Black Prince ruled a successful court in Aquitaine, Spain was at war with itself. In 1350, Alfonso XI, King of Castile, died of plague. Alfonso had been historically loyal to France – supporting it in sea-battles against the English at Sluys and Winchelsea. Despite this, he had exercised some diplomacy with England – the ill-fated marriage alliance that resulted in Princess Joan dying of plague en route to wed his son Pedro. Alfonso was a successful diplomat and popular King; he kept the peace in Castile by allying with neighbouring Aragon. He was also well-liked in Christendom after waging continual war against Muslims in the south of Spain – where he died whilst besieging the Moorish stronghold of Gibraltar.[15] Upon Alfonso's death, the crown passed to his son, Pedro I, who promptly began to unpick his father's policies and jeopardise peace by antagonising Aragon. A jealous man, Pedro murdered his half-siblings and later executed their mother, Alfonso's longstanding mistress. To posterity, he became known as Pedro the Cruel.[16] His half-brother Enrique survived and fled to France, where he served as a loyal mercenary biding his time to return to Castile for revenge.

Over a decade later, Enrique managed to forge an alliance with Pere III, the King of Aragon. Pere had a contentious reputation. According to a chronicle he wrote about himself, he was a peace-loving monarch. Yet another story goes that, following a rebellion in Valencia, the Aragonese King forced the burghers of the town to drink the molten metal of the very bell that had rang out across the town to signal the uprising.[17] Nonetheless, he was a natural ally for Enrique, and together they intended to usurp Pedro and restore the peace between neighbours, as enjoyed in the reign of Alfonso. Pedro soon discovered the plot against him and allied himself with the Muslim King in Granada and Charles of Navarre, fracturing Spain and also calling in foreign allies. In 1362, Pedro I signed a peace agreement with Edward III at St Paul's Cathedral, officially switching Castile's allegiance from France to

England. However, this did nothing to prevent his own people closing in on him. To Pedro's horror, the Castilian nobility flocked to the Aragonese – furious with Pedro's alliance with Granada. By 1366, King Pedro I of Castile was deposed and his half-brother, Enrique Trastámara, was celebrated as the new King of Castile. Later that year, the despondent ex-monarch arrived in Aquitaine and threw himself on the mercy and protection of the Black Prince, expecting him to honour the alliance Pedro had agreed with Edward III. The complicated fraternal feud had spilled out of Spain and into France and England, drawing both sides into the argument and into another decisive battle.

Bertrand du Guesclin was the most famous soldier and hero in France. A Breton knight, du Guesclin inspired epic romantic literature, poetry and theatre. He was considered such an icon in France, the physical embodiment of French chivalry and valour, that, following his death, du Guesclin's body was cut up, boiled and parts were dispatched to various churches and shrines.[18] In 1365, he rode to Bordeaux to visit the court of the Black Prince. He hoped to persuade the Prince to permit an expedition into Spain, to rid France of the Companies. Although the English army had moved out of France in 1360, many rogue soldiers and mercenaries had remained and joined the feared Companies. These French, English and German freebooters – including Eustace d'Auberchicourt – lingered throughout the country, raiding, pillaging, raping and extorting towns and villages. After years of continuous harassment, France was more devastated by the Companies than it was by the Black Death. Jean Froissart emphasised the urgency of the situation, suggesting that if they were not removed from the country, 'they would destroy the noble Kingdom of France'. To the French, the Companies were a nightmare, and brought with them destruction and terror akin to the Riders of the Apocalypse. Charles V was desperate to rid his country of their persistent atrocities – whatever the cost.

It was decided that the best method was to direct the Companies' interest elsewhere. With funding from the Pope in Avignon and the King of France, they were effectively paid to leave the country. Bertrand du Guesclin was tasked with leading the Companies over the Pyrenees and into Spain, where they would ride south and fight the Moors in Granada. As some of soldiers within the Companies were pledged to the Black Prince, du Guesclin was forced to seek his approval at Bordeaux. Aware of the devastation the Companies were causing, the Black Prince sanctioned the planned exodus. Bertrand du Guesclin, however, had not informed the Prince that the Companies were intended for a crusade against the Moors in Granada. As Granada was an ally of Pedro, and Charles V supported Enrique, the Black Prince was incentivised to support Pedro in reclaiming his throne. By proxy, he resumed war against Charles V by opposing his sworn ally.

Charles V loathed Pedro I. In 1353, Pedro had married Blanche of Bourbon, the sister of Charles's wife Joanna. Pedro treated her appallingly, publicly humiliating her as a form of entertainment, leaving her desperate and despairing in Spain. Pedro, in the face of warnings from the Pope, chose to live openly with his mistress, Maria de Padilla. The situation came to a head when Blanche died in suspicious circumstances in 1361, the year before Pedro signed his alliance with Edward III. Rumour circulated that Blanche of Bourbon had been murdered by her husband, prompting Charles V to support Enrique's claim to the Castilian throne aided by the Companies. The payment for the Companies' services – and removal from France – was split three ways: between the Pope in Avignon (Urban V), Charles V and Pere III of Aragon. With full pockets, the Companies, led by du Guesclin, marched out of France via the coastal Languedoc and towards Montpellier and Perpignan. Around 12,000 soldiers entered Spain at the end of the year and, by that spring, Pedro I had fled.

John of Gaunt was at the Savoy Palace, occupied with royal administration, around the time he was told of Pedro's flight to Aquitaine.[19] Pedro offered the Black Prince lands in Castile, jewels and money, along with payment for the cost of the campaign, in exchange for help in regaining his throne. Edward III granted the request and chose John of Gaunt to take troops and supplies to Aquitaine to support the Black Prince and Pedro I against Enrique and the Companies. Gaunt spent the summer preparing for the campaign. He borrowed from the Crown, pledging land and property as collateral for the loan. After six years of managing his estates and running diplomatic errands for the King, John of Gaunt was eager to set sail and join his brother on their own campaign. Around the end of November, he set sail from Plymouth into a rough, windswept sea.

Crossing the Channel was often a challenging journey. A strong current and changing winds pushed the English fleet back, delaying landing. Finally, John of Gaunt docked at St Mahé in the Duchy of Brittany – held by English ally Duke John IV – where he went 'on his way commanding and maintaining a great company'.[20] The crossing to France and subsequent journey to Bordeaux was the first time Gaunt had independently led an army. He intended to meet his brother at Dax – south of Bordeaux – where the majority of the army had mustered. On the march south, Gaunt stopped at Bordeaux where he was met by Princess Joan and his brand-new nephew, Richard.

Richard – the second son of the Prince, his firstborn being named Edward – arrived on the Feast of Epiphany (Wednesday 6 January) and was christened two days later. According to Chandos Herald, the heavily pregnant Princess Joan did not want her husband to leave on campaign. He claims that she was so distressed at the Prince's imminent departure that she went into labour and 'grief delivered' the future Richard II. The Black Prince was overjoyed at the birth of his son and saw it as a blessing for the campaign ahead. Shortly after Richard's christening the Prince marched away with an army of 1,000 soldiers.

John of Gaunt did not stay long at Bordeaux. Eager to see his brother and bring the anticipated reinforcements, he left quickly for Dax where the Black Prince rode out to meet him. They embraced each other warmly, and with clasped hands spoke of home and their family.

Around the same time that Gaunt arrived in Bordeaux, Bertrand du Guesclin and Enrique Trastámara met Charles of Navarre at Santa Cruz de Compezo on the Castilian-Navarrese border. Charles switched his allegiance to Enrique and swore to block the path of the Black Prince, forbidding him to enter Spain through Navarre. Aware of the English intention to invade Castile, du Guesclin began to prepare for an attack; closing off the Prince's most obvious point of entry – through the Pyrenees by the Roncesvalles pass and into Navarre – had been his first strategic move. This necessitated the support of the slippery Charles, for whoever had his co-operation enjoyed the fastest passage into Spain.

Archers, men at arms, horses and wagons filled the small town of Saint-Jean-Pied-de-Port at the foot of the Pyrenees. This was normally occupied by pilgrims, travelling across the mountains to the holy city of Santiago de Compostela. The road through the mountains was notorious for thieves. Margery Kempe – a mystic from Bishop's Lynn in East Anglia – even avoided the Roncevalles Pass on her way to Santiago, choosing to sail instead, for 'she was very afraid then that they should rob her and take her gold'.[21] Roncevalles, a hamlet along the pass, was the site of the famous defeat of Charlemagne and the death of Roland at the hands of a mighty Saracen army. The battle is remembered and romanticised in the *Song of Roland*, an eleventh-century epic poem. As the Black Prince needed to take the Roncevalles Pass into Spain he was forced to persuade Charles of Navarre to permit their passage across the Pyrenees. Whilst at Saint-Jean-Pied-de-Port, John of Gaunt was sent by his brother to escort Charles of Navarre to a meeting with the Prince. It is unknown whether Charles revealed his previous agreement with the French, or whether the Black Prince already knew his path was blocked. Nonetheless, the Prince clearly offered agreeable terms; not only did Charles of Navarre grant the English army access, he even swore to fight on their side. With this endorsement, the journey across the Pyrenees could begin.

The misty, snow-covered mountaintops piercing the sky were a beautiful sight, but crossing in winter was not advised. For the army, thieves were less of a threat than the terrain, which during winter was icy, snow-bound, with bears and wolves prowling amongst the trees. The journey was almost impossible. With only nine hours of daylight to cross seventeen miles, they had to move fast and then remain still on the icy path when darkness fell. To reach the summit of the pass, the army had to stumble up an incline of over 1,000 metres, battling rain, wind and hail. The path was narrow, so the army was split into three formations that made the journey over seven days. John of Gaunt went first, leading the vanguard up the slippery path, alongside John Chandos. The Black Prince and Pedro, forced to wait after a turn of bad weather, followed five days later, followed by the last formation led by the Count of Armagnac. According to Chandos, 'no one stopped for his companion, not even a father for his son, for there was such a great cold, snow and frost there that everyone was afraid. But by God's mercy the crossing was made'. Memory of the terrifying journey across the icy Roncevalles Pass might have lingered with John of Gaunt, for he later supported three hospitals of Our Lady of Rouncivall in London. The hospitals were established under the same name as the 'Saint Mary Monastery in the mountains' and Gaunt donated to their cause, perhaps in gratitude for 'God's mercy' and his safety on the journey.[22] The army united, relieved and exhausted, and was permitted a week at Pamplona to recover from the arduous journey as the Prince dispatched spies to gather information on the terrain and Enrique's movements.

The Black Prince had not forgotten the Gascons and the Englishmen who rode with the Companies, and who had made their way to Spain with du Guesclin. Some had homes in Aquitaine and owed fealty to the Prince. Unwilling to let his own men fight for the opposing side, he sent John Chandos to track them down. They were faced with an ultimatum: non-compliance with the Prince's terms would result in the loss of their personal property in England and Aquitaine, and the reward was more than Enrique could match. As mercenary soldiers – one of whom was the infamous freebooter Eustace d'Auberchicourt – these men would always follow the best deal, and so they happily trotted back to join the Black Prince's coalition, leaving Enrique and Bertrand du Guesclin with a depleted force.

Charles of Navarre had honoured his latest change of allegiance and allowed the Black Prince to enter Spain. The English then rode west to Vittoria, where Enrique Trastámara held the Castle of Zaldiaran, an imposing fortress positioned on the crest of a mountain. Enrique waited for the Black Prince at Vittoria where he intended to block the Prince's passage south into Castile by trapping him at the base of the mountain. However, despite the obvious advantage of higher ground, Enrique would not face the Black Prince in battle, even after the Prince challenged him to fight. Tempted though Enrique may have been to face his enemy, Bertrand du Guesclin – accustomed to English tactics – advised him to be patient and ignore the bait.

As dawn broke and sunlight crept up the mountain pass at Vittoria, riders stealthily slid down the valley wall. Horses then thundered down the pass towards the unsuspecting enemy. The horsemen were lightly armoured and the cavalry was fast. Clouds of dust billowed in the morning air as they picked off their first victims: English foraging parties looking for breakfast. As the camp woke, preparing for the day and awaiting the arrival of food, thousands of enemy cavalry burst into their camp and attacked. On agile horses, they weaved around tents, 'launching javelins, spears and lances', and cutting down soldiers who were struggling to arm.[23] Woken by the noise, John of Gaunt stumbled to his feet with his sword and armour and ran to the nearest hilltop, where he raised the standard of the Black Prince to summon his men. Panicked troops rallied around the banner and arrayed themselves for combat. The Black Prince then ordered his men to counter-attack, as the Spanish light cavalry, chosen for the ambush, were driven back up the pass; without the advantage of surprise they proved no match for heavy horses and armoured knights. The story of the English army's bravery lived on in local folklore, and the place of the attack is still known as *Inglesmendi*: 'the English hill'.

The army clung together, anticipating a resurgence of Spanish and French troops, but no further attackers appeared on the hill above. The sky began to spit and the Prince decided to retreat in order to take a better route into Castile. The new path took the army through the mountain to La Guardia over the River Ebro, where they emerged in the heart of Castile. Here, the Black Prince intended to meet Enrique Trastámara and Bertrand du Guesclin in pitched battle. Enrique anticipated the Prince's change of plan and also moved south, crossing the Ebro close to the English army. The Black Prince, Pedro and John of Gaunt made camp in the green vineyards near Nájera, to the west of the River Najerilla, and waited.

There were two chroniclers present at the Battle of Nájera, on opposing sides. During the battle, Pero Ayala, a Spanish chronicler, carried the banner of the Order of the Sash – an elite faction of the Castilian army – and fought for Enrique. Chandos Herald was on the side of the English, witness to the Black Prince's entire Spanish campaign. Both give an account of what followed.[24]

The Spanish army was largely made up of the same Castilian and Aragonese light horsemen – known as 'ginetes' – who had ambushed the English at Vittoria.[25] As both armies prepared for combat, the Black Prince and Enrique exchanged letters carried by heralds moving between opposing lines in an attempt to come to some sort of agreement. The Prince wrote to Enrique, addressing him as the *Count* of Trastámara, and accusing him of unlawfully usurping the crown from the rightful heir. In a final diplomatic gesture to avoid battle, he urged Enrique to surrender his claim and even offered to reconcile Enrique's lands should he submit. But Enrique was eager to fight. He rebuffed the Black Prince's accusation, arguing that Pedro had been a poor King and that the people of Castile suffered under his rule. He emphasised Pedro's immorality in a stark statement: 'He killed his own Queen'.

According to Ayala, Enrique was an honourable man, and it is likely that the Prince did indeed want him restored to a favourable position, without compromising English gains. However, with Pedro and Enrique firmly at odds, a decisive battle remained the only option. Bertrand du Guesclin – who accompanied Enrique to Nájera – warned him about open combat with the English, but Enrique was determined to defend his crown. Antagonised by the Black Prince's message, Enrique moved his men over the River Najerilla and prepared them for battle. The move was impulsive. By crossing the river, he lost a good defensive position: the river now stood behind his army rather than ahead of them. What followed was one of the famous English victories of the Hundred Years War, and John of Gaunt's formative experience of pitched battle.

Shortly before dawn on 3 April 1367, the Black Prince ordered his army to take up position on a steep ridge overlooking the plain, in the middle of which ran a principal road between Nájera and Navarette. Enrique had expected the English to move up the main road, and with the Najerilla behind him, he positioned his army in the centre of the road, blocking the Prince's path.

On the Spanish side, the remainder of the Companies was in the vanguard – the front and centre – commanded by Bertrand du Guesclin. On the wings were Enrique's brother, Tello – notoriously unreliable – and an Aragonese nobleman named Don Alfonso, Count of Denia. Enrique commanded the division to the rear of du Guesclin's mercenaries, and behind him stood Spanish infantrymen.

On the English side, John of Gaunt led the vanguard. He controlled the first line of the attack – men at arms from England and Gascony – and he was accompanied by John Chandos and two marshals of the English army, Steven Cusington and Guichard d'Angle. It was necessary to station an experienced warrior and commander on the front line to supervise John of Gaunt. Having fought with the Black Prince in every campaign, John Chandos was a natural choice. Prince Edward was in the formation behind Gaunt. At the wings were their Navarrese allies; Charles of Navarre, however, was nowhere to be seen. Earlier in the campaign, he had been – conveniently – captured by the French, and was content to be imprisoned in Aragon, safely awaiting the result of the battle. He would eventually make his escape and return to Navarre, shirking responsibility for his part in the war.

As was traditional chivalric practice before a battle, selected soldiers – usually young noblemen – were ceremoniously knighted on the battlefield. In addition, Sir John Chandos trotted forward and asked the Black Prince to bless his banner. The Prince, Pedro and John of Gaunt unfurled the banner and said, 'God grant you honour thereby', before Chandos went to take his position in the vanguard. The Prince turned to his army and made a speech. He implored his men – who were hungry after days of hard marching – to 'conquer them with blow of lance and sword', in order to reap the benefits of their ample food supplies. The army roared for 'St George', whose cross they bore on their surcoats, as the Prince turned to Pedro and said: 'Sir King, today you will know if ever again you will have Castile'. Battle began as dawn broke and the sun rose over the horizon. As Enrique Trastámara looked out over the empty plain ahead, there was no English soldier in sight, until cries emerged from the left flank of his army. The cross of St George appeared a few hundred yards away to the left – it became clear that the Prince had launched a surprise attack.

Chandos Herald claims that the vanguard of the English – led by John of Gaunt – initiated the battle. Pero Ayala credits the right wing of the Spanish with taking the opportunity to advance at great speed towards the English left flank. Whoever advanced first, it was not long before both vanguards collided, resulting in a dramatic mêlée of steel, blood and sweat. John of Gaunt was determined to prove himself on the field and Chandos describes him as fighting 'full of valour . . . so nobly that everyone marvelled, looking at his great prowess . . . no creature, rich or poor, adventured himself so far forward as he did'. As soldiers shoved, hacked and stabbed at each other, Spanish slingers hurled rocks into the advancing English army, forcing men from their horses and delivering fatal blows to advancing soldiers. Still, the English longbows – the deadliest and most famous weapon of the Hundred Years War – could not be beaten. Chandos describes archers shooting 'thicker than rain falls in winter', wounding men and horses with more efficiency than the slingers or crossbows the Spanish brought to the battle. Castilian and Aragonese soldiers turned and fled, with many dispatched by longbowmen and infantry as they ran for their lives towards the River Najerilla. The river had once been seen by the Castilian forces as a defensive asset, but as the end of the battle closed in, it was overrun by men clamouring to escape, and the river transformed into a watery death-trap. By dusk, it ran 'red with the blood that flowed from the bodies of dead men and horses'. Those who safely crossed ran towards the town of Nájera, but were soon plucked from their hiding places and killed. Both chroniclers believe around 400-500 men lost their lives in their flight from battle, by either sword, arrow or drowning. The Battle of Nájera was a victory for the Black Prince, Pedro and John of Gaunt. Enrique escaped to Aragon despite attempts to hunt him down, and Bertrand du Guesclin was captured and ransomed for a vast sum. The restored King of Castile, Pedro the Cruel, dropped to his knees before the Black Prince and John of Gaunt, blessing his victory and Castile.

Despite Pedro's emphatic gratitude, he soon fell out with the English Princes over the treatment of prisoners. Both brothers were expected to uphold and defend the code of chivalry. As part of this code, prisoners were treated fairly and well until a ransom was received for their release, or they were lawfully tried for any crimes and dealt with accordingly. John of Gaunt upheld this code ardently during his lifetime – honour was priceless.

From a knight to a King, captives had significant ransom value. A prisoner taken in war could be a lucrative asset to his captor, depending on his rank and status. Pedro approached his English allies with an offer to pay the going ransom rate for the Castilian prisoners. But his intention was not to release them, but rather to butcher them. Both the Black Prince and John of Gaunt were horrified. The Prince made Pedro pledge his word that he would not touch the prisoners taken at Nájera.

One of the captives was Inigo Lopez de Orozco, who had previously favoured Pedro and supported his rule, before defecting to Enrique. He was now the prisoner of a Gascon soldier who would profit handsomely from his ransom. Pedro brutally attacked de Orozco and stabbed him to death. The Gascon knight was furious and took his frustrations to the Black Prince. Pedro defended himself but, to mitigate the Prince's rage, suggested that he pay the asking price for more blood; it soon become clear that Pedro the Cruel was true to his sobriquet. The Black Prince denied Pedro 'a thousand times what each prisoner was worth' and suggested that instead he pardon them and seek their alliance.[26] Reluctantly, Pedro gave his pardon. The Spanish captives – rather than serve a murderer – managed to escape to Enrique, who was regrouping his army in southern France.

Relations with the newly restored Pedro then went from bad to worse. One month after the battle, the English Princes rode into the Cathedral of Santa Maria in Burgos, to witness Pedro reaffirm his promise to repay the cost of the expedition and grant the Black Prince territory on Spain's northern coast near the Bay of Biscay. Despite this, the promised lands and wealth never materialised and the English army remained in Castile. As they waited, the weather grew hotter. The fierce Spanish sun beat down on the now demoralised army and the Black Prince fell sick, possibly inflicted with agonising dysentery – a common ailment for soldiers in cramped, unhygienic conditions with little access to clean drinking water. The Prince became so unwell he retreated to Aquitaine to await the promised funds from Pedro in the comfort of his own Duchy. Frustrated with Pedro's lack of honour and the unfortunate turn of events, the Black Prince had even plotted to take Castile himself; a plan he likely discussed with John of Gaunt on the long march back to Aquitaine. However, the Prince's sickness was worsening and his plans for Castile were sidelined – neither brother ever saw Pedro again.

After the Battle of Nájera, the ransomed Bertrand du Guesclin returned to Spain to continue the offensive against Pedro. The Constable joined forces again with Enrique Trastámara and led an army back into Castile to oust Pedro for a second time. In 1369, Enrique and du Guesclin trapped and captured Pedro near the Castle of Montiel, south of Madrid. Whilst held prisoner in the French camp, Pedro finally came face to face with Enrique in one of the most dramatic fraternal showdowns in history. They fought, man on man, until finally Enrique – and a band of his followers – stabbed Pedro to death in the same brutal manner that Pedro had used upon others. The reign of Pedro the Cruel was over and Castile was wholly Trastámaran. The death of Pedro I marked a temporary closure of Plantagenet interest in Iberia.

The initially successful campaign, and the Battle of Nájera, left a lasting impression on John of Gaunt. Under his patronage, Walter of

Peterborough composed an epic rhyming poem about the battle: 'the wars of high born brothers I declaim / few lines have bred a stock of greater fame'.[27] Gaunt was proud of the victory at Nájera. It conferred the sort of prestige, honour and chivalric glory that, so far in his life, he had witnessed only from the sidelines. Although the Black Prince's suggestion of a further Castilian invasion was likely borne out of frustration and anger with Pedro, a seed was planted for John of Gaunt. Nájera was a victory for Gaunt equal to Poitiers for the Black Prince and Crécy for Edward III. The prospect of victories like Nájera, territorial expansion and perhaps even kingship, crystallised in an obsession with Castile – a desire to further the King's wish of a 'Plantagenet Empire'. John of Gaunt would cling to this idea, and, for the next twenty years, occupy himself with the conquest of Castile. He persistently laid out his ambition before Parliament, seeking support for another expedition to succeed the English victory in 1367.

That summer, though, Gaunt began the journey home, riding high on his success at Nájera. Yet this momentary glory would soon be overshadowed by a personal tragedy: the death of his beloved Duchess.

FIVE

DEATH, DUTY AND DYNASTY

'Allas, death, what ayleth thee
That thou coldest have taken me
Whan thou toke my lady swete
That was so fair, so fresh, so fre
So good that men may well se
Of al goodnesses she had no mete'.

Geoffrey Chaucer, *The Book of the Duchess*

IN *THE BOOK OF THE DUCHESS*, THE 'MAN IN BLACK' IS
shrouded in grief. He is consumed by sadness, becoming a personifica-
tion of sorrow. 'White' is lost, a fact the Man in Black cannot accept.[1]
The Man suffers from grief-induced insomnia and finally falls asleep
reading Ovid's story of Ceyx and Alcyone; he slips deep into a dream
vision of hope beyond darkness. In the dream he is led into a clearing
in a wood where spring returns to the earth and flowers grow abundant. He is shown that the darkness of winter does not linger but moves
into spring.

On 12 September 1368, John of Gaunt's 'very dear wife', Blanche of
Lancaster, died at Tutbury Castle, either following childbirth-related
complications – possibly the birth and death of an infant called Isabel
– or from the plague. At twenty-six, the Duchess had already given

birth seven times, with three babies surviving infancy by the time she died. Although Blanche had a relatively short life, she was revered at court for her kindness, beauty and grace, prompting Geoffrey Chaucer to compose the dream vision, *The Book of the Duchess*, between 1369 and 1374, when her tomb was constructed. It is in part through this book that we can begin to understand John of Gaunt's grief over the loss of his young wife. Within the narrative, Chaucer offers an intimate understanding of the process of grief and moving on from the trauma of loss. The character of the Black Knight is trapped in sorrow, cutting the promise of hope short with 'she ys ded'. He sits bereft at the foot of a tree, contemplating the loss of his wife: 'I have of sore so get won, that joy gete I never non, Now that I see my lady bryght which I have loved with al my myght is fro me did and ys agoon'. *The Book of the Duchess* is the first narrative poem in the English language to begin with 'I', placing Chaucer as a subject – an observer of his patron's emotional distress. Although the relationship between patron and vassal is distinguishable in *The Book of the Duchess*, Chaucer's relationship with John of Gaunt did not develop exclusively through literary patronage. Chaucer was employed by John of Gaunt as a soldier – he possibly even accompanied Gaunt to Aquitaine in 1369–70 – and his son Thomas also had a flourishing career in Gaunt's service. Despite Chaucer's verse being regularly associated with John of Gaunt, it was rarely commissioned by him. The only poem Chaucer produced in connection to Gaunt was *The Book of the Duchess*.[2]

The Duchess of Lancaster's body was carefully carried to London from Tutbury with a guard of 1,000 horsemen and interred in an alabaster tomb in St Paul's Cathedral. Black cloth was draped across the walls of the cathedral and her tomb surrounded by men in white and blue hoods – the Lancastrian colours – holding burning torches. In the same deeply pious manner as her father's Leicester funeral, Blanche was respectfully laid to rest. An altar was erected with a chalice and missal – a book containing the prayers, important chants and instructions for the mass – and two chaplains were paid to sing masses for her soul. For the rest of his life, John made sure that Blanche – the lady he loved with 'all his myght' – was remembered. The anniversary of her death was commemorated annually, a tradition that continued even into the reign of their son, Henry IV.

After Blanche's death, Gaunt suffered further personal tragedy. In 1368, his brother Lionel of Antwerp, Duke of Clarence, remarried, his first wife having died in Dublin five years earlier. Violante Visconti was the daughter of the Italian nobleman Galeazzo Visconti, Lord of Pavia and Duke of Milan. The Visconti family was extremely wealthy and Lionel's marriage was meant to secure an Anglo-Milanese alliance between Edward III and the Italian dynasty. The marriage was lucrative: Violante's dowry was so large it took two years to negotiate. Finally, the couple married in Milan in June and the ceremony was followed by an elaborate thirty-course banquet. There was apparently enough food left over to feed 1,000 men. Four months after the wedding Lionel died at Alba in Piedmont. It was rumoured that the prime cause was excessive consumption at the wedding feast.

The death of Lionel of Antwerp prompted his deputy commander, Edward le Depenser, to threaten war on the Visconti family, in the belief that gluttony was not the real cause: le Despenser was convinced the Visconti had orchestrated the murder. Nothing came of his accusations and Edward's grand plans for royal rule in Italy were thwarted. Lionel was initially buried in Pavia before being moved to England. He was reinterred at the convent of Austin Friars in Clare, Suffolk, beside his first wife, Elizabeth de Burgh.

Following the death of Blanche, John of Gaunt spent the last months of 1368 working closely with his father at court to broker a new marriage for himself. In another attempt to secure an alliance with Flanders, John was proposed to Margaret, the daughter of its Count; it was effectively the same marriage agreement that he had previously tried to achieve for his brother, Edmund of Langley. Again, this was refused and Margaret eventually wed the Duke of Burgundy, Charles V's brother. The rivalry between England and France was catalysed by the marriage. And even as the French won the alliance with the Count of Flanders there were growing hostilities in Aquitaine. The Black

Prince was losing control of his territory and faced an uprising from the Gascon nobility.

Prince Edward lay sick. Bedbound at his court in Bordeaux, he was attended by the leading physician Pierre de Manti. The Spanish campaign that proved so spectacular for John of Gaunt had taken its toll on his brother. The illness, possibly dysentery, that began in Spain had worsened and the fouage – the tax enacted to fund the Spanish campaign – had unsettling consequences back in Aquitaine. With Pedro dead, the Prince was never reimbursed. The nobility previously loyal to the Prince in Aquitaine began to air their grievances to Charles V. According to Chandos Herald, 'those who he held as friends now became his enemies'.

The Black Prince's failure to inject funds back into his Duchy following the expenses of the Spanish campaign presented an opportunity for the French King, eager as ever to undermine English influence in Aquitaine. Charles V invited Gascon noblemen to appeal against the fouage, promising protection against the Prince should he try to punish them. Some were cautious of Charles's suspiciously generous olive branch; others were quick to accept his proposition. Despite the Prince living and ruling in France, many French aristocrats loathed him and his family. Louis, Duke of Anjou – an ally of the Spanish King, Enrique – commissioned a tapestry as a visual representation of his animus towards the Plantagenets. In an allegory woven into the tapestry, Edward III, the Black Prince, John of Gaunt and Edmund of Langley were all demonised as a single beast surrounded by a swarm of locusts emerging from a thick black smoke.[3]

The writer and courtier Christine de Pisan observed that 'wars were better fought by the power of the mind than by brute force'. Her observation rang true for Charles V. John of Gaunt dismissed him as a 'lawyer', a politician rather than a military leader. Charles managed to plant seeds of doubt in the minds of the Prince's allies, recruiting the Count of Armagnac, the Count of Perigord and the Lord of Albret in his mission to oust the English from Aquitaine. The Treaty of Brétigny had stipulated that Edward III would renounce his claim to the French throne after the ransom for John II was paid. By 1369, the French had not paid the ransom in full and Edward III had not formally renounced the title King of England and France. With some English soldiers – deserters who joined the Companies – still wreaking havoc in France, Edward III too found himself in breach of the terms of the Treaty, which stipulated that the English had to remove all their fighting men from the country. This gave Charles V the opportunity to attack the Prince whilst he was in a weak position, by arguing that Brétigny was invalid, and Charles V was still the ultimate ruler of Aquitaine. Such a position would inevitably result in a renewal of war. With Gascon nobles refusing to pay the Prince's fouage, 800 English soldiers prepared to sail to Aquitaine to help the Prince restore order. In a secret arrangement the Gascon lords, formerly loyal to the Prince, swore allegiance to Charles V in exchange for his protection against the English in Aquitaine. In November, the Black Prince received a summons to the Parlement of Paris on 2 May 1369, to answer appeals made against him by the Gascon lords in response to the fouage. According to Chandos Herald, he angrily stated: 'if God gives me comfort and I can get up from this bed, I will cause them harm enough yet'.

The Prince never made it to Paris. Despite his determination to defend his honour, title and authority, he was struggling to maintain control of his lands. The tax in Aquitaine had been described by the *Anonimalle Chronicle* as an 'intolerable burden'. John Chandos delivered a letter to Edward III in which the Black Prince attempted to defend himself against the growing accusations, stipulating: 'I have written so forwardly about this, because it affects me and my honour and standing so closely . . . I ask you, most honoured Lord, for the sake of such little power I have to serve you, to take these matters entirely to heart . . . for I will always be ready to carry out your orders as best I can'. The French closed in on the Prince, as the Duke of Anjou began recruiting troops across the Languedoc, intent on attacking before English support could arrive.[4]

Edward III called a Great Council at Westminster to determine the best course of action in France. He summoned the most powerful lords in the realm, including John of Gaunt; at almost sixty years old, Edward III was preparing for the 'second war'. The objective was to help the ailing Black Prince and save Aquitaine from falling into French hands. Plans for a new campaign were formed, with John of Gaunt chosen to lead the English army into France for the first time. Following the success of Nájera, Edward III trusted Gaunt as a leading commander, offering a chance of victory in France akin to the Black Prince at the start of the Poitiers campaign. Over the spring and early summer of 1369, a muster of troops, arms and supplies was arranged with the intention of sailing to the garrison at Calais, from where Gaunt could conduct a fresh invasion.

As the army gathered at Southampton and prepared for the crossing, John of Gaunt was appointed Lieutenant in the March of Calais. The King sent 'milord John of Gaunt, Duke of Lancaster, and the Earl of Hereford and the Lord of Mauby and other great Lords, along with a powerful force of valiant men, beyond the sea to Calais'.[5] After landing, Gaunt advanced south at the head of 6,000 men to Picardy, then stopped in the valley at Tournehem. He planned to defeat the French in a surprise attack. According to a cleric from Rouen, the Duke of Burgundy, known as Philip the Bold, rode north from Rouen to face Gaunt, following the orders of his brother, Charles V. The French King's leading advisors were his three brothers: the Dukes of Burgundy, Anjou and Berry. They were his lieutenants in the war against the English, and in the following years led the French efforts against the Black Prince and Gaunt.

In early August, Philip the Bold left Rouen after attending a council held by the King. A week later, he arrived in Tournehem, where John of Gaunt and the English army were encamped. Gaunt and his men were dining in the camp when Philip the Bold led his army towards them. Taken by surprise, not having anticipated any French opposition at Tournehem, Gaunt dropped everything, crying out 'To arms!' before ordering the army into a defensive formation, 'arraying their divisions and units skilfully'.[6] Then, according to the cleric from Rouen, John of Gaunt refused pitched battle with the French, barricading his army from any possibility of attack: 'the Duke of Lancaster and the English, who were very subtle and crafty in war, fearing the great chivalry and strength of the French, had fortified themselves in such a way that none could approach them'.[7] The *Anonimalle Chronicle* argues the opposite, that Gaunt was eager for combat but the French refused him. Despite having the advantage by trapping the English in the valley, the French did not press their attack. Philip the Bold may have wished for combat but was under strict instructions from Charles V not to engage with the English in pitched battle. As part of his defensive plan, Charles adopted his former strategy: to avoid battle and wait for the English to run out of supplies, and for morale to plummet. With both armies locked in stalemate, Philip the Bold received information that John of Gaunt was expecting reinforcements. Edward III and the Earl of Warwick were due to arrive at Tournehem, having embarked from Sandwich in Kent. After a month of tension between John of Gaunt and Philip the Bold at Tournehem, the latter fled before the English reinforcements could arrive.

After the enemy appeared to move off, Gaunt and his men carefully took stock of their abandoned camp. It was clear the French had indeed vanished in a hurry, for they left behind a feast: 'a good sixty tuns of wine and as many of beer, and plenty of bread and a great plenty of fresh and salted meat and of fish'. Despite Gaunt's failure to engage the French, he managed to damage the morale of one of their leading noblemen, and 'thereby did the realm of France suffer great shame and great harm'.[8] John of Gaunt did well at Tournehem. The Rouen chronicler's assertion that he deliberately avoided battle with the French is probably untrue. Following his experience of months teasing the French to fight, it is unlikely that Gaunt would have missed the opportunity with men who were fresh out of Calais and eager for war. But neither did he give up his defensive position to pursue the Duke of Burgundy. Although he lost the opportunity for a grand victory like Poitiers, Gaunt demonstrated strategic nous, patience and level-headed command.

Despite his intention to meet his son at Tournehem, Edward III never joined the campaign in France, sending the Earl of Warwick in his place. In August 1369, as Edward was preparing for departure, the Queen, Philippa of Hainault, 'who had such boundless charity for all humanity', died at Windsor Castle. According to Jean Froissart, who was in the Queen's service: 'when the good lady perceived her end approaching, she called to the King, and, extending her right hand from under the bed clothes, put it into the right hand of the King, who was very sorrowful at heart, and thus spoke: "We have enjoyed our union in peace and prosperity."' In her final moments, Philippa implored the tearful King to care for the legacies that she had charitably endowed and, finally, she requested that upon his death, he 'lie by my side in the cloisters of Westminster'.

The Queen was mourned throughout England, but Froissart describes John of Gaunt in particular as 'greatly afflicted' after he received the news whilst camped at Tournehem with his army. Moving out, he marched his men through Picardy raiding, burning and pillaging, although he never achieved any formal combat. Thomas Walsingham, the Benedictine monk of St Albans, chided in his chronicle account of the war that there was a lack of direction in Gaunt's campaign. Gaunt arrived at Harfleur and immediately attacked. He ordered wave after wave of assaults, but could not breach the walls as the defenders of the city rained crossbow bolts down on his men. John of Gaunt had the time and the means to take Harfleur but disease – dysentery and possibly plague – now spread through his camp like wildfire, killing the Earl of Warwick, who had come to Gaunt's aid at Tournehem. Forced into a stalemate after only four days outside Harfleur, Gaunt marched back to Calais through the smoking landscape he had created. By December 1369 he was back in Westminster, where he found the court in deep mourning for the Queen.

The Black Prince was informed of his mother's death in late September. His mood, along with his health, was rapidly deteriorating and he began to delegate power to those he trusted, particularly Sir John

Chandos. However, in the New Year the Prince was crushed by another loss.

As Gaunt led the offensive in the north of France, another wave of fighting broke out on the borders of Aquitaine, between the French – in alliance with defecting Gascon nobles – and the English with loyal Gascon nobles under the Black Prince. In defence of the Prince's territory, John Chandos orchestrated an ambush against a group of French soldiers. On the road between Limoges and Poitiers, there was a bridge near the village of Lussac in Poitou spanning the Vienne river. John Chandos prepared to ambush the French party before they could cross the bridge. As they approached, Chandos and his men – who outnumbered the French – blocked their path at the foot of the bridge. Chandos, wearing a 'great robe, richly emblazoned' dismounted and ordered his banner to be unfurled and waved before the French troops. He strode confidently towards the French and proudly announced, 'I am John Chandos, look at me well, for, if God pleases we will now put to the test, your great deeds of arms that are so renowned'. In the middle of winter, the ground was sheeted with a thin layer of ice and John Chandos suddenly slipped, tripping on the heavy material of his robe and falling to the ground. Before Chandos could collect himself, the French party advanced and the ill-fated knight received a lance blow directly to his face, having had no time to pull down his visor. And so, the 'noble John Chandos' met an ignoble end.

Chandos was one of the most effective English military commanders in Aquitaine and the Prince's closest friend. After his death Edward III dispatched John of Gaunt to Bordeaux to help his brother manage its defence. Around 1,000 men travelled to Aquitaine with Gaunt, largely recruited from the Lancastrian retinue. With a resurgence of the war, the English coastline was vulnerable again and Edward III needed to keep part of the army at home to protect the realm. John of Gaunt landed at Bordeaux with his relief force in the middle of August 1370. He marched to Cognac where he met with his younger brother, Edmund of Langley, and the Black Prince. This was the first time Gaunt had seen his beloved older brother since the end of the Nájera campaign and he was forced to face the fact that the Black Prince was crippled with illness. After he arrived in Cognac, John of Gaunt embraced the Prince, who was carried in a litter to greet him as he did not have the strength to walk.

The Black Prince and John of Gaunt launched a new strategy to reassert control in Aquitaine. They agreed to reward loyalty by redistributing the lands belonging to defecting lords to those who had remained faithful to the English. The Prince also offered a second chance to deserters by 'pardoning their crimes' and permitting them to return to his service.[9] He also suggested that John of Gaunt should be granted the full power of Lieutenant in Aquitaine, for he was unable to lead his men, let alone fight.

The first course of action for the brothers was to reclaim the city of Limoges, which had fallen to the French through the disloyalty of its bishop, a man the Prince had previously trusted.

Limoges was a wealthy city in the heart of Aquitaine, situated between Poitiers and Bergerac, and on the right bank of the Vienne river. The city was well fortified, wrapped in a defensive circuit of high walls built in the twelfth to thirteenth centuries, with over twenty towers and eight portcullis gateways. It was also split into two: the cité and the chateau. The cité – on the lower ground of Limoges – was occupied by the clergy and formed a religious community with a monastery, a convent, the Bishop's residence and the Basilica St Etienne. Above the cité was the chateau, which had a burgeoning enamel industry, a busy food market and a castle – the Place de la Motte. There was also another church in the chateau, the church of St Michael. The population of Limoges was around 15,000 and was controlled by its bishop, Jean de Cros, who – previously on good terms with the Black Prince – had been appointed godfather to his firstborn son, Edward. In August 1370, Limoges surrendered to the Duke of Berry, a brother of Charles V. The Duke of Berry was a renowned aesthete. He collected fine things: art, jewellery, expensive artefacts and chateaux, and commissioned tapestries and exquisite books of hours such as the *Très Riches Heures*, designed by the esteemed Limbourg brothers. The Duke adored excess; he had over 1,000 hunting dogs, and a menagerie with a camel, a leopard and a monkey.

On 21 August, the Duke of Berry marched his army outside Limoges and set up camp in the suburbs of the town amongst the vineyards. For the next three days, the Duke opened negotiations with the defender of the town, Jean de Cros. The Bishop was easily persuaded to submit the cité to the Duke, for, on the lower ground and with no garrison, it was in a weaker defensive position than the chateau that loomed above. The residents of the chateau, however, were not convinced and agreed to stand firm, loyal to the Black Prince. Having promised the Duke of Berry control of the town, Jean de Cros pleaded with the citizens of the chateau to surrender. In his desperation he fabricated a rumour that the Black Prince was dead. The citizens of the chateau were unconvinced, continuing their stand against the Duke of Berry. With the gates of the chateau firmly closed, Berry had two choices: to besiege the hostile part of the town, or leave. With the English army on the march, he chose the latter and prepared to move out. Having surrendered the cité, Jean de Cros begged the Duke of Berry to stay and defend Limoges from the advancing English, to no avail. Instead, Berry donated a division of soldiers to the Bishop's defence. Soon afterwards, he fled.

From the moment Black Prince had heard that Limoges had been seized, he was determined to reclaim it. With an army of 4,000 soldiers, the Prince and John of Gaunt marched out. The army was a mixed bag of Gaunt's men, noblemen from Aquitaine who remained loyal to the Prince and some of the Companies, including Eustace d'Auberchicourt. On 14 September, the English army arrived at the walls of Limoges, behind John of Gaunt. The Black Prince delivered orders from his litter. What happened next is subject to contention, Jean Froissart's interpretation of the events at Limoges has tarnished the reputation of the Black Prince as a violent aggressor. However, recent evidence suggests that it went the following way.[10]

John of Gaunt led the offensive against Limoges in a siege that lasted five days. After discovering that one part of the city wall was built on soft ground, Gaunt ordered his men to tunnel beneath. As they dug,

the French defenders of the town – left by the Duke of Berry –
responded by digging their own mine in retaliation. Gaunt was caught
inside the tunnel as the two sides encountered each other in a messy
hand-to-hand underground skirmish, forcing Gaunt and his men to
back out. Gaunt then had siege engines wheeled outside the walls,
launching missiles that took down part of the external wall, allowing
him to lead a small force of men at arms into the city through the
breach. As the English and Gascon soldiers charged, Jean de Villemur,
commander of the small French garrison left by the Duke of Berry,
charged straight at John of Gaunt. Froissart describes the two men
fighting hand-to-hand until Gaunt, highly impressed by his opponent's
swordsmanship, paused to ask him his name.

At the end of the first wave of the attack, the lower wall outside the cité
collapsed, and the full might of the English and Gascon army was able
to push through the cité towards the gate of the chateau. The people of
the chateau had remained loyal to the Black Prince and, as the English
approached, they opened the gate. The French garrison, furious that
the citizens of the chateau compromised their defence, perpetrated the
massacre of the people of Limoges that followed. As the English flooded
in, they pursued the French soldiers into the main square where John
of Gaunt led the advance. Outnumbered and with no alternative, the
French surrendered and a few were taken prisoner, including Jean de
Villemur. Terrified, Jean de Cros was brought before the Black Prince's
litter. Seething with rage at the man who had betrayed him, the Black
Prince was tempted to show him no mercy; however, true to his vow of
clemency, the Bishop was spared.

At the end of September, the Black Prince wrote to the Count of
Foix to inform him of the recovery of Limoges, stipulating that 100
soldiers and 200 civilians had been killed in the fighting as Limoges
was reclaimed by the English. The Black Prince also granted a pardon
to the citizens and the clergy of Limoges. He wished to 'not see them
further punished as accomplices in this crime, when fault lay clearly
with the bishop'.[11] The account of the siege of Limoges as delivered by
Jean Froissart has been, until recently, the principal account of the

massacre of the people of the chateau. It suggests that the Prince, cruelly and sparing none, slaughtered the innocent citizens of Limoges. By this time, Jean Froissart – previously in the employ of Queen Philippa of Hainault – had come to France under the patronage of Guy II, Count of Blois. This allowed him to write book two of his chronicles, but Guy – who was for a time held hostage in England after the Treaty of Brétigny – was hostile to the Black Prince. Froissart's account of Limoges naturally painted the Prince as a monster to appease his patron, but the slaughter of innocent citizens was actually conducted by the Duke of Berry's men. For Charles V, Limoges was a disaster. Appalled at the ineptitude shown by his brother, Berry, the King stripped him of military authority.

The Black Prince, John of Gaunt and their army returned to Cognac where the Prince received another devastating blow: his eldest son, Edward, only five years old, had died of plague at Angoulême on 29 September. The Black Prince was no longer able to cope with the pressures of leadership in Aquitaine. Chronically unwell and heartbroken at the loss of his little son, he passed all authority over to Gaunt and granted him the Lordship of Bergerac. According to Jean Froissart, the Prince parted with the Lords of Aquitaine with a sorrowful speech, 'during the time that he had been their prince, he had always maintained them in peace, prosperity and power, as far as depended on him, against all their enemies; but that now, in the hope of recovering his health, of which he had great need, he intended to return to England; he therefore besought them earnestly to put their faith in, and to serve and obey his brother, the Duke of Lancaster, as they had before served and obeyed him; that they would find him a good and courteous Lord'.

In what was known as an *homage de bouche*, a ceremony in which the Lord or sovereign receives a kiss from the nobles of Aquitaine which binds them to fight for him in the defence of his lands, John of Gaunt was accepted as the new Lord of Aquitaine. This was formalised in an agreement with the Black Prince granting John the title Lieutenant of Aquitaine. The Black Prince – again carried in a litter – embarked from Bordeaux with his grieving wife, the Princess Joan, and their surviving son, Richard. Their situation was so bleak they were unable to stay for Edward's funeral, a responsibility taken on by Gaunt who ensured that it was a magnificent affair. Despite the prestige that came with his new responsibility, Gaunt was not content with the position. He agreed to take on the Prince's role only on condition he was released the following summer. To mitigate his request, the Black Prince offered John the town and Castle of La Roche Sur Yon – an offer he accepted.[12] Aquitaine was in a bad state of affairs: it would be a complex and incredibly difficult job to return the English territory to the profitable province it had once been.

The Black Prince's relationship with the Lords of Aquitaine was precarious. As the Prince had lost his grip over his territory, the nobility were forced to choose between remaining loyal to England and the Prince, or defecting to the French. Consistently loyal to his brother, and to the Crown, John of Gaunt took his authority in Aquitaine seriously and set about recovering the land that had been lost. He started with a small walled town east of Aquitaine called Mont Pon. William, Lord of Mont Pon, had been a loyal subject of the English. As the Black Prince's position grew weaker, however, he went over to the French, permitting the Duke of Anjou entry into the town. William's betrayal was an example of the consistent defection of disloyal lords in the latter part of the Black Prince's leadership of Aquitaine, which Gaunt now sought to mitigate. Gaunt led an army against Mont Pon. Anticipating punishment, William fled, leaving only four knights to protect the castle. John of Gaunt arrived at Mont Pon and 'with great vigour' led an offensive siege against the castle. His force scaled its walls and quickly forced the small contingent of French knights to surrender. According to Froissart, John of Gaunt initially refused to take prisoners and wished to make an example of the disloyal William of Mont Pon, and any man who had aided his flight. The four French soldiers captured by Gaunt's men appealed to the Duke for their lives and were eventually successful in changing his mind. Gaunt set about repairing the damage caused in the brief attack on the walls and left shortly after, installing two knights as governors and forty soldiers to keep the peace.

The rest of the year went a similar way for John of Gaunt. He spent most of his time trying to restore the financially crippled government in Aquitaine and, even after informing the King of the situation, was still largely left to deal with the problematic territory himself. During the final year of the Black Prince's reign in Aquitaine, over half of the army had deserted due to lack of payment. To prevent the inevitable pillaging, raping and torching in English territory, John of Gaunt paid the restless soldiers himself. On 23 September 1371, he formally resigned his post into the hands of the Prince's officers and planned his journey home. Of the 800 men who came with him from England, fewer than half remained. Those who did were his retainers and held lands in the Duchy of Lancaster. John of Gaunt had completed the time he promised the Prince he would spend in Aquitaine and was eager to pursue his own promising cause: to take back Castile and there, crown himself King.

The idea of invading Castile and taking the throne probably mani-fested itself during the time John of Gaunt was based in Aquitaine in the early spring of 1371. Froissart claims that it was the barons of Aquitaine, whom Gaunt had come to know well, who suggested the idea of marrying the eldest daughter of the murdered Pedro the Cruel. Gaunt had, by this time, been a widower for over two years and a new marriage was inevitable. He had been occupied – up until then – governing Aquitaine and demonstrating loyalty and obedience to the will of his family. However, he was tempted by the opportunity to become King of Castile through Pedro's daughter, Constance.

Following the death of their father, the daughters of Pedro and his mistress Maria de Padilla (whom he secretly married prior to Blanche of Bourbon) were kept at Bayonne. With nowhere to go, Princesses Constance and Isabella lived under the protection of the Black Prince, having initially served as collateral for Pedro's promise of payment. The payment never came, and the Princesses now lived in exile as potential heirs to the throne of Castile. According to Froissart, Sir Guiscard d'Angle approached Gaunt with the idea of marrying into Castile: 'My Lord, it is time you should think of remarrying. We know of a very noble match for you, one from which you or your heirs will be Kings of Castile. It will be a charitable deed to comfort and advise damsels who are daughters of a King, especially when in such a pitiable state as those ladies are. Take therefore, the eldest as your bride'. It is possible that John of Gaunt had already considered Princess Constance as a poten-tial wife: in his will Pedro had stipulated that the husband of his eldest daughter would have a rightful claim to the throne.

John of Gaunt sent four knights to bring both princesses to Bordeaux. However, he was impatient to secure the match. Rather than waiting and marrying Constance in a grand court ceremony, he rode out to meet her on the road. On 21 September 1371, thirty-one-year-old Gaunt married seventeen-year-old Constance at Roquefort, near Mont de Marsan, and she became the new Duchess of Lancaster. By the time Gaunt relinquished his Lieutenancy in Aquitaine in September, he was eager to return home and introduce his new wife to his family, and to the realm. Around the end of the month he sailed from Bordeaux with Constance and her sister Isabella on a salt ship, requesting the ship's master remove a cargo of bay salt to make the ship available for their voyage. Having shouldered a significant financial burden in Aquitaine, John of Gaunt had little wealth to spare on the luxury of a fine ship; when they arrived in England, Constance was even forced to pawn some of her belongings. Two weeks after landing, John of Gaunt returned to the Savoy Palace and to Westminster, where he was remu-nerated and described the desperate situation in Aquitaine to the King. He insisted that if the territory were properly defended it would invite a return of loyalty from the lords who had deserted the Prince. It is likely they also discussed his new objective – to reinvade Castile and take the throne.

On his way to Westminster, Gaunt left Constance at Hertford Castle, close to London, one of his favoured country residences. It was a small castle, but crenelated and fortified with a large outer wall and spacious keep. Hertford was a comfortable but safe location from which the new Duchess could familiarise herself with England. After three months in England, Constance of Castile was formally and publicly received in London as the new Duchess of Lancaster; she was also pregnant. Constance was greeted with a procession through Cheapside, and the Black Prince rose from his sickbed to escort his new sister-in-law to the Savoy Palace, where John of Gaunt intended to formally install her as his Queen of Castile. When Constance gave birth to a baby girl, Catherine, in 1372, the future looked promising for the new couple. Their union, however, was purely political and never developed into a loving or close relationship. The marriage survived out of ambition and hatred: John of Gaunt's ambition for the throne, and Constance's hatred for her uncle, Enrique. However, the real thorn in their marriage was John of Gaunt's continuing love affair with another woman – Katherine Swynford.

SIX

CAT OF THE COURT

'With that there ran a rout of rats at once,
And small mice with them, more than thousand,
And came to a council, for their common profit;
For a cat from the Court, came when he liked
And o'er leaped them lightly, and caught them at will,
Played with them perilously, and pushed them about.
For dream of divers dangers, we dare not look about;
If we grumble at his game, he will attack us all,
Scratch us or clutch us, and in his claws hold us'.

William Langland, *Piers Plowman*

IN A DRAWN-OUT COUNCIL MEETING, JOHN OF GAUNT WAS formally endowed with the title 'King of Castile and Leon' by right of his wife. He was addressed as 'Monseigneur d'Espagne' and adorned Constance with jewels – emeralds, rubies, pearls and a gold circlet (a small thin crown) – in the fashion of a Queen. He also expanded his retinue to include a body of Castilians, some even becoming part of his inner circle.[1] It was probably around this time, as Gaunt settled into his new position of power at the Savoy, that he also began a long-term love affair.

Katherine Swynford and John of Gaunt met whilst she was in the service of his first Duchess, Blanche, as a chamber servant.[2] During this time, the two women were on close terms, for Katherine's own daughter, Blanche Swynford, was placed in the same chamber as both Philippa and Elizabeth – the daughters of Blanche of Lancaster – and Gaunt was appointed as her godfather.

Katherine was married to one of Gaunt's retainers, Sir Hugh Swynford, who held a manor in Kettlethorpe in Lincolnshire.[3] 'Beyond the seas on Thursday after St. Martin in the Winter last' Hugh Swynford suddenly died, whilst serving John of Gaunt in Aquitaine. He left Kettlethorpe in the possession of Katherine and his son and heir Thomas, who was four years old.[4][5] Hugh Swynford's land and house were part of the Duchy of Lancaster, and as his Lord, John of Gaunt dutifully ensured the welfare of his family. He employed Katherine in his household as a 'maistresse' – a governess – to his daughters, and appointed her sister, 'the well loved damoysele, Philippa Chanse', to serve the new Duchess, Constance.[6][7] 'Philippa Chanse' was Philippa Chaucer, the wife of Geoffrey. It is possible that Philippa and Geoffrey met the same way as Chaucer and Gaunt: through Elizabeth de Burgh, who also employed a 'Philippa Pan' in her service – perhaps the daughter of Paon de Roet.[8] The Chaucers' service and loyalty were important to John of Gaunt. He sponsored their children Thomas and Lewis and placed their daughter, Elizabeth, in an esteemed nunnery, St Helen's in Bishopsgate. Gaunt also sent Philippa gifts such as a hanape, a large drinking goblet, made by his favourite goldsmith, Rauland.[9]

In spring 1372, shortly after John of Gaunt paraded Constance through London, he gifted Katherine a generous sum of money.[10] This is the first record of his direct association with her, and it is likely that around this time she became his mistress. In 1373, their first son, John, was born and given the surname Beaufort after Gaunt's French lands, Montmorency-Beaufort. Following his birth, Gaunt granted Katherine more money as well as a lucrative marriage agreement for her daughter Blanche.[11] Critics of Gaunt scorned the relationship, whispering that it had begun before Blanche of Lancaster's death. This is not the case. Nearing the end of his life, John of Gaunt confirmed to the Pope that he had never committed adultery with Katherine whilst

Blanche – or Katherine's husband, Hugh – had still been alive.[12] Their relationship was a very public affair, inviting the gossip and bad favour. From the Abbey of Saint Albans, Walsingham regularly chastised the Duke for his scandalous relationship, calling him a 'fornicator and adulterer'.[13]

Ignoring the whispers and criticism that circulated around the affair, John of Gaunt remained wholly focused on the development of his new title and carrying out domestic responsibilities on behalf of the King. Gaunt maintained his own court – independent to his father's – at the Savoy Palace. Described by Thomas Walsingham as 'a house unrivalled in the Kingdom for its splendour and nobility', the Savoy was emblematic of Lancastrian leadership. The Palace stood between Westminster and the City, on a road named 'La Straunde' and built on a slope that led down to the Thames.[14] The original house, built of limestone, had been crenelated and fortified by Edmund, Earl of Lancaster, and later filled with spoils of war by Henry, Duke of Lancaster.[15] The Palace boasted battlements and towers, and was protected by a portcullis and surrounded by domestic buildings. There was a great hall at the Savoy – the key feature of a medieval manor house or castle – and a chapel. Gardens and orchards stretched from the Palace walls to the foot of the river, maintained by a well-paid gardener, Nichol.[16]

Through the 1370s Gaunt conducted the majority of his administration from the Savoy Palace, peppered with short visits to Hertford Castle.[17] As part of establishing the Savoy as his principal power base, Gaunt invited influential Spaniards into his retinue and the Savoy Palace took on some of the glamour of a continental court: dazzling, wealthy and European. As he established his 'Castilian' court, his position at his father's court developed and Gaunt was requested to conduct a series of diplomatic missions and sign documents on behalf of the King, whilst also seeing to his extensive Lancastrian lands.[18] As Edward III's dependency on Gaunt increased, so did Gaunt's power and, in 1373, he was again trusted to lead his own expedition into France to try to remedy the dire situation in Aquitaine.

A year after Gaunt had relinquished his Lieutenancy in Aquitaine, Poitou and Saintonge – the two most productive provinces in the region – fell to Bertrand du Guesclin.[19] On 17 July 1373 Gaunt crossed the Channel with a force of 6,000 men at arms and archers, together with Henry Percy, the Earl of Northumberland, and followed by the Duke of Brittany. On landing at Calais, the army split into two columns and marched through France, taking separate parallel routes south, then reunited on the Somme near to the town of Bray. The army rested near the River Avre where John of Gaunt wrote a furious letter to Charles V. He warned the French King, 'do not be surprised if I come now to injure you and your supporters and avenge the wrongs you have done to me'. Despite Gaunt's antagonism, Charles V continued the trope of avoiding pitched battle against the English on French soil. Gaunt could not persuade Charles to fight and much of his army was picked off by French raids as it marched 500 miles through the already barren countryside, from Calais to Bordeaux. As Gaunt's army moved closer to Aquitaine, the French tried to contain it at Moulins, where a small stone bridge formed the only crossing into Bordeaux. In a pincer move, Bertrand du Guesclin followed Gaunt into Moulins from the rear, the Duke of Burgundy directed his army towards Moulins from the south-east and the Duke of Anjou raced south from Paris with a large force, intending to enter the town from the north. As the French closed in, Gaunt desperately tried to push his army over the swelling river to avoid annihilation.

Finally, the English army safely crossed, but the wagon train filled with supplies was left sinking in the mud. The close encounter at Moulins prompted a truce: Charles V permitted the Duke of Anjou to discuss terms with John of Gaunt.[20] As part of traditional chivalric diplomacy, a truce was agreed until the following spring, to be followed by a battle on Easter Monday on land at the confluence of the rivers Garonne and Tarn. Having avoided battle during every English incursion since Poitiers, the French believed that this time they could defeat Gaunt on the field.

Respite from the hard march was needed. By December, the fatigued and dwindling English army lay in tatters. They had lost their armour

– thrown off to escape its weight – and they were thin, exhausted and many had been taken as prisoners or killed during French ambushes along the march to Bordeaux. When John of Gaunt and his army finally reached Bordeaux – many them on foot – they found the city devastated by famine and plague. Wealthy English landowners who had accompanied Gaunt on campaign were forced to grovel for scraps of food on the streets. In England, the campaign was thought to be running successfully, for in the opening of Parliament in November 1373 the Chancellor, Sir John Knyvet, referred to Gaunt's expedition: 'by their good and noble governance and feats of arms, great damage and destruction have been done to the enemies overseas'. It was not until January 1374 that the terrible gravitas of the situation was made known, when Gaunt's messenger arrived in Westminster. As Edward III came to terms with the failing campaign, Gaunt waited in Bordeaux for funding – desperately needed to gather an army that would be fit to fight in the spring.

Neither funding nor reinforcements arrived. The King did order money sent to Gaunt to pay the soldiers' wages, but his ministers never followed through – they claimed they did not know where to send it. With no resources coming in from England, John of Gaunt directed his intentions towards Castile, and travelled to Dax for a meeting with Charles of Navarre and Gaston Phoebus, the Count of Foix. He wanted to discuss passage to Castile through the Pyrenees. Whilst John of Gaunt was in talks at Dax, the Duke of Anjou was waiting for troops sent by Enrique Trastámara in Castile. Enrique was marshalling an army on the other side of the Pyrenees to aid Anjou in the forthcoming battle at the rivers. As the agreed time for battle approached, however, the promised Castilian army was not ready. Reliant on Castilian support to achieve a victory, the Duke of Anjou panicked and pulled out of the battle. John of Gaunt returned to Bordeaux, still with his mind set on an invasion of Castile with the promised support of the Count of Foix and the King of Navarre, and crucial funding from England. However, within a month the Count's support had waned, Charles of Navarre had reneged on his promise and no support had arrived from England. Forced to accept the failure of the campaign, Gaunt returned home.

The Duke of Lancaster returned to a country teetering on the brink of political breakdown. Threads had come loose from what was once a tightly woven infrastructure of monarchical power in England. The King was growing older and the Black Prince was incapable of managing the country. John of Gaunt was thrust into the position of being a leading authority in the realm, and was expected to deal with the fallout of a failed war and face emerging political unrest. The political tension that mounted in the first part of the 1370s manifested in what became known as the Good Parliament.

The Good Parliament of 1376 changed the course of English politics for a decade, shifting political power from the King and aristocracy in favour of the Commons. By spring 1376, Parliament had not sat for three years – the longest period of adjournment since the beginning of the century. A single roll of thirty-two membranes (vellum pages) survive as a record of the Good Parliament – more than for any other English Parliament of the period. There are also two chronicle accounts, the *Anonimalle Chronicle* – whose writer may have been present, or at least in Westminster, when the Good Parliament took place – and that of Thomas Walsingham.[21] Both accounts are generally in favour of the Commons, but Thomas Walsingham's is particularly partisan against John of Gaunt. Walsingham was a Benedictine monk from the monastery at St Albans who was clearly well-informed regarding the proceedings.[22]

By 1376, aged sixty-three, Edward III retreated further and further away from active participation in Parliament. For over ten years, the King had been embroiled in an affair with the Queen's lady in waiting, Alice Perrers. Alice was considerably younger than the King – and eight years younger than John of Gaunt. Edward III was besotted. Alice provoked the clergy and the nobility by conducting herself like a Queen, dressed in cloth of gold and dripping in the jewels that the doting King had gifted her – some of which had belonged to the late Philippa of Hainault.[23]

The Black Prince was sicker than ever, and primarily kept himself away from court politics, living at Kennington Palace in Vauxhall with Princess Joan and their son and heir, Richard. This left John of Gaunt the authority at court, acting as a go-between for the King and his Council. Ordinarily, any actions of the King, his Council and his immediate family would be raised in Parliament should they be cause for concern – the upcoming Parliament would prove no exception. The King's governance, once revered and celebrated, had become a liability and so, by 1376, tensions ran high in anticipation of what was expected to be a catalogue of grievances from the Commons.

The Commons – knights and burgesses – sat in a separate chamber from the Lords (the nobles and high clergy). On 28 April they gathered in the King's Chamber at Westminster Palace, in the presence of the King and of the Black Prince, who had come to the opening session before sailing back across the Thames to his palace, too sick to witness the full proceedings. Edward III – who had avoided calling Parliament for the previous three years but was now in desperate need of funds – soon made himself scarce. He was acutely aware of the bubbling tensions. Instead of facing the inevitable backlash over his actions and those of his councillors, he left John of Gaunt as his representative, as 'lieutenant of the King to hold Parliament'. In *Piers Plowman*, William Langland characterises John of Gaunt as 'the cat of the court', borne from the belief of many – following his actions during this very Parliament – that he was devious and not to be trusted. The Good Parliament would prove to be a test of his diplomacy as well as of his loyalty to Crown and family: with the King's interests at odds with the Commons', Gaunt would inevitably be making enemies.

After the opening session of Parliament, the Commons were reminded of their duty: to enhance the position of the realm in the face of continued war in France, or elsewhere. With the power to agree or withhold taxation, they had the final say over the continuation of the war effort. The Commons left for the Chapter House at Westminster

Abbey to conduct their discussions, and the lords and clergy vacated to the White Chamber. The King's taxation request was discussed for around ten days, and the outcome was not in his favour. The Commons concluded that Edward would not be in such financial difficulty as to need further funding for his campaigns had he not been so poorly advised. It was common practice in the Middle Ages for the blame for mismanagement of the realm to be directed towards the King's 'wicked advisors', resulting in baronial rebellions and uprisings, such as the attack on Piers Gaveston in the reign of Edward II. As the King was regarded as being divinely appointed, he escaped direct culpability. Any explicit attack on the King would leave a person open to a charge of treason, with dreadful penalties to follow. In 1376, this pattern continued, for the Commons targeted Edward III's close advisors, accusing them of deceit and corruption. In order to represent their views, they chose from amongst themselves the first ever Speaker of the House of Commons, someone well able to withstand scrutiny and pressures from the nobility. Peter de la Mare – the 'rat of renoun' in *Plowman* – was a knight of the shire for Hertfordshire and a steward of the Earl of March. For the next three months the 'rat of renoun' stood in staunch opposition to the 'cat of the court'.

The Commons made their way from the Chapter House at Westminster to the Palace, where the general assembly was to be held. When they arrived they were shocked to discover the ageing King nowhere to be seen, but in his place sat John of Gaunt. He spoke uneasily: 'Which of you has the task of setting out what you have decided among yourselves?' Peter de la Mare stepped forward to accuse some of the King's closest advisors of crimes against the Crown. Those named were William Latimer, the King's chamberlain; John Neville of Raby, the steward of the household; and Richard Lyons, Warden of the Mint – all were accused of deceit and fiddling the Crown's purse. The King's mistress, Alice Perrers, was also accused of stealing the shocking sum of almost £3,000. Peter de la Mare stated, 'It would be a great profit to the Kingdom to remove that lady from the King's company so that the King's treasure could be applied to the war'.[24]

The greatest charges were brought against the corrupt and expedient advisors, Latimer and Lyons. They were blamed for selling licences to merchants that allowed them to export wool without taking it first to Calais, the location of the Staple.[25][26] They were also accused of taking a cut of loans that had been arranged between the Crown and the Exchequer and of conspiring with the French, resulting in the loss of territory. The last accusation caused such a ruckus in Parliament that the accused, William Latimer, was challenged by a knight who had once owned part of the land that Latimer lost in France. This was the first time the Commons brought legal action against lords, who of course traditionally held more power and influence than they. This assertion of the people's rights was, for its time, radical.

Initially, John of Gaunt tried to co-operate with the Commons, adhering to their requests and grievances. He agreed to the imprisonment of Lyons and the stripping of land and title from Latimer, as well as the removal of Alice Perrers. After gentle persuasion by John of Gaunt, the King agreed to exile his mistress from Court following the Commons' inquest into her squandering of Crown funds. This – for a time – halted their long-term affair. It is unlikely that John of Gaunt approved of Alice Perrers and following her exile – in an attempt to permanently force her from the King's bed – he made a private arrangement for a senior courtier, William Windsor, to marry Alice.[27] The wedding took place later in the year but was made public only after the King's death. Despite ensuring the removal of the King's unpopular mistress, Gaunt was furious that the King's dirty laundry had been aired before Parliament. He argued for the preservation of royal dignity and freedom. In arguing for such dignity and freedom on behalf of his father, it is possible that Gaunt was also defending himself. In his account of the Good Parliament, Thomas Walsingham accuses John of Gaunt of moral hypocrisy, for despite the King's exile of Alice Perrers his own relationship with Katherine Swynford sailed on.

While John of Gaunt was becoming increasingly unpopular in his defence of the Crown, the Black Prince – from his sickbed – continued to command the admiration and love of the people. He had little

involvement in the Good Parliament, but made a personal effort to see
that Alice Perrers was removed from the King's side. Once the model
of an uxorious King, Walsingham describes a man in old age 'drawn
downward with lechery and other sins'. During Parliamentary proceedings, the Black Prince had Alice privately investigated, suspecting that
she was guilty of witchcraft with the help of an 'evil magician dedicated
to evil doing'. After the Prince discovered that Alice employed a physician, the accusation spiralled and she was accused of initiating her
affair with the King with the help of a necromancer.[28] Alice's 'magician'
was in fact a practising physician from the Order of Preachers – now
the Dominican Order. Following the accusation, John of Gaunt
dispatched two knights to fetch the physician from Pallenswick, Alice
Perrers' estate near London. He was arrested and brought before Gaunt
who transferred the man into the care of the Archbishop of Canterbury,
where he narrowly avoided being burned at the stake for heresy. The
physician was forced to answer accusations that he 'made wax effigies
of the King and Alice' and used juices of magical herbs and words of
incantation to enable Alice to get whatever she wanted from the King.
After Perrers was informed that her physician had been arrested,
Walsingham describes her to 'be very afraid and her face fell'.

Alice Perrers, a 'shameless, impudent harlot' of 'low birth' had
significant influence over the King.[29] She was not a member of the
nobility; she came from a family of goldsmiths and was representative
of the body of merchant classes that had infiltrated court and
Parliament. John of Gaunt heavily resented the growing influence of
characters like Alice. She had risen in power, but so had the Commons
who opposed her. To the Duke of Lancaster, they were the same entity
that threatened the authority, autonomy and sanctity of the Crown,
which he sought to defend.

On 8 June 1376, in the middle of Parliamentary proceedings, John
of Gaunt was faced with a deep personal loss, on top of the strenuous
inquisitions and demands of the Commons. The Black Prince – 'the
flower of chivalry' – passed away at Westminster Palace. He had finally
lost his battle with the illness that had plagued him over the previous

eight years. It is uncertain exactly what killed him; he was described by Thomas Walsingham as having a 'bloody flux', which left him weak and often drifting in and out of consciousness.[30] It has been supposed that he was afflicted with dysentery, contracted whilst in Spain at around the time of the Battle of Nájera, for the illness was rife amongst the army on that campaign. However, this is unlikely. Death by dysentery comes fast and agonisingly, whereas the Black Prince suffered for years before his final decline. It is possible a form of cancer was the real cause.[31] The King was grief-stricken at the loss of his eldest son and heir, and left for his countryside castle at Havering, whilst John of Gaunt continued to represent him at the Good Parliament.

The Black Prince's death devastated John of Gaunt. They had lived together, fought together, and Gaunt had been trained in war, chivalry and duty by him – they were quite literally brothers in arms. The Prince had been the most influential figure in his life and Gaunt dearly loved and respected him. This was made evident when he took on the enormous task of trying to repair the situation in Aquitaine in 1370. John of Gaunt always came to his brother's aid, but faced with his death amid a precarious political period, he was left little time or space to mourn.

Despite the death of the Prince, John of Gaunt continued with his role in Parliament, provoking further suspicion regarding his intentions for the future of the realm. Only weeks after the Prince's death, his son and heir Richard was brought before Parliament, after the Commons requested that he be endowed with the title Prince of Wales. This was a clear stab at John of Gaunt, whom they suspected had designs on the Crown himself. The distrust was unfounded. John was unbendingly loyal to his brother, his family and the Crown – he would not compromise his honour, and there is no hard evidence that he ever considered trying to subvert the line of succession. At the Black Prince's bedside he swore to his brother that he would oversee Richard's ascent to the throne.

After over three months of proceedings, new councillors were appointed and the Good Parliament finally broke up on 10 July. The

Commons held a feast to celebrate the end of Parliament and the ousting of corrupt court officials. The younger sons of the King respectfully attended; however, John of Gaunt, notably, did not, confining himself to the Savoy.[32] Perhaps this was out of spite, arrogance and rage that the Commons had prevailed; however, John of Gaunt had also just lost his brother, whilst managing the most politically fraught Parliament of the reign of Edward III. It is more likely that he suffered emotional exhaustion, frustration and immense grief.

The Commons dispersed, feeling safe in the knowledge that their requests had been upheld and a better future lay in store for the remaining years of Edward III's reign. However, over the next two months, John of Gaunt developed a bitter animosity towards the decisions implemented at the Good Parliament and began to undo all that it had achieved.

In November 1376, the King took a turn for the worse, possibly suffering a minor stroke. To the horror of the Commons Alice Perrers was restored to his bedside: John of Gaunt had revoked her banishment. Alice returned to the King – according to a furious Thomas Walsingham – 'as a dog to its vomit' and the Speaker of the Commons, Peter de la Mare, was imprisoned in the cold, dark cells of Nottingham Castle. He had been arrested on Gaunt's orders, probably to prevent him protesting as Gaunt set about undoing the actions of the Good Parliament.

De la Mare's employer, the Earl of March, was also removed from his post as Marshal of England, to be replaced by Henry Percy, the future Earl of Northumberland.

In under six months, John of Gaunt began to unravel the actions of the Good Parliament, with the intention of undermining the Commons and restoring dignity and freedom to the Crown. Thomas Walsingham stated that he was 'under pretence of responsibility which he bore for the realm'.[33] However, Gaunt was under no pretence; he was the only member of the royal family who was truly able to reinvigorate the authority of the monarchy – but the cost was to his personal reputation and the liberty of the Commons.

During this time, John of Gaunt's standing went from bad to worse in the court of public opinion. His actions over the previous four years had a cumulative effect. In London he grew increasingly unpopular, yet within the Duchy of Lancaster he continued to protect the interests of the people.[34][35] By the end of a politically fraught year, Gaunt's projection of Crown authority against the revolutionary free will of the Commons resulted in what would be an explosive outcome.

In the New Year, another Parliament was held, and this time John of Gaunt's official, Sir Thomas Hungerford, was appointed Speaker. Gaunt was accused of 'packing' the Commons with his loyal supporters, replacing those who sat the previous year. However, there is no evidence of an obviously pro-Lancaster Parliament; there may have been even more Lancastrian retainers present in the Good Parliament.[36] A poll tax was implemented by this Parliament and, in celebration of the King's jubilee, a general pardon was extended to those who had committed criminal offences.

The only person in the realm excluded from the pardon was William Wykeham, Bishop of Winchester and Chancellor of England.[37] After the Good Parliament, William Wykeham was appointed to the Royal Council and given the post of chancellor to replace the impeached Lord Latimer. However, as part of John of Gaunt's reversals, he was soon charged with financial mismanagement and relieved of his position: the post was returned to Latimer. This chain of events chipped away at the Church's good feeling towards John of Gaunt and infuriated Wykeham's fellow bishops.

The feud was catalysed after the Bishop of London brought a priest called John Wycliffe to trial for heresy. Wycliffe was an Oxford theologian whose reformist sermons were attracting growing interest across England. Wycliffe attacked Church wealth, denied the doctrine of transubstantiation – the transformation of bread and wine to the body and blood of Christ during the Eucharist – and promoted the idea that the Bible should be translated into English from Latin. The Lollards – the name deriving from the Dutch word *lollaert*, 'to mutter' – were the religious group that emerged under Wycliffe. Their style of worship was based on reading scripture and they too would be accused of heresy for denying Catholic doctrine. The Lollards propagated Wycliffe's controversial views and, by 1377, he had gained popularity and John of Gaunt's patronage. In the early 1370s, Gaunt acquired a reputation for supporting Lollards, probably out of mutual concern over clerical wealth. Emotive rhetoric condemned Wycliffe and his supporters as dangerous 'heretics' in the medieval Christian world. Wycliffe – known to contemporaries (even critics) as the 'Flower of Oxford', and to posterity as the 'morning star of the Reformation' – paved the way for the religious reform that was to turn the world upside down in the sixteenth century.

A crowd gathered outside St Paul's Cathedral in the City of London on 19 February 1377 to witness the trial of John Wycliffe before an assembly of bishops. He was charged with speaking against Church endowments. The priest had been brought to trial by William Courtenay, Bishop of London, for two reasons: he wished to make an example of Wycliffe and his Lollard views, and to attack John of Gaunt, Wycliffe's patron. It is unclear exactly what John of Gaunt's motivations were in his open support of Wycliffe. He had always displayed conventional piety: charity for the poor, funding schools, colleges and hospitals, bequeathing land and various expensive and ornamental furnishings to a variety of religious houses, including St Paul's.[38] [39] [40] He traditionally patronised the Carmelites, an Order which prioritised careful contemplation and simple piety and provided all of his confessors.[41] John of Gaunt was not a religious reformer, but he did sympathise with the humble ranks of clergy and made gifts to various churches in need.[42] However, in the 1370s, he developed a reputation for anticlericalism. This was largely political. Gaunt disliked the wealth, power and influence the clergy had over the Crown and government; through his patronage of Wycliffe, he likely sought to mitigate this power. Yet the chronicler Henry Knighton offers another perspective: 'he believed them [Lollards] to be holy, because of their appealing speech and appearance, but he was deceived as were many others'. As a monk in Leicester – a Lancastrian town – Knighton's reading would inevitably be a generous one. Lollardy was, for a time, popular in Leicester and even Knighton's own Abbot, Philip Repingdon, was an enthusiastic follower of Wycliffe until the 1380s when Wycliffe came under investigation for heresy. By 1382, Gaunt had also rejected Lollard views – thus avoiding being labelled a heretic – and returned to a conventional form of piety in his support of the Carmelite Order. It appears that his temporary interest in Lollardy was largely political and Wycliffe's doctrine was too radical for Gaunt who, in the end, upheld orthodox worship.

However, in February 1377, John of Gaunt was prepared to fight Bishop Courtenay and summoned four doctors of divinity to defend Wycliffe against the attacks of the clerical court gathered at St Paul's. Gaunt also installed the Marshal, Henry Percy, to oversee the proceedings and maintain order amongst the crowd clamouring to witness the action. As the trial began Henry Percy advised Wycliffe to sit down, for 'there were many questions to be answered, he would need a soft seat'.[43] The Bishop of London objected, demanding the priest remain standing. As an argument broke out, John of Gaunt furiously stormed into the Lady Chapel of St Paul's Cathedral with an armed following. Before the shocked convocation of clergymen, he threatened to drag Bishop Courtenay outside by his hair.[44]

Wycliffe managed to escape further questioning but John of Gaunt's threat against the Bishop of London proved incendiary in the City. Following the conflict with Bishop Courtenay in Saint Paul's, John of Gaunt dined with Henry Percy on fresh oysters in the City. As they ate, Gaunt received news that angry rebels were seeking him out at that very moment, threatening to kill him. He apparently jumped up so fast he banged his shins on the table, before they both made a quick getaway by boat, down the Thames to Kennington, where they sought refuge with Princess Joan.

The situation escalated. In a small-scale but violent rebellion, angry Londoners attacked Gaunt's men, besieged the Savoy and hung his arms reversed, the sign of a traitor. Gaunt's arms were also reversed at St Paul's Cathedral, the resting place of Blanche. And a new rumour circulated through the City, possibly begun by the slighted William Wykeham: that Gaunt was not the true-born son of Edward III, but rather the offspring of a Flemish butcher, who had been snuck into the birthing room in a switch for a stillborn girl.[45] John of Gaunt was warned in a letter from Maud (the former maid of his daughter, Philippa) that he was being maliciously slandered by 'various friars and preachers'.[46] This new accusation represented a deeply personal attack, for it brought into question the legitimacy of the very royal heritage that defined him. In order to avoid anarchy, Bishop Courtenay tried to calm the angry mob as John of Gaunt – furious with the Londoners for attacking his property, his men and his honour – was soothed by his sister-in-law. Princess Joan successfully moderated the situation and persuaded Gaunt to take the moral high ground, rather than seek revenge.

The Good Parliament precipitated years of tension and animosity between John of Gaunt on the one hand and the Commons and the people of London on the other. Under the pressure of a political revolution, Gaunt tried to salvage the reputation, rights and privileges the royal family was accustomed to. He wanted the royal family to be respected and loved by the people – whose rightful place he considered to be far beneath them – and to protect his nephew's traditional rights as future King.

John of Gaunt never sought to disallow the Commons a voice; in fact he endeavoured to hear their pleas. However, he would not entertain the notion that someone could rise so far above their birth station as to impose their will upon a King. Despite the actions of Latimer and Lyons and the corrupt coterie that circled King Edward, John of Gaunt chose to pardon them, in order to rehabilitate royal authority. Alice Perrers, however, was a compromise. Initially, Gaunt attempted to remove the King's mistress for good, through his pact with William Windsor. But, eternally loyal to his father, Gaunt complied with his dying wish for Alice's return, again to the detriment of his reputation.

With the animosity between the City and John of Gaunt still fresh, a speaker on behalf of the Londoners sought an audience with ten-year-old Prince Richard at Kennington Palace, where he was living with his mother. They asked him to assure them that, in his kingship, he would 'defend their liberties'. Richard was beloved by the people – he was a prince they believed would make a good King. With the Black Prince dead, the Duke of Lancaster was Richard's leading advisor and protector. In a gesture of goodwill and hope for a peaceful future, John of Gaunt also came to see his nephew at Kennington. On his knees he requested that Richard pardon the citizens for their crimes against him. In an effort to control a situation spiralling out of control, Peter de la Mare was freed and William Wykeham restored. John of Gaunt had made enemies, but he ensured that Richard's reputation remained golden and that, as Edward III became weaker, the people were ultimately loyal to their future ruler.

John of Gaunt's loyalty to his family, to the dying request of the Black Prince and to the authority of the Crown meant sacrificing his reputation with the people. His actions at what became known as the Bad Parliament, however clumsy, or explicable, were never forgiven or forgotten. He was able to enhance the love, respect and security of his nephew Richard among the people, but he could never redeem himself.

SEVEN

ENEMY OF THE PEOPLE

'Let's purge this choler without letting blood.
This we prescribe, though no physician.
Deep malice makes too deep incision.
Forget, forgive; conclude and be agreed.
Our doctors say this is no month to bleed.–
Good uncle, let this end where it begun'.

William Shakespeare, *Richard II*, Act I, Scene I

ALICE PERRERS WAS DRESSED IN ERMINE AND DRIPPING IN new jewels as she sat beside the dying King. Edward III was now confined to his bed at his palace in Sheen, quietly deteriorating, away from the crowded court and the demands and politics of Westminster. In his final days, Alice Perrers was again his dearest companion. Thomas Walsingham paints a cold picture of Alice as unscrupulous and greedy: an ambitious mistress with many enemies. He accuses her of peeling precious rings from Edward's frail fingers as he gasped his last breath before escaping, laden with stolen riches, leaving just a single priest to console the dying King. It is not known exactly who was with Edward III in his final moments, but it is most likely that his three surviving sons – John of Gaunt, Edmund of Langley and Thomas of Woodstock – were present as the King received the last rites.[1] On 21

June 1377, in the fifty-first year of his reign, the sun began to set in the sky and King Edward III finally passed away, suffering what was likely to have been a fatal stroke. The King's body was covered in a shroud and remained within a black-draped chamber at Sheen, while elaborate funeral arrangements were made. Nearly two weeks later, an enormous procession left the palace, the King's coffin at its centre.

Onlookers in London could see the horizon flickering with firelight as 400 torch-bearers walked solemnly beside the coffin as it was carried into London – through Wandsworth, Southwark, across London Bridge – finally resting at St Paul's Cathedral. The procession was enormous. Over 1,000 participants, including the King's entire household, followed the coffin through London, dressed in mourning, and thousands more lined the streets to lament the death of the warrior King.

When the coffin reached St Paul's, it was set carefully on a platform at the heart of the cathedral, so mourners and clergy could pray and perform mass: a ceremony which went on throughout the night. At dawn, people began to line to the streets again, from St Paul's to Westminster, in part to publicly mourn the King, but also to receive the generous alms that were dispensed as part of the funeral procession as it passed. It was here that John of Gaunt joined the procession with his brothers, accompanying their father's body to its final resting place, Westminster Abbey. The King lay in state at the abbey for one night, and the following day he was interred, resting peacefully amongst the Kings who came before him and beside his dutiful and beloved Queen, Philippa.

The solemn spectacle of the King's funeral was followed soon after by another deeply sacred but celebratory event – a coronation. In deep mourning for his beloved father, John of Gaunt was hurled into the enormous amount of administration required for Richard's crowning. With rumour and suspicion circling around his loyalty to the young King, Gaunt would crucially need to place himself at the forefront of proceedings as a staunch supporter. He even ensured that Richard's coronation proceedings were officially documented in the Close Roll – an official chancery record.[2]

A week before Richard's coronation, John of Gaunt sat in the White Hall of Westminster Palace, near to the King's chapel, dealing with the business necessary to ensure the smooth running of the day's events. One of Gaunt's many titles was Earl of Leicester, and as such he claimed the office of Steward of England; as the Duke of Lancaster he was to hold the King's sword, 'Curtana', during the procession and ceremony, and finally, as Earl of Lincoln, he would perform the task of carving meat for the new King at the feast following the coronation.[3] John of Gaunt had an irreplaceable role in the ceremony, that was dutifully fulfilled.

By 16 July, the day of Richard's coronation, the City was heaving with visitors who had flocked into London to witness the momentous occasion: this was the first coronation in almost fifty years. With an influx of people, crime levels rose and visitors reported being attacked and mugged.[4] The stiflingly hot, dangerous and busy streets were an unpleasant environment to be in, but nevertheless buzzed with festivity.

Celebrations were stretched over two days in order to accommodate the necessary formalities. The day before his coronation, Richard processed through the streets from the Tower of London to Westminster Palace, accompanied by an entourage made up of German mercenaries, noblemen from Gascony and England, and knights dressed in white robes. All of this was to demonstrate the force that Richard – although only ten years old – held at his command. They followed the traditional processional route through Cheapside, Fleet Street and along the Strand, passing elaborate spectacles in each vicinity. In Cheapside, the conduit flowed with wine, and near to Fleet Street, in the turrets of a mock-up castle, girls waited to shower the new King with tiny gilt scrolls and offer wine as he passed by. Richard was at the back of the train, enjoying – and possibly overwhelmed by – the lavish attention cast upon him. At the front, cutting his way through the throngs of eager spectators, was John of Gaunt, whose job it was to make a path for the royal train. However spectacular, opulent and exciting the preceding events were, the coronation itself was even more so. A deeply sacred and momentous occasion, it was steeped in centuries of tradition, following the coronation of Kings since William the Conqueror on Christmas Day in 1066.

On the day of the coronation, the procession continued from Westminster Palace – where it had paused the night before – a short distance from Westminster Abbey. On a dais at the centre of the abbey, the throne of England was placed for Richard to take up his role as King. John of Gaunt carried Curtana aloft, at the forefront of the procession. Otherwise known as 'the sword of mercy', it played a symbolic role in the coronation of English Kings, to demonstrate the monarch's power and presence. Gaunt would never hold this sword as King, and this act was a direct and pertinent response to those who accused him – publicly and in secret – of traitorous designs on the throne; during the course of the ceremony he would present the sword to Richard before the entire congregation.

On his entrance into the abbey, Richard was led to the altar and, on his knees, swore on the sacrament to uphold the laws and customs of his ancestors, to protect the Church and clergy, and to do justice and uphold the laws of the people. After prayer, the consecration ceremony began: the most important and sacred part of a coronation. Screened from view by cloth of gold, the young King's shirt was removed and he was touched on the hands, chest, shoulders and head with holy oil – the means to officially anoint him before God. The young King of England was then transported to the celebratory feast by his tutor, Simon Burley: in the excitement he lost a shoe.[5] Exhausted from the pressure, the attention and the festivities, Richard had to be carried to bed on the first night of his official kingship by his loyal tutor. John of Gaunt had faithfully and respectfully buried his father and fulfilled his oath to his brother – he had overseen Richard's peaceful succession.

It was around this time that Gaunt became particularly public about his relationship with Katherine Swynford, who had recently given birth to their third child, Thomas. He was frequently spending time with her at Kenilworth Castle, rather than with his wife. The public and liberal relationship that Gaunt and Katherine enjoyed after 1377 was due to Gaunt's shift in position after the death of Edward III. He was the uncle of the King, the most powerful noble in the country, a Prince, and even a King himself; he was powerful enough to conduct the affair without fearing the consequences.

Katherine accompanied John of Gaunt that summer as he toured his extensive Duchy lands – the towns and villages where he was most at ease and felt confident in the love of the people. According to later local folklore, John of Gaunt went out riding one day, from Market Bosworth to Leicester, with just one servant for company.[6] He passed through the parish of Rathby where villagers were playing sports in the fields. Intrigued by their activity, and as a lover of sport, he went to join them, asking their reason for celebration. The villagers answered that it was the end of meadow mowing day; an ancient tradition practised in unison at the same time of year. Happy to see people enjoying themselves on his lands, he briefly joined them in their sports, before asking them to come to Leicester Castle, where he would grant them a gift of livestock or land. Gaunt promised to seal his grant in a service performed at St Mary's Church in Leicester, with the sermon dedicated to the hospital founded by his late father-in-law, Henry, Duke of Lancaster. The villagers could not believe their luck and around fifteen took up the generous offer.

John of Gaunt was in Leicester around this time, seeing to the development of the town's defences. He invested in the security of the town – as his Lancastrian predecessors did before him – and spent considerable time at the castle, so much so that he developed the kitchens and wine cellars in order to provide for his extensive retinue.[7] However, Leicester was not the jewel in John of Gaunt's crown. Over the summer, he was eager to visit Kenilworth Castle, his newest and most elaborate building project, overseen by Henry Yevele, his favourite architect. However, whilst Gaunt was absent from court, the new royal infrastructure was being sorely tested.

On 29 June, a force of French and Castilian ships sailed into Rye and destroyed the port and the town, leaving it in ashes. They subsequently attacked the west coast, hitting Dartmouth, Plymouth, Weymouth and

Rottingdean with a mighty force. Their fleet briefly sailed back to Harfleur, before launching another offensive, attacking Poole, Southampton and the Kentish coast; they even extracted a lucrative ransom from the people of the Isle of Wight. Whilst Edward III had been incapacitated and the nobility and Commons had been fighting amongst themselves around the time of the Good Parliament, the French had been preparing to resume war, with the intention of clawing back territory lost to the English crown. The French carefully strengthened their alliance with Castile, gaining the support of the powerful Spanish navy. They also spent considerable time and money building and repairing their own naval force, previously defeated by Edward III. The English, meanwhile, had little to spend on their own fleet, which now amounted to a mere five usable warships: poor defence against the fifty French vessels now careering around the coastline. The French seemed unstoppable, even taking the major defensive forts of Calais in a dual land and sea attack. They retreated from the main garrison, according to chronicle accounts, only due to the marshy ground, perilous for an army to cross.

Gaunt's youngest brother Thomas of Woodstock, now Earl of Buckingham, was sent to personally manage the defence of the Devon coast, a principal French target. As defensive measures were put in place along the south coast by Thomas of Woodstock, John of Gaunt remained in the north touring his lands. This led to criticism from Thomas Walsingham for not defending his coastal property, Pevensey Castle in Sussex. The chronicler accused the Duke of ignoring the pleas of his men to protect the castle, instead enjoying himself in the north, 'sporting and hunting'.[8] Contrary to Walsingham's claims, evidence suggests that John of Gaunt maintained Pevensey Castle as well as all his ducal estates – he looked after his property and invested in its upkeep. In 1381, Gaunt appointed William de Fiennes and William de Battison to protect Pevensey in the event of a hostile incursion following the Peasants' Revolt.[9] It seems unlikely that Gaunt would treat the threat of French invasion any differently.

*   *   *

Lords and Commons gathered at Westminster in October 1377 for the autumn Parliament, where proceedings were opened 'as if it were a sermon' by Archbishop Simon Sudbury, who implored the Members to 'rejoice' in the young King's ascension to the throne.[10] Before matters of the realm were brought to Parliament's attention, John of Gaunt publicly addressed the enduring rumour regarding his desire for the throne. He 'rose in Parliament and kneeling before our said Lord the King requested most humbly that he listen to him a while, concerning an important matter'.[11] John of Gaunt had decided that now was the time and the forum in which to address formally the whispers that continued to circulate. He demanded that the ill-will against him stop, insisting on his loyalty to King and Crown. He pointed out that as a prince, great magnate and man of authority, position, and a good and loyal subject of the Crown, he had the right to seek justice and resolution against those who had traitorous intentions against him. Gaunt threatened 'if any man, of whatever estate or condition, were so bold as to accuse him of treason, or other disloyalty, or any other deed prejudicial to the Kingdom, he would be ready to defend himself by his body'. Before Richard II and Parliament, John of Gaunt made a spectacle of his plea, and the lords and prelates rose to their feet and eagerly applauded him; they called for the punishment of the Duke's accusers.

This display of honour was genuine but, nonetheless, suspicion endured. As Richard was ten years old, the natural course of action would be to appoint a regent until he came of age. Only one child had formerly succeeded to the throne since the Conquest – Henry III.[12] In that instance, William Marshal, 'the greatest knight', acted as regent for the young King. John of Gaunt, the natural and perhaps only choice of regent, was snubbed, probably to his disappointment and likely due to London's vociferous hatred of the Duke. It was decided that Richard II was capable of ruling and authenticating documents himself. He would be overseen by a series of councils, known as 'continuous councils'. Nine members were elected, some of whom had originally served the old King, but most of whom were closely associated with the Black Prince. Notably absent from the councils were all the King's uncles; they were instead given a general supervisory role.[13] The nine councillors – although in an esteemed position – were forbidden to use their position to better themselves by 'wardship, marriage, rent nor nothing else pertaining to the King'. Richard insisted that 'jurisdiction over which matters shall belong to the King himself, and his uncles of Spain, Cambridge, and Buckingham'. This was a diplomatic solution during Richard's minority, which distinguished the authority of the King's uncles from that of the councillors making decisions on the young King's behalf. The continual council was a fresh initiative. Its members represented the orders of landed society: a combination of prelates, earls, barons and knights. The precedent for this structure had come with the new council nominated during the Good Parliament.[14]

The pressing issue was the urgent action required to defend the country against the French. With little to spend on war, government looked to the Commons to aid the King in his first military challenge as a reigning monarch. The merchant oligarchs of London – essential for their financial clout – gave a generous grant to the Crown as a show of goodwill to the new King, but their funding came with terms attached. The money was to be spent on war and security alone and, to ensure this, two members of the mercantile elite in London were to be appointed treasurers: John Philipot and William Walworth.

Despite the goodwill towards Richard II, the Commons made a threat regarding the abuse of royal power. As part of proceedings, fourteen items from the common petitions – a statement of grievance and request for reform – were presented before Parliament, taken verbatim from those of 1311, in Edward II's reign. The Ordinances of 1311 were a series of regulations imposed on the King by the nobility and the clergy to restrict his overexertion of monarchical power.[15] Some of the clauses in the Ordinances evoked Magna Carta, including the clear stipulation that the Church's liberties must remain unimpaired. A generation later, in the 1377 Parliament, someone was keen to remind powerful royals that a price would be paid for overexerting their authority – this was likely directed at John of Gaunt.

Ignoring the warning, Gaunt began to put his best men into prime positions within government, most notably Richard Lord Scrope, who shot into the position of Lord Chancellor, taking his place on the 'woolsack' for the rest of his career in Parliament. Gaunt also rewarded his retinue and friends well, and Geoffrey Chaucer was promoted into a role that suited his skills: custom control over the wool export in the port of London, where Chaucer was expected to 'write the rolls with his own hand'.[16] This was an important job, since wool continued to be England's greatest export. As the revenue from wool sales was the main source of income for the Crown, the controller had to be a trusted loyal servant. Since Chaucer was married to Katherine Swynford's sister, Philippa, he and Gaunt were more familiar with one another than ever. It was likely through Gaunt's influence and suggestion that Chaucer was employed in such a major administrative role. It was not only the Lancastrian affinity who benefitted during Richard's minority. John of Gaunt himself was on the receiving end of a series of royal grants, including the ratification of the town of Bergerac along with its castle. Richard's support of his uncle allowed Gaunt to act as he pleased, particularly with his mistress. It was certainly at the request of John of Gaunt, within weeks of Richard's ascension, that Katherine was granted two wealthy manor estates for life, in exchange for Gaunt's county of Richmond.[17] This generous gift – at the cost of his own property – is testament to Gaunt's respect and love for Katherine Swynford in the late 1370s.

Six years after John of Gaunt assumed the title of King of Castile and Leon, he was yet to make this a reality and claim his crown on Spanish soil. Despite his personal ambition, Gaunt's close domestic involvement in the early years of his nephew's kingship prevented him making a move overseas. During Richard's minority, Gaunt was forced to put his Spanish ambitions on hold and focus his diplomatic and military efforts elsewhere: on the Scottish borderlands, where imminent threats required urgent attention. Early in Richard's reign, Sir Thomas Musgrove, the keeper of Berwick-upon-Tweed, led a raiding party into Scotland, whereupon he was attacked by a party of Scots, taken prisoner and held to ransom.

The relationship between England and Scotland remained fractious. Northumberland was harried by the Scots at any opportunity and attacks on the border came frequently. The Scots were a source of continual frustration for Edward III, who – like his predecessors – treated them harshly. With the ascension of a new, young King, the Scots saw the chance to push at the boundaries of English power. The fragile situation required skilled diplomacy, from someone of significant status. With his experience in Scotland and superior position in England, John of Gaunt was the natural choice to conduct serious negotiations with the Scottish nobility. He was dispatched with the order to arrange a march day (a formal meeting) with the Scottish leaders and come to terms. In the New Year, Gaunt met with the Earl of Carrick – the son of the Scottish King, Robert II – and embarked on the first of a long series of negotiations that would occupy him for years to come.

With Scottish talks underway, plans to regain territory lost in France were being put into action. In the summer of 1378, John of Gaunt led a fleet to the Breton port of Saint-Malo, a high granite-walled town at the mouth of the River Rance in Brittany, held by the French and surrounded by the sea on either side. The intention was to seize the town and leave behind a garrison, as a stronghold to reoccupy territory that had, until recently, belonged to England. However, the French were on high alert, aware of the English threat. They had fortified the town well and were led by the exemplary commander Bertrand du Guesclin.

Although siege engines surrounded the walls of Saint-Malo, threatening total destruction, the English army was continuously beaten back by the French defenders as Gaunt ordered waves of attacks; coaxing the French into open combat had never previously worked. The only option was to continue to bombard the town with siege engines whilst, over a month, carefully excavating under the walls – a tactic Gaunt had employed at Limoges. When the French defenders succeeded in collapsing his mine before it could be blown to create a breach, the siege was doomed. The humiliated John of Gaunt was forced to sail his army back to England.

On his return from Saint-Malo, in a further sting to his reputation, Gaunt was faced with the news that John Philipot – the merchant in charge of the administration of Richard's war funds – had captured a notorious Scots pirate ship, a small but significant victory against Scottish belligerence. John of Gaunt had little time to stew over the military successes of others, for in London another testing political situation emerged, described by a furious Thomas Walsingham as 'the pollution of Westminster Abbey'.

Back in 1367, at the Battle of Nájera, two knights, Robert Hawley and John Shakwell, had captured a Spanish grandee, the Count of Denia. As a reward, the Black Prince agreed that the knights could keep the Count as their prisoner with the prospect of a lucrative ransom. The Count managed to persuade all concerned that his son, Alfonso, should take his place as captive, and he promised the enormous ransom would be paid. Hawley and Shakwell returned to England with their prisoner. In 1371, they came to the attention of Crown officials, who now wished to repatriate the Count of Denia's son, still held in London as the ransom money remained outstanding.[18]

The Count was a powerful figure in Castile, and the return of his son may have been suggested by John of Gaunt in order to create some good faith, or possibly because an alliance with the Count of Denia would be an asset to any future campaign there. However, Hawley and Shakwell were not willing to give Alfonso up – holding out for the full ransom. They tried to hide him, but were caught and imprisoned in the Tower of London. Both men managed to escape and fled to Westminster Abbey where they sought sanctuary. The Royal Council secretly sent fifty men to the abbey, led by Sir Alan Buxhill and Sir Ralph Ferrers, to oust the runaways and drag them back to the Tower. In his chronicle, Thomas Walsingham describes Buxhill and Ferrers as 'men worse than atheists' for the 'agents of Satan ... burst into a church ... polluting that very temple of God'. As Hawley and Shakwell – unarmed – tried to escape, a fight broke out. According to Walsingham, the King's men held all clergy present at the points of their swords as they surrounded Robert Hawley. The interception turned into a brutal fight – Hawley was struck on the back of the head and killed instantly and one of the clergymen mortally wounded. The relationship between the Crown and London following the Good Parliament had remained fragile, and although John of Gaunt was not present during this dramatic showdown, he found himself in the midst of the furious argument that followed.

The clergy grouped together following the murder in the abbey and demanded vengeance. Simon Sudbury, the Archbishop of Canterbury, publicly announced that all involved in the sacrilege were to be excommunicated, with the exception of the King, Princess Joan and John of Gaunt. Bishop Courtenay – Gaunt's adversary – continued to proclaim the act of excommunication during worship at St Paul's, despite Richard II's requests that he desist; he also refused a royal summons to a council at Windsor. During this council, John of Gaunt was made aware of the situation and was incensed. Antagonised by Bishop Courtenay's refusal to adhere to the King's request and invitation, he threatened to ride to London and 'drag' the Bishop to Windsor. This once again filled Londoners with rage. The Duke called them 'rascals' and pushed for the October Parliament to be moved outside the capital to avoid further conflict. His wish was granted and Members of Parliament were forced to make the journey to Gloucester, where proceedings were held in the great hall of the Benedictine Abbey of St Peter's, Gloucester Cathedral, where Edward II was buried. The cathedral was close to the town and the Lords and Commons were forced to talk over the constant noise of ball sports and buskers outside.[19]

John of Gaunt took the opportunity to invite John Wycliffe to speak against the laws of sanctuary, stipulating that they cannot protect 'debtors'.[20] The Commons were nonetheless furious over the murders inside Westminster Abbey, offering the Abbot of Westminster support and empathy when he spoke up against the Crown. Coupled with new requests for further financial aid, it resulted in bitter tension. Speaker Sir James Pickering voiced the Commons' despair that Richard II needed more funds and scrutinised the Crown for improper expenditure, since the money given for the war effort was all gone, and yet the

King was still in debt. The Commons suspected John of Gaunt of fiddling with the allotted funds and misspending them; the Crown pointed out that John Philipot and William Walworth, the appointed treasurers, were the only ones with access to the funds.

Unsatisfied, the Commons continued to examine the situation, demanding that the accounts be laid out for a detailed assessment. The accusation was not taken lightly and Gaunt's temper in response to the Commons' suspicions was recorded: he branded his accusers as 'liars and gossips . . . back-biters, [who] resemble dogs who chew raw meat. For the said false back-biters thus do this when, with their evil words, they devour raw good and loyal people, who do not dare to protest at anything or adopt an angry countenance before the aforesaid good people.'[21] Following Gaunt's outburst, the situation was pacified. The Commons offered some financial aid, more Crown jewels were used as collateral for a loan and Walworth and Philipot were removed from their posts as treasurers.[22]

Amidst all of this, there was one issue that both sides could agree on: supporting the Pope in Rome, Urban VI, against the Pope in Avignon, during the Schism that polarised the Catholic Church in 1378. It was to rumble on into the following century. Pope Gregory XI returned to Rome in 1377 after almost seventy years of the Papacy being housed in Avignon. Upon his death, the Italians were eager to elect a new Pope who would support Rome as the Holy See. As a result, Urban VI – a loyal Roman – was elected as Pope, but he alienated many of the cardinals who originated from Avignon. In response to the Pope's rebuff, a faction of esteemed cardinals vacated Rome and returned to Avignon, having elected a new Pope from amongst themselves – Clement VII. This was significant as it gave the English a new and influential ally against the French, who supported Clement. Crucially, the Schism also furnished John of Gaunt with an opportunity to take the Kingdom of Castile, under the guise of a crusade in support of the Pope in Rome. Throughout the Gloucester Parliament, Gaunt was called 'King of Castile, Duke of Lancaster', when previously the titles had been the other way around.[23] The reversal was significant:

perhaps his Spanish ambitions were not far from his mind, or he now felt the need to assert regal authority in Parliament. Nonetheless, his persuasive diplomacy was once again required on the Scottish borders before he could implement any of those long-considered plans for a Castilian campaign. Intermittent aggression from the Scots convinced the King that military intervention in Scotland was sorely needed. In February 1379, John of Gaunt was appointed Lieutenant over the Marches towards Scotland. However, that spring, a turn of events in Castile grabbed his immediate attention.

In the town of Santo Domingo de la Calzada, in the northern Iberian Peninsula, Enrique Trastámara fell ill. The Castilian King had travelled to Santo Domingo to discuss an alliance with the slippery King Charles of Navarre. The meeting was a successful one, resulting in the Treaty of Briones. Enrique spent the week feasting and celebrating before he suddenly passed away. His dying wish was for his son, Juan, to be always loyal to France.

The death of Enrique Trastámara marked the start of a new phase of English interest in Castile. The succession of Enrique's son to the throne of Castile raised the prospect that John of Gaunt's kingship – which had lain dormant for seven years – could now be revived. Gaunt was eager to act. However, he had pledged to help Richard manage negotiations with the Scots. If he reneged on this duty he would be subject to a backlash in Parliament, and would certainly be denied the necessary support and funding to launch a Castilian campaign. Forced to remain in England, Gaunt focused on his greatest building project to date, Kenilworth Castle, which he forged as the centre of his displaced Castilian kingship.

The castle, in the town of Kenilworth in Warwickshire, was a small part of John of Gaunt's Lancastrian inheritance. A castle had stood at Kenilworth since the Normans and it had developed into a powerful fortification under King John, during the Barons' War. After John, Simon de Montfort held the castle and it was subsequently besieged during the Second Barons' War. Kenilworth finally made its way into Lancastrian hands through Edmund Crouchback and then Thomas of Lancaster, who built its first great hall. The castle had the makings of a perfect fortress and John of Gaunt intended to make it a palace fit for a King, even a rival to Westminster.

Prior to Richard's coronation, Gaunt had begun to invest in the renovation of Kenilworth, with work beginning in 1374. He developed the kitchens, creating a split kitchen in order to cater for large parties. It was twice the size of a regular aristocratic kitchen, complete with a bread oven and large cauldron. He also built a larder, buttery, pantry and scullery, and a storeroom to house precious plate. However, his great masterpiece was Thomas of Lancaster's great hall, which was extensively developed. The great hall was a projection of Gaunt's kingly status, the focal point of his development, boasting modern design, vast windows and expensive decoration. It was an impressive architectural feat, split into two levels; the undercroft below to store wine and ale, and the hall above. They were joined by a large staircase which led up to the hall from the keep. The undercroft had access to the outside of the castle through a small square portcullis, where a servant received incoming supplies to feed the Lancastrian retinue.

The great hall, ninety feet long, was accessed by a flight of stairs with an impressive carved frieze at the top. There were six window bays fitted with vast perpendicular glass windows stretching up towards the huge vaulted ceiling. The hall was enormous, kept warm by six carefully positioned and ornately carved fireplaces, with colourful tapestries hanging above – probably depicting hunting or Biblical scenes. The floor was colourfully tiled and there was a dais at the end – distinguished by elaborate floor tiles rather than a traditional raised platform – where John of Gaunt's long head table would preside over the rows below, warmed with further fireplaces behind. To the left and right of the dais sat a side room, taking up an entire bay window, which had its own private fireplace. Here Gaunt held private conversations and conducted various negotiations. As a diplomat and politician, it is unsurprising that he saw this as a necessary feature in his great hall.

After putting on a grand feast, John of Gaunt provided ample entertainment, hosting music and dancing; he considered this a priority at
Kenilworth, building a brand-new dance floor in the hall. There was a
private passageway behind the dais, leading to Gaunt's personal apart-
ments and to the tower. The tower was private and overlooked the lake
that surrounded the castle. A romantic setting, it was laced with tapestries, ornate furniture and jewels. Yet Gaunt was still expected to share
the garde robe (toilet) on the ground floor. It was in the tower that he
entertained private guests, most commonly Katherine Swynford.
Katherine usually stayed with Gaunt at Kenilworth whilst Constance
remained largely at Hertford or Tutbury Castle, far away from her
husband.

For John of Gaunt, Kenilworth Castle was an unbridled expression
of power, kingship and wealth. He even employed the same master
carpenter, William Wytherington, and carpenter, Henry Spencer, who
had worked on Windsor Castle. He paid acute attention to detail and
spared no expense on its construction; Gaunt even ordered vaulted
carvings in the ceiling of the pantry, a place no guest would ever visit.
The castle was not only a way to solidify the public perception of his
kingship; it was an expression of his personal creativity, for John of
Gaunt was an aesthete as well as a practical ducal overlord. He enjoyed
music, art and literature, and Kenilworth Castle was a vehicle where he
could exhibit them all. In 1379, Gaunt spent Christmas and New Year
at Kenilworth, despite the great hall still being under construction. It
was away from London, away from his enemies and away from Richard:
it was a palace in which, finally, he could be a King.

That year's festivities at Kenilworth ended when John of Gaunt was
forced to make the journey to Westminster, in pouring rain, to attend
Parliament and receive bad news about the state of the realm. Around
a quarter of a million pounds had been spent to secure the country's
defences, but there was little to show for it. A naval expedition under
the leadership of Sir John Arundel was wrecked off the Irish coast, and
it was rumoured that the cause was drunkenness. The tax that had
been implemented in 1379 had not raised enough funds to cover the

costs of running the country. The dismal weather pre-empted a dismal situation – the Crown was broke.

As rain pattered down outside Westminster, Parliament gathered inside the Painted Chamber to hear what the Lord Chancellor, Richard Scrope, had to say. The main concern continued to be the safety of the realm from foreign attack as well as the protection of English garrisons over the Channel. Scrope explained 'armed might [is needed] to safe guard the town and strong places in the March of Calais, the castle and the town of Brest and the castle and the town of Cherbourg'. He argued that 'it cannot be borne without your aid', imploring the Commons for further loans.[24] Adding to this, due to continual civil unrest in Flanders, there was no profit on the subsidy on wool. Speaker Sir John Gildesborough announced the Commons' disappointment and, this time, blamed Richard's elected advisors, the continual council. The decision was made to disband the council forged at Richard's ascension, for 'their greater ease and to relieve the King of their costs . . . our Lord the King is now of great discretion and handsome stature'.[25] Parliament believed that, at thirteen, Richard was by now old enough to rule the Kingdom himself. The Commons granted financial aid through another tax, on condition that the money was used only for an expedition to Brittany led by the Earl of Buckingham – Gaunt's youngest brother Thomas of Woodstock. Lord Scrope was ousted from his position as chancellor and replaced by the ill-fated Archbishop of Canterbury, Simon Sudbury. It was agreed that there would be no further rise in tax for at least eighteen months and Parliament disbanded, in the belief that perhaps, this time, the realm had sufficient resources to strive for a more positive future.

EIGHT

THE RISING

'When Adam delv'd and Eve span,
Who was then the gentleman?'

John Ball, 1381

THE RAIN BEAT HARD ON THE WINDOWS OF ST ANDREW'S
Priory as Lords and Commons poured into the hall for the opening of
another Parliament. Writs were dispatched in early December, ordering Members of Parliament to meet at Northampton. The choice of
location was unconventional, but it was necessary, given the tension
between John of Gaunt and Londoners that still lingered. The Lords
and Commons begrudgingly made the journey to the Cluniac Priory,
an important monastic house, but not the impressive and imposing
Westminster. After enduring the long journey through driving rain
and floods – weather representative of the last Parliament – the grum-
bling Lords and Commons assembled to hear what Lord Chancellor
Simon Sudbury had to say as he opened proceedings.

The news was bad; in fact, the situation was dire. The heavily relied-
on wool revenue no longer existed due to civil war in Flanders, seriously damaging a trade that had provided a safe income for England
for generations.[1] The wool trade was so crucial that it prompted the
lasting tradition of the Chancellor sitting on a woolsack in Parliament.

Sudbury glumly announced that the French continued to pose a threat, circling in the English Channel and intimidating coastal towns and villages. There was also civil unrest in Ireland and the Scots had once again attacked the northern borderlands – a situation John of Gaunt was currently trying to deal with. Yet again, the Crown was broke and Simon Sudbury was given the awkward task of not only declaring the gravity of the situation, but making a request for financial aid amounting to over £160,000.[2]

The Commons reluctantly agreed to grant £100,000, accrued by another tax on the people of the realm. This was set at three groats per person over the age of fifteen – three times the usual rate. It was targeted primarily at the labouring classes who, it was believed, were able to bear the brunt of the hike. Once it was decided that the clergy were expected to pay the remaining sum, the resolution was made to implement the new tax in the spring, leading to financial security by the summer.[3] With all in satisfactory agreement, proceedings moved on; however, the decision of November 1380 to economically cripple the poor was one of the worst political misjudgements of the Middle Ages. It would result in the largest rebellion the country would ever see.

John of Gaunt was not amongst the men who gathered together in Northampton. In September he was placed at the head of a border commission to forge a truce with Scotland.[4] In summer 1380, sailors from Newcastle upon Tyne and Hull set off from the coast to deter pirates who were active around the North Sea and threatened trading ships that worked out of Newcastle. Thomas Walsingham states that on their mission, the crew came across a Scottish ship which they commandeered. Provoked, the Scots retaliated, 'eager to take vengeance in their turn upon the Northumbrians' and attacked the borderlands. 'They entered our land with a large number of their savage race and attacked the people of Westmorland and Cumbria . . . it was said they went everywhere rampaging, everywhere slaughtering and consigning whatever they could to the flames'. The Earl of Northumberland, Henry Percy, was keen to stage an attack in response, but with no funds to support a campaign, let alone a war, John of Gaunt was sent to find a way around the situation. So whilst the Lords and Commons were gathering in wet Northampton, he was receiving Scottish delegates in Berwick-upon-Tweed, carefully managing the precarious Anglo-Scottish relationship to avoid further costly warfare. By the time the decision over the poll tax had been settled, he was on his way to Northampton, having successfully agreed a truce of thirteen months. Gaunt would naturally be expected to attend Parliament and was eager to make it there for a murder trial that was due to take place at the end of the proceedings.

On 25 August 1379, Janus Imperial was standing on the doorstep of his lodgings in Acon Lane in Cheapside when two men walked past and picked a fight. His men were with him and quickly retaliated. One of the antagonists – a man named John Algor, a mercer from a merchant guild – stamped on Imperial's feet and the other, John Kirkeby, stabbed Imperial twice in the head. This unsurprisingly proved fatal. But this was no ordinary street skirmish; it attracted the attention of the Crown and the assailants were quickly arrested by former mayor John Philipot. Imperial was a Genoese envoy and representative of the Doge of Genoa; he was in England under the protection of the Crown and his murder enraged John of Gaunt, who pushed hard for the charge of treason and the full punishment that went with it – a brutal traitor's execution. After deliberation in the January Parliament of 1380, the trial was set to take place during the later November Parliament. It is likely this is one of the main reasons that proceedings were to take place in Northampton: to avoid the backlash of Londoners enraged at the prosecution of two of their own men, especially on the orders of John of Gaunt.

The murder of Janus Imperial was the result of ongoing hostility between Gaunt and the people of London, who believed the Duke extended his authority well beyond his remit. Imperial's unfortunate fate was the result of a rumour that Gaunt, with Imperial's help, was seeking to move England's main trading port to Southampton. Such a move would spell catastrophe for London's merchant oligarchs, stripping them of their authority and wealth and therefore their influence at court. Yet, despite the apparent benefits to this arrangement for Gaunt, there is nothing to suggest this plan was actually in the making: it was all likely rumour and speculation.

In 1380 mercantile London was divided between two opposing factions. Mayor William Walworth was allied with former mayors Sir Nicolas Brembre and John Philipot in staunch support of the Wool Staple and opposition to the government-sold licences that allowed wool merchants to avoid paying tax. These licenses lined the Crown purse but cut out the merchant oligarchs of London in the process. Opposing them was John Northampton, a maverick who promoted the interests of the vulnerable, and radicalised the allocation of power in the City. He wanted the poor to have a say in who represented them in Parliament and to end mercantile corruption. John of Gaunt backed him in both aims, to their mutual benefit; Northampton needed powerful support against Brembre, and Gaunt needed an ally in the City against the merchant elite that had too much power over the Crown. The tension between Gaunt and the London merchants came to a head through the trial of John Algor and John Kirkeby.

In order to reach Northampton in time for the trial, John of Gaunt made a swift journey south from Scotland, stopping only briefly at his estates as he travelled. He finally reached Parliament during the last week of November and prepared to sit for the trial of the accused murderers, due to take place in early December. The first defendant called before the jury was John Algor. After originally testifying that the murder was the result of a coincidental argument between the men, Algor changed his testimony to admit that he and John Kirkeby hunted down Janus Imperial in the belief that he sought to destroy the wool merchants in London. Despite Philipot personally arresting both Algor and Kirkeby, this admission provided evidence of a potential coup – with Philipot at its head. John Algor was emphatic he had not killed Imperial, laying the blame at the feet of his accomplice, John Kirkeby – the classic cut-throat defence when two stand accused. Algor remained in prison but Kirkeby was charged with treason and condemned to the gruesome fate of being hung, drawn and quartered at Northampton. To John of Gaunt, justice was done and the Crown's authority endured.

As John Kirkeby's butchered body became a feast for crows in Northampton, Parliament rose and the Lords and Commons rode home to begin Christmas celebrations and rest after the arduous month of negotiation and politics. It was believed that the country would be restored and its borders strengthened with the new revenue from the poll tax: the future looked bright.

The Rising of 1381 was cataclysmic for England. It polarised towns and villages and exposed the divisive alliances that tore communities, even families, in two. There was no simple 'side', for men and women from various backgrounds and social classes banded together to advocate for change. For some it was a revel, an opportunity for anarchy, and for others it was a revolution. For some it was peaceful and, for others, exceptionally violent.

The year began with the first round of harsh tax collection, as initiated by Northampton's November Parliament. Bailiffs and sheriffs around the country were charged with the unrewarding task of extracting extraordinary sums from labourers. By March, the first wave of collection had not achieved the expected sum. The government still desperately needed income so a new treasurer was appointed – Robert Hales, Master of the Hospital of St John of Jerusalem, a military-religious order based in London. It was soon decided that tax collection would no longer be split between January and June, as previously agreed. The entirety would be taken in one crippling deduction, enacted by specially appointed tax collectors around the country. The people were under immense financial pressure, and when they began to avoid the tax collectors, the government dispatched commissioners of enquiry to extort funds by brutal interrogation and threats. With this aggressive strategy, it was not long before the collectors faced backlash and, by April, London sheriffs were refusing to conduct collections, in terror for their lives.

Despite the stirrings of trouble, the nobility continued its daily lives without change or marked concern. John of Gaunt spent a large part of early 1381 mustering an army, to be led by his brother Edmund of Langley, Earl of Cambridge, to aid the Portuguese against the Spanish in an ongoing Iberian war. Gaunt had previously floated the idea of a Portuguese alliance as a way of protecting the English coastline and Brittany, for the Portuguese would be in a position to block any French or Spanish warship from heading through the Straits of Morocco and up towards the English Channel. With the constant threat of attack from the French and Spanish, who had already spent Richard's reign intimidating the English coastline, an alliance with the Portuguese was of considerable benefit. If Castile could then be taken by Gaunt's forces, England would be in a powerful position. John of Gaunt soon mustered his military retainers, to 'serve the Duke in peace and war, and to go with him to war wherever he wishes suitably arrayed for war'. Their payment would be ten marks a year.[5]

This campaign was Gaunt's opportunity – sanctioned and funded by the Crown – to claim Castile with the support of the Portuguese; this alliance was crucial to his ambition. The military force assembled for his campaign accounted for a large part of the country's debt, as exposed by Archbishop Sudbury in the November Parliament. The labouring classes were essentially paying for John of Gaunt's pursuit of the Castilian throne. Gaunt was enormously invested in the Portuguese campaign, but despite his natural inclination to lead it himself, duty to King and country came first. As ships set sail for Portugal, John of Gaunt prepared for another trip to Scotland, to secure the truce that he had implemented the previous autumn.

In May 1381, John of Gaunt – having spent much of his time at the Savoy Palace gathering forces and orchestrating the administration of the Portuguese campaign– left for Edinburgh, unaware that this was the last time he would see his beloved London home.[6]

Various chroniclers describe the events that followed in colourful detail. Thomas Walsingham, Jean Froissart and Henry Knighton, as well as the Monk of Westminster, all depict a period of massive civil unrest and an attack on London by the common people. All concur that it was unprecedented and violent. The *Anonimalle Chronicle* has been considered the most accurate and detailed source for the Rising that took place in the summer of 1381, and it is possible that the chronicler was even witness to the events as part of the King's entourage.[7] Thomas Walsingham describes the start of the uprising as the labourers making an attempt to 'clamour for liberty . . . a conglomeration of plebeians that no one could remember seeing or hearing of the like' and only weeks after John of Gaunt's departure from the Savoy an uprising began in Brentwood, Essex, sparking what later became immortalised as the Peasants' Revolt.

John Bampton – a tax collector in Brentwood – fled for his life as the people of the town turned violent at his attempts to extort payment. The confrontation between John Bampton and the people of Brentwood snowballed and unrest now bubbled up in Kent. Soon, two vast rebel groups were making their way to London, united in fierce opposition to the brutal tax and those who inflicted it upon them – namely the closest advisors of the King, including the Duke of Lancaster.

'We may all be united together', articulated John Ball, a priest of minor orders and protagonist of the Rising, 'there be no villeins not gentleman . . . the Lords be no greater masters than we be'.[8] John Ball was described in the *Anonimalle Chronicle* as 'a chaplain of evil disposition', a type of prophet to the rebels, counselling them that they were equal to those who subjugated them. A band of 60,000 farmers, low order clergy such as parish priests, roofers, reeves, bailiffs, men and women formed a powerful army, collecting followers as they razed towns and villages to the ground, unless the people contributed to the cause. They threatened to kill lawyers, jurors and servants of the crown, and those they did catch met a bloody end. The rebels who emerged out of various parts of Kent gathered together at Dartford where they held counsel. They agreed that 'there were more Kings than one and that they would neither suffer nor have any King except King Richard'.[9] This was a direct reference to John of Gaunt and his assumption of the title King of Castile. The people resented Gaunt's foreign court, Spanish ambitions and, above all, his influence on the King. It was also still rumoured that Gaunt had designs on the throne of England. As a result, anyone found wearing Gaunt's livery was mercilessly attacked and their property destroyed.

The rebel groups from Essex and Kent now charged down the old London Road towards Rochester Castle, an imposing Norman edifice that guarded the River Medway. Rochester Castle had already endured one siege, during the Barons' War of 1215, when King John attacked the rebels garrisoned within. King John did everything he could to conquer the bastion, even blasting the south tower with fire fuelled by boiling pig fat. The siege ended only when the defenders were starved out. On 7 June, over 150 years later, rebels from Kent and Essex also attempted to lay siege to the fortress. By 1381 Rochester Castle was being used as a prison, held by the Constable, Sir John Newton.

The castle was as a prison should be – impenetrable. The rebels had rallied the Medway towns and streamed over the crumbling bridge to the foot of the castle gate. They lacked the sophisticated equipment needed for a siege – trebuchets or siege engines – yet coercion and threats proved enough for Sir John Newton to capitulate and open the gates. As the rebels streamed into the castle, they took Newton hostage and made for the dungeons. Their main objective was to release the prisoners, including a man called Robert Bellyng. This implies that the attack on Rochester was planned specifically to release Bellyng, who probably immediately joined the rebellion. After the attack on Rochester Castle, the Kent faction of rebels elected 'Watt Teghler' as their leader, 'indeed a tiler of houses, an ungracious patron'.[10] So the leading protagonists of the Rising emerged as Wat Tyler, the preacher John Ball and a rebel from Suffolk, Jack Straw.[11] The rebels now travelled towards London by way of the pilgrims' road to Canterbury, where they attempted to have the Archbishop of Canterbury re-elected – for 'he who is archbishop now is a traitor and will be beheaded for his iniquity'.[12] Unsuccessful in their attempt, they went on to London where, on the road, they encountered the King's mother, Princess Joan. Froissart recounts that the Princess was startled and, although they did not harm her, they treated her 'rudely'.

Kent and Essex rebels arrived at Blackheath, accompanied by various other supporters they had recruited along the way. From Blackheath the rebel force could see the Tower, where the King had taken refuge along with the terrified treasurer, Robert Hales, and the Archbishop of Canterbury, Simon Sudbury – both were wanted by the rebels.

Tyler chose the rebels' prisoner – Sir John Newton – to deliver their terms to the King at the Tower of London. They stipulated that it was their desire to 'save him and destroy the traitors to him and the Kingdom'. Richard agreed to hear their grievances at Blackheath the following day, the eve of Corpus Christi (on this year, 12 June), where the rebels – elated and hopeful for their meeting with the King – duly gathered, carrying the banners of St George. As promised, on the day of Corpus Christi, Richard embarked on a royal barge at the Tower and sailed towards Greenwich, where he could address the rebels from the safety of the river. It was a warm June day and the barge glided easily down the Thames, the breeze carrying a stench of smoke in the air. As they approached Blackheath, the scale of the rising became apparent. Thousands of armed rebels provided an intimidating spectacle. On one side of the river were 50,000 Kent rebels; on the other side, another 60,000 from Essex, all united under one cause.[13] Unprepared for such a massive confrontation, the King's councillors implored him to retreat. Shocked by the magnitude of the rebellion, the barge hastily turned about in the direction of the Tower. The rebel commons were aghast: they expected to parley with their King but instead they watched him run away. Richard was back safe in the Tower, but his rapid departure had added fuel to the fire. The march on London continued and thousands now descended on the City, chanting and baying for the heads of the traitors who sought to oppress them.

The Kent Commons, led by Wat Tyler, surged over London Bridge, torching a brothel run by Flemish women before pushing towards the gate at the end of the bridge, where they demanded entry into the City. The mayor, William Walworth, had ordered the gate secured against their entry, but, as the crowd gathered beneath the city walls, the keepers of the bridge, anxious for their lives, conceded to the demand of the mob. They unlocked the chains, lowered the rattling bridge and allowed the rebels to pour into the City.

Many Londoners were sympathetic to the rebel cause, and it provided an opportunity to seek revenge en masse against John of Gaunt in particular, after years of tension and animosity. More recruits were gathered and, together, they stormed Fleet Prison, the property of the Master of the Hospital of St John in Farringdon, and Temple's Round Church, which was based on the Church of the Holy Sepulchre in Jerusalem – the supposed site of Christ's burial. The rebels broke in and headed for the treasury where they found ornate manuscripts, scrolls and records pertaining to the sacred history of the church, wealth and privilege and the current legislation that oppressed them. All the parchment and books they could claw from the treasury were brought outside the Round Church and hurled into a furnace.

As the fire cracked and black parchment floated in pieces into the sky, the rebels made their way towards 'La Straunde' and their main target: the Savoy Palace.

At around four o'clock on 13 June, the rebels broke into the Savoy Palace with ease. With John of Gaunt absent, the delighted rebels found their way inside his rooms and destroyed cloth, coverlets, books, beds, a valuable headboard decorated with heraldic devices, napery and jewels.[14] They found jewellery set with precious stones which they smashed with axes and ground into dust, they threw silverware into the river and shredded garments pulled from chests in the wardrobe.

The rebels were enraged to find that Gaunt was not at home – they had hoped to make an example of the hated Duke. Instead, their revenge was material and they made do with a mock puppet of his person. Having obtained his jakke (jacket), they impaled it on the end of a lance and shot arrows at it, before hacking it to pieces with their axes. Gaunt's belongings were collected and carried into the great hall where they formed a pyre. The point of the destruction was to show the wealthy the limits of their power, but some rebels were tempted by the riches they found inside the Savoy. Arms laden with stolen goods, they tried to escape but summary justice came swiftly: they were struck down and immediately executed; the revolutionaries swore they were not there to steal from the rich, but rather to destroy the rich.

As the great hall was filled with Gaunt's belongings for the fire, a party of around thirty rebels went exploring in the cellars. To their delight, they came across Gaunt's supply of wine, barrels enough to keep his household from going thirsty for months. Delighted with their discovery, they began a revel, a Bacchanalian orgy beneath the palace whilst an inferno (fuelled by Gaunt's property) blazed in the hall above. As the rebels in the cellar became drunker and drunker, two barrels were rolled onto the pyre in the hall. It was believed the barrels were packed with riches but, in fact, they were filled with gunpowder. The inevitable explosion ripped through the building. To the horror of the rebels, the Savoy Palace, 'unrivalled in the Kingdom for its splendour and nobility', was consumed in flames that could be seen throughout London.[15] All that remained were the ill-fated drunken rebels trapped in the cellars as the Savoy Palace came crashing down above them.[16]

The best view of the City was from the Tower of London, the imposing edifice built by William the Conqueror that loomed over the streets. From a small window, the King watched helplessly as flames engulfed his uncle's home and many other great buildings in the City and beyond. It was decided among the councillors who shared Richard's sanctuary in the Tower that he must meet with the rebels, hear their grievances and put an end to their violence. After he had fled from Blackheath, the brutality escalated into a series of ruthless beheadings in the City. Richard now agreed to meet the rebels at Mile End and on 14 June he left the Tower, accompanied by the Earls of Buckingham, Kent, Warwick and Oxford as well as Thomas Percy, Robert Knolles and William Walworth. His mother followed behind and Richard was escorted by his half-brothers, Thomas and John Holland. Sir Aubrey de Vere carried the royal sword, an emblem of kingly authority that served to remind the rebels whom they were addressing. As threats had been made on the lives of the Archbishop and the Treasurer, it was deemed appropriate that they remain in the Tower for their own safety.

The sword did not have quite the desired effect. As the royal entourage progressed through Aldgate on its way to Mile End, a cabal of rebels met and surrounded the party. One man – the London captain, Thomas Farringdon – even made a grab for the reins of Richard's horse, demanding justice against the Treasurer, Robert Hales. As the mob became increasingly intimidating, Princess Joan turned and fled back to the safety of the Tower. The King – likely shaken by the altercation in Aldgate – finally reached Mile End, an expansive area of fields, where the road ran east directly through the middle of the green.

The rebels were waiting for him, some eager to finally make terms and request reasonable justice and some seeking violence; others stayed near the City, circling the Tower of London like bloodhounds. Richard was faced with the same rabble that had waited for him on the banks of the river near Blackheath, although this time they sported various heads on spikes, as trophies from their rampage through the City. Those keen to negotiate waved flags and banners overhead that rippled in the breeze and demonstrated some loyalty to the King.

Their terms were reasonable: men should be free from servitude and pay a fixed rent of four pence per acre of land. Richard agreed to this, eager to appease them. However, as the King was speaking to the rebels at Mile End, another party of Kent rebels by the Tower of London soon took justice into their own hands. One of them was a woman named Joanna Ferrour. In a throng of 'terrifying uproar' the rebels made their way into the Tower, according to Thomas Walsingham, through the gate. The Tower of London was designed as a prison as well as a garrison and it had never been breached. The keep of the Tower was protected by causeways, drawbridges, portcullises and gates, as well as an armed guard. The only way the rebels could possibly gain entry was if they were let in. The rebels had strength in numbers but they lacked the superior weapons it took to storm a bastion like this. The rebels accessed the Tower by the same method they employed at Rochester – coercion.

Simon Sudbury was kneeling in the chapel of St John, an original part of the White Tower, as the rebels broke into the keep. The eyes of

St Edward and St John, gleaming from the stained glass, bore down on the Archbishop as the shouts and chants of the rebels outside echoed through the windows. Simon Sudbury continued to pray until, inevitably, the mob burst into the chapel, delighted to find Sudbury on his knees. 'Welcome my children', he said, 'look here, I am the archbishop whom you seek, but I am no traitor, and no plunderer'.[17] His attempt to reason with the rebels was fruitless; they dragged him from the altar outside onto Tower Hill where they struck off his head in eight clumsy, bloody blows. Robert Hales, the Treasurer, was also dragged from the altar to meet the same fate, as was Brother William Appleton, a physician in the service of John of Gaunt.

As the three men were brutally executed, another remarkably survived. When John of Gaunt rode north to Scotland, he left his son, Henry Bolingbroke – aged fourteen – in the company of the King. As Richard rode out to meet the rebels that day, he left Henry in the Tower for his own safety – as the son of John of Gaunt he was a prime target for the rebels. Henry Bolingbroke quietly hid in a cupboard in the Tower and waited for the rebels to leave: miraculously they never discovered his hiding place. The councillors to the King were not so fortunate. Their severed heads were taken to London Bridge, where they were impaled on spikes as trophies of justice. The killing spree continued as rebels dragged men from their homes, from churches and even from Westminster Abbey to be beheaded, until Richard released a proclamation for all men to come and meet with him again, this time at Smithfield.

On 15 June, the rebels gathered and confidently faced the King and his men. William Walworth rode forward from the King's party and demanded the rebel leader make himself known. Wat Tyler approached the King and asked for liberty and equality, stating that 'all men should be free'. The day was hot and, as Tyler pleaded his cause to the King and his men, he suddenly became thirsty and requested a jug of water to wash his mouth out. Tyler swilled the water and spat it out in front of the King. To the nobility, this small and seemingly insignificant act was symptomatic of the crudeness and ill manner of Tyler and the rebels he represented. A valet in the King's retinue scoffed that Tyler was no more than a thief, prompting a violent rebuff from Tyler. In response to his rudeness, William Walworth moved to arrest him, prompting Tyler to lunge forward and try to stab the mayor. Tyler's attack was thwarted and Walworth ran him through; as the crowd of shocked rebels watched the scene unfurl, Wat Tyler died at the King's feet . . . and his cause died with him. Some claim Tyler escaped, only to be dragged from his sickbed and executed, but others state that the mayor had him beheaded there and then, and his severed head exhibited as the consequence of rising up against the Crown.

The rebels were poised to attack and they greatly outnumbered the King's party; however, they hesitated. Richard acted quickly and seized the opportunity to quell the inevitable bloodshed: he rode out before them and spoke as their King. Richard was safe; despite their grievances he was still considered the divinely appointed monarch and their saviour. The fault lay with his advisors and his uncle. Richard believed in his own importance; it was his armour. He performed the role of a benevolent King, merciful to his people and bade them leave peacefully. He swore that he would grant their wishes and no harm would come to them. And so, the Rising was over and the rebels were granted their request. As they swarmed out of the City, London still burned and bodies that lay in the streets were pecked at by hungry birds and gnawed on by stray dogs.

The Rising was over, but had scorched the country. The full extent of the destruction was yet to be revealed and many were still none the wiser regarding the week's events. Only two days later, John of Gaunt received the news that his home and his property were destroyed.[18]

As London burned, news of the Rising spread like wildfire. More rebel groups rallied together throughout the country and attacked John of Gaunt's property. Leicester, as the seat of Lancastrian power in the midlands, was a prime target.

Henry Knighton was in Leicester when news reached its mayor that a mob had taken up arms against John of Gaunt and was fast approaching to destroy his property.[19] Over 1,000 citizens collected any weapon they could find – axes, pikes, scythes and swords – and gathered upon nearby Gartree Hill, ready to defend their town and their Duke. A clerk of the wardrobe at Leicester filled a cart with Gaunt's belongings and had it pulled to Newark Abbey, the structure carefully built by Henry, Duke of Lancaster, to represent Lancastrian piety, wealth and power. The cart arrived as the Abbot was hurriedly preparing the abbey for attack. Unwilling to risk his life to house the Duke's belongings, he turned the cart away and bolted the door. The desperate clerk had little choice other than to direct the laden cart into the churchyard of St Mary de Castro – a smaller church close to the castle – and pray for divine protection. Despite the panic and preparation for attack, the rebels never came to Leicester. The rumour that had made its way north from London that a band of armed rebels was marching to attack was just that – a rumour. Rebellion did spill out of London and riots ensued in Saint Albans, Norwich, Beverley and Lincolnshire, but Leicester remained unaffected. However false, the myth of an army seeking Gaunt's blood continued to travel north. Five days after the sack of the Savoy, the news of the Rising reached John of Gaunt at Berwick-upon-Tweed.

The Duke of Lancaster was in the process of finalising a successful negotiation, a three-year truce with the Scots, when he received news of the Rising in London and the attack on his property. The Savoy lay in ashes, the King had sanctioned the rebels' desire to bring the 'traitors' to justice and his loyal servants had been murdered – Brother William Appleton's head decorated London Bridge. After he absorbed the news, John of Gaunt did not appear surprised.[20] He was aware of the malice of Londoners – the Savoy having previously been a target for their rage – but he had underestimated their capability and the extent of their ruthlessness. Gaunt was hurled into a compromising position. With the truce in Scotland – the product of his careful diplomacy and skill – on a knife-edge, news of such significant civil unrest in England could undo everything he had achieved, or, worse, trigger a Scottish attack. He decided to keep the news of the Rising quiet until the truce was concluded. Unfortunately, Scottish spies were quickly informed of the situation and the next day, as Gaunt met with Robert II's son Carrick at Ebchester to seal indentures, he was forced to lay his cards on the table. With no news from the King, John of Gaunt was left at the mercy of the Scots. To make matters worse, he was informed 10,000 rebels were marching north to seek their revenge against him – the same rumour that initiated the defensive force at Leicester.

John of Gaunt found himself in a precarious situation. He was reliant on the goodwill of the Scots who had been, until recently, enemies of the Crown. Furthermore, with no news from Richard, Gaunt was uncertain of the King's position towards the rebels who demanded his blood. Both Simon Sudbury and Robert Hales had lost their heads; there was no reason for John of Gaunt to escape the same fate should the King permit it. Responsible for his entire household as well as his mission in Scotland, Gaunt had little time to plan his next move. His initial actions were to order the strengthening of his properties that were under threat of rebel attack. He ordered Sir Walter Ursewyck, the Constable of his castle in Tickhill on the Nottingham/Yorkshire border, to defend it 'with twenty men at arms and archers [and] buy victuals detailed in the enclosed bill to stock the castle'.[21] Gaunt intended to remain in the north – the further away from London he was, the better. His initial plan was to travel to Bamburgh, then on to Pontefract Castle where his household was located, and he dispatched an order for the castle to be stocked with 'enough wood for the household during the Duke's stay' and for goods and wine to be brought up from Leicester – possibly the same goods stuck on the cart at St Mary de Castro. In the end, this did not matter, for Gaunt did not reach Pontefract as he had carefully planned. Instead he was forced to submit to the authority of the Earl of Northumberland, Henry Percy.

As negotiations were brought to a peaceful conclusion with Scotland, John of Gaunt planned to dine with Percy at Alnwick Castle on his way south. In light of the danger he was in, Gaunt needed an ally and travelled to Alnwick in haste with a skeleton of his usually bulging entourage. He had sent most of his men back to their homes to protect their property or assess the damage that had already been done, so his force was far from imposing. As Gaunt's depleted retinue approached Alnwick, northern Lords Sir John Hotham and Sir Thomas Motherby met him on the road to hand over a letter from Henry Percy, Earl of Northumberland, clearly stipulating that Gaunt was no longer welcome to dine with him. In addition to this snub, speaking on behalf of the King, Percy forbade the Duke to travel to any other castle in England, including Pontefract – even to collect his belongings. It is uncertain whether Henry Percy was actually following Richard II's orders, or whether he saw Gaunt in a vulnerable position and seized the opportunity to undermine him. Percy's refusal of hospitality and aid resulted from the animosity he had harboured ever since Gaunt had been made Lieutenant of the Scottish Marches – Percy's domain. Leaving the powerful Duke of Lancaster entirely powerless was the best revenge Percy could take.

This came as a significant blow, leaving John of Gaunt with no ally in the north. He was forced to turn his demoralised party around and head back towards Scotland. Sixty miles north they were met at the magnificent Melrose Abbey near Roxburgh by the Earls of Douglas, Moray and Mar and an impressive escort of spears. They had been sent to accompany Gaunt to Holyrood Abbey in Edinburgh, where he would be welcome to stay under the protection of the Scots, despite the newness of the truce. A sojourn in Edinburgh was an opportunity for Gaunt to consolidate, and he was offered remarkably generous hospitality during this time; testament to the Duke's fairness and diplomatic skills in his consistent negotiations over the years and, possibly, to the respect fostered by having been – for however short a time – a candidate for the Scottish throne.

Whilst at Holyrood, Gaunt began to contemplate his fate, namely questioning what – or who – was responsible for his poor fortunes. After days of no word from the King, he became anxious that God was punishing him and he landed on the most obvious sin, adultery: his blatant infidelity with Katherine Swynford.[22]

The relationship between Gaunt and Katherine was public. He treated her with admiration, love, generosity and spent considerably more time with Katherine than he did with his wife Constance. During the revolt, Katherine had gone into hiding – possibly in an abbey or convent. She had property and land in Lincolnshire, left to her by her late husband, Hugh Swynford, but as she was known to be Gaunt's mistress it was unlikely that she fled to the place she was best known. It is possible that Katherine was already at Pontefract with John of Gaunt's household – where he had intended to travel after completing negotiations with the Scots. Katherine still had responsibility for Gaunt's daughter, Philippa, and they had four children together – John, Henry, Thomas and the youngest, Joan, who was only two years old. Nonetheless it is clear that the events of 1381 put an end to their love affair. Both Thomas Walsingham and Henry Knighton state its termination was necessary to placate 'the Lord's anger' and, in doing so, John of Gaunt 'humbled himself in every respect'.[23] Henry Knighton recounts that Gaunt vowed to God to 'remove that lady from his household, so that there could be no further offence', and it appears that, after 1381, Katherine was no longer in his employ.

The termination of the relationship was not painless for John of Gaunt. He ended their affair out fear of the repercussions if it continued and to restore amity with his enemies and critics – namely, the Church. Continuing their adultery after the violence of the Rising – the murder of his men and the destruction of his property – could invite further rage, attention and attacks on his character, possibly even jeopardising the welfare of Katherine and their children. The priority – following the Rising – was to mend old feuds, not fuel them and according to Henry Knighton, Gaunt did his best to redeem himself in the Church's eyes. He did, however, offer Katherine his continuing friendship, protection and dutiful care; neither she nor their children would want for anything and she continued to command his respect thereafter. Katherine eventually left her home at Kettlethorpe and took a house in Minster Yard, Lincoln, an isolated and secure home for herself and her children near a monastic community. She and Gaunt remained in contact and she continued to receive gifts and grants from him, such as wine for her household.[24] There is a lacuna of information regarding John of Gaunt's relationship with Katherine Swynford – as there is for most women in the Middle Ages – but it is clear that their separation was sudden. The emotional effect on Gaunt appears in the sources the following month, after the dust of the Revolt had settled. On 23 July, John of Gaunt had a chapel built in Knaresborough. It was dedicated 'to St Katherine' – a parting gesture for the patron saint and namesake of the woman he dearly loved.[25]

As Gaunt terminated his relationship with Katherine, his attention was drawn to the welfare of his wife, Constance, who was waiting for him in a state, 'smitten in her heart for great fear' at Knaresborough Castle after a stressful journey north.[26] As rebels sacked the Duke's property in London, Constance fled nearby Hertford to avoid possible capture. As her safety became compromised in the south, the Duchess quickly left for Pontefract Castle – likely knowing that this was where the Duke's household had assembled. As she reached the gates of the castle after a long and dangerous journey, she was shocked to find her entry barred. Refusing the Duchess of Lancaster would be a punishable offence in normal circumstances. As Constance was vulnerable after fleeing Hertford, it could only be under extraordinary circumstances that she was turned away, suggesting that the guards at Pontefract – on high alert – were expecting an imminent rebel attack. There is no reason why the same rumour that reached John of Gaunt of a 10,000-strong merciless army had not reached his household in Pontefract, terrifying those who were duty-bound to defend it. If the rebels believed Gaunt's wife to be inside, the defendants would likely lose their lives protecting her. Constance was forced to continue travelling through the night to the nearest Lancastrian stronghold, Knaresborough, with only torchlight to guide her way, until she finally reached the castle and was admitted by its keeper, Richard Brennand.[27] Constance was understandably terrified.

As his wife waited in Knaresborough, John of Gaunt, still a guest at Holyrood, anxiously awaited news and reassurance from Richard II, who was achingly slow to send word. Gaunt was exceedingly grateful, humbled by the Scots' hospitality. He requested wine and spices as well as money from his lands in Lancaster to be sent to him immediately, and gave a golden salt cellar in the shape of a dove to the Earl of Douglas's son.[28] Thankful as he was for Scottish goodwill, Gaunt was eager to remind them that he was also still powerful. The generous gifts he bestowed on his hosts were likely a diplomatic reminder of his position in England – however precarious it seemed in that moment.

Despite the generosity of the Scots, and their persistent offers to support him on the battlefield against the rumoured force moving north, Gaunt was desperate to return to England, and he wrote to the young King for his good grace. According to Walsingham, Gaunt was in such a vulnerable position that he threw himself on the mercy of his nephew, even offering 'if the King prescribed it . . . to leave the realm and go into exile'. In the end there was no need. Richard finally dispatched a letter to his anxious uncle which stipulated that he was needed in London, putting his mind at ease and assuring him of his goodwill. At the end of July, Gaunt was finally able to travel and, with over 500 men, he set out to collect Constance from Knaresborough. When they were reunited, a penitent John of Gaunt dropped to his knees and begged forgiveness for his adultery with Katherine Swynford. Constance graciously forgave the affair and they spent the evening together, celebrating their reconciliation.

Richard was obviously eager to have his uncle returned safely, for he dispatched orders to all lords north of London to escort the Duke of Lancaster to meet him.[29] As John of Gaunt moved south, one of the first lords sent to escort him – as directed by the King – was the bashful Henry Percy.[30] Percy's earlier disdain towards Gaunt had not been forgotten and any opportunity to rebuff the Earl would be relished. When Gaunt was met on the road with an entourage specifically gathered to escort him south, he had the chance to return Percy's hostility, haughtily thanking Richard for his order to the Earl of Northumberland but declining his aid. Embarrassingly for Percy, he was forced to turn around and take his troops home. John of Gaunt was proud and Henry

Percy's dismissal at Alnwick had dealt him a significant blow. The animosity between the two men started a feud that would rattle the highest echelons of government and threaten the repair of the realm, following the largest rebellion in its history.

As Richard had directed, the nobility flocked to aid Gaunt on his journey towards London, a gesture that may have helped soothe a badly bruised ego. 1,000 spears were dispatched to escort him to Reading Abbey, where he had married Blanche. The King was pleased to see him, and according to Henry Knighton showed his uncle 'the greatest respect, and did all that he could for his comfort'. Richard may have gushingly welcomed the fugitive John of Gaunt, but his motivations after the Revolt are questionable. Why did he make his uncle, advisor and greatest protector wait in fear and anxiety for his position, even for his life, for so long? After the rebels dispersed, Richard had immediately ridden out to his mother, Princess Joan, before commanding that the lords, nobles and sheriffs of the land enforce the peace by whatever means.[31] In London, further rebels were caught and executed and in Essex – the root of the rebellion – Richard personally oversaw a merciless pacification. After rebels were arrested all around the county, some were hung from trees, some drawn and quartered and others beheaded.

At the age of fourteen – in accordance with medieval tradition – Richard had reached the end of his childhood.[32] Without the imposing, powerful and authoritative voice of John of Gaunt, Richard saw the wake of the Revolt as an opportunity to exercise his kingship. He was filled with a sense of God-given importance, that self-importance that had given him the reckless courage to stand before an army of angry rebels and trust in their natural worship of him. The moment the rebels surrendered to fourteen-year-old Richard was the moment he began to believe anybody would, and should.

John of Gaunt – under oath to his brother on his deathbed – had protected Richard's interests and his crown, yet Richard allowed his loyal uncle to stew in Scotland, having lost property and men, under the precarious protection of England's old enemies who could as easily have murdered the Duke as given him hospitality. It was only after Richard was finally advised to bring his uncle back to London that he acted and sent word. Perhaps this was for Gaunt's safety, with small-scale rebellions still active throughout lands in the south as minor continuations of the Rising. However, it is more likely that Richard was too distracted managing the aftermath of the Revolt – and perhaps the delay was a way of avoiding Gaunt's counsel. By 1381, John of Gaunt was aware of what kind of King the young Richard might eventually become and began to lose trust in his nephew. Despite this, he was still bound by unbreakable duty to the Crown – and above all to family.

NINE

NOBLE UNCLE, LANCASTER

'A little more than kin, and less than kind'

William Shakespeare, *Hamlet*, Act I, Scene II

500 ARMED MEN MARCHED ON THE WALL THAT WRAPPED around the City of London. As they approached, the watchmen who guarded the City gates identified them from their Lancastrian livery. At the head of the column was the Duke of Lancaster. He had come from the north, through Leicester – possibly to assess the damage caused by the Revolt – before making the journey to London to attend the November Parliament at Westminster.[1] The citizens of London were especially cautious of Gaunt in the wake of their sacking of the Savoy Palace. Armed Lancastrian retainers could provoke violence in the City, which in turn could escalate into further civil unrest, potentially even civil war. Gaunt's argument, however, was no longer with the Londoners, or even the merchant guilds; nor was it with the King or the Church, but with the single Lord who recently humiliated and shamed him in his weakest moment, whilst the commons of England rose up in their thousands. His argument was with Henry Percy, Earl of Northumberland.

Shortly before Gaunt arrived for Parliament, Henry Percy led his own armed retinue towards the City walls. As an adversary of the unpopular Duke of Lancaster, Percy was considered an ally of the Londoners. He was welcomed and even granted citizenship.

John of Gaunt followed Henry Percy and arrived outside the gate wearing armour: he had prepared himself for a hostile reception. This was Gaunt's first appearance in London following the Revolt. The Savoy lay in ruins and the City gate remained firmly closed to him and his men. Angry and humiliated, he was forced to march his army west around the City wall, to the Bishop's palace in Fulham, where he stayed as a guest for the duration of Parliament; with no London residence of his own, he was left with little choice.

The rift between Gaunt and Percy had been threatening the stability of the country for months. Two powerful nobles at odds offered the opportunity for another rebellion, compromising the government as it carefully monitored the country's precarious situation. Following the Revolt, Richard made it his personal mission to punish the rebels in Essex and Kent and instructed Gaunt to oversee pacification in the north.[2] By the end of summer, the government was heavily focused on restoring order. According to Henry Knighton, Gaunt requested that Richard be largely merciful. Although Knighton generally provides a generous account of John of Gaunt, there is still no evidence to suggest the Duke sought to punish rebels in the same manner as Richard II in Essex, and instead focused his attentions on repairing his properties.[3][4] However, Gaunt did not extend the same clemency to Henry Percy.

John of Gaunt was quick to inform the King of the rebuff outside Alnwick. He described the Earl as 'disloyal' and 'disagreeable'.[5] The matter was raised again at a council in Berkhampstead, where Henry Percy defended himself belligerently against Gaunt's accusations. Percy, boiling with rage, removed his glove and slammed it on the table in front of the council; this was a challenge directed at John of Gaunt. By the time of the November Parliament both men had arrayed themselves for battle and brought to London their own armies, threatening the freshly restored peace. The simmering City posed so much of a threat that the King postponed the opening of Parliament to try to end

A portrait of John of Gaunt dating from the sixteenth century.

A 1340 Gold Noble depicting Edward III crowned, with a sword and shield, and on board a ship, following the Battle of Sluys.

The Battle of Sluys in 1340, from a fifteenth-century manuscript copy of Jean Froissart's *Chronicles*.

The tomb of Edward, Prince of Wales, the Black Prince, at Canterbury Cathedral. The Prince's heraldic 'achievements' (shield, helm and crest, jupon, scabbard and gauntlets) are preserved in a glass case nearby, but modern copies of these appear above his tomb.

Above left: Blanche, Duchess of Lancaster. The first wife of John of Gaunt and daughter of Henry of Grosmont, Duke of Lancaster, a detail from John of Gaunt's tomb.

Above right: Constance of Castile, Duchess of Lancaster with John of Gaunt. Constance was the second wife of John of Gaunt and the daughter of Pedro of Castile ('the Cruel') and Maria de Padilla.

Katherine Swynford's tomb at Lincoln Cathedral.

Geoffrey Chaucer, by Thomas Hoccleve, from *The Regiment of Princes* (1412).

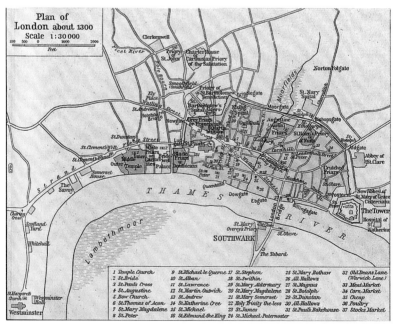

London as it may have appeared at the start of the fourteenth century.

Above left: Pontefract Castle in West Yorkshire. Gaunt's main castle in Northern England and where Richard II was incarcerated and killed in 1400.

Above right: John of Gaunt's Cellar, Leicester, one of the only surviving parts of the original Leicester Castle.

Kenilworth Castle, John of Gaunt's main building project and favourite residence from 1377.

Left: John of Gaunt as depicted in the St Cuthbert window of York Minster. He is shown kneeling before a prayer-desk (prie-dieu), facing the large figure of St Cuthbert, with his hands raised in prayer.

Above: The Lancastrian linked 'esses' livery collar, worn by John of Gaunt's retainers and also adopted by his son, Henry IV.

Left: Richard II, the Westminster Portrait depicting Richard crowned and enthroned. This is one of the earliest and most famous examples of portraiture in the fourteenth century.

Below: One of two original volumes of John of Gaunt's Register, held at the National Archives in Kew, London.

Above left: John of Gaunt's seal prior to his change of arms to King of Castile and Leon.

Above right: John of Gaunt's seal following his change of arms to King of Castile and Leon. Quartering the arms of Castile (castles) with the leopards of England and fleur-de-lis of France.

Left: A fifteenth-century manuscript depiction of the Battle of Nájera in 1367, from Jean Froissart's *Chronicles*.

Below: *The Trial of John Wycliffe*, a nineteenth-century interpretation by Ford Maddox Brown (1886). John of Gaunt is depicted crowned and wielding a sword before the Bishop of London.

Left: The Peasants' Revolt in London. Richard confronts the rebels in a miniature from a fifteenth-century manuscript copy of Jean Froissart's *Chronicles*.

Above: John of Gaunt's supposed surcoat, kept at Rothwell Church in Yorkshire.

Left: The tomb of John of Gaunt in old St Paul's Cathedral, London. The tomb was destroyed in the Great Fire of London in 1666, along with the rest of St Paul's. This drawing is by Wenceslaus Hollar (1607–77). Gaunt is depicted with his first wife, Blanche of Lancaster. One hand is in prayer and the other clasps the hand of his wife.

the feud. He ordered that neither Gaunt nor Percy could enter Westminster Palace armed.

The Lords and Commons convened at Westminster in early November to hear John of Gaunt – the jilted uncle – make his case against the Earl of Northumberland. It was agreed that they would take turns to speak, despite Henry Percy's desperate interjection, during which he was embarrassingly silenced by the King. The dispute had lingered on longer than Richard was willing to indulge, and before Parliamentary proceedings could begin he was determined to put the issue to bed. Gaunt wanted an apology but Percy refused to acknowledge his fault in the matter, laying the blame on the men who rode out to deliver the message to Gaunt in June. These Lords, John Hotham and Thomas Motherby, were duly arrested and taken to the Tower, imprisoned on the charge of disobeying their orders. However, Percy had not accounted for the possibility that his original letter was still in existence. Furious, the men disputed their arrest and produced the Earl's orders for all to see. Within three days, the humiliated Earl was forced to apologise to Gaunt and they exchanged the kiss of peace. Finally, Parliament could begin and Gaunt and Percy were left to quietly despise each other.

Richard was keen to demonstrate that he was no longer a child in need of councils and guidance: he was determined to rule by his own accord. The King had gained confidence and authority after overpowering the masses; the only piece missing from Richard's kingly image was a Queen. As the country recovered after the Rising, its future Queen, Anne of Bohemia, travelled from Flanders to Dover. Her arrival marked the end of a turbulent year and the start of a hopeful future. Parliament was adjourned early, and John of Gaunt was sent to greet the new Queen, for with his cool charm and gallant nature it was expected that he would make her feel most welcome in her new country.

Anne had gravitas in her lineage. She was the sister of Wenceslas IV, King of Bohemia (the present Czech Republic) and Emperor-Elect of the Holy Roman Empire (formed out of the largest portion of territory in western and central Europe). Her aunt Bona was the former Queen of France, her uncle was the Duke of Luxembourg and her sister was the Queen of Poland and Hungary. The Holy Roman Empire had been unbendingly allied to the Pope in Rome since the Schism of 1378. A powerful Imperial alliance was an attractive option to Richard II's advisors and, before the Rising, John of Gaunt had been working hard to secure the match, hosting Wenceslas at a banquet at the Savoy Palace.

The marriage was prestigious, but it was also too good to be true, for Wenceslas of Bohemia was broke. Instead of benefitting financially from the traditional dowry, the Crown purse was expected to loan Wenceslas £12,000, on top of a £4,000 payment in honour of Richard's new wife.[6] The *Westminster Chronicle* described the new Queen as 'a tiny portion of meat', implying that she was perhaps small and fragile, or that she came with little financial weight. On 18 January 1382 she was escorted into London, seated upon 'a great charger', with John of Gaunt at her side.

The crowd of Londoners who cheered the Queen into the City presented a stark contrast to those who had torched its buildings only the summer before. Fourteen-year-old Anne and fifteen-year-old Richard were wed at Westminster Abbey two days later by the recently appointed Bishop of London, Robert Baybrooke, and the teenage marriage grew to be genuinely loving. Anne was crowned shortly afterwards by the Archbishop of Canterbury – John of Gaunt's adversary William Courtenay, who replaced the murdered Archbishop Simon Sudbury. The new Queen was treated lavishly and showered with generous gifts – Gaunt gave her a silver enamelled ewer on an elaborate stand. Jousts were held at Smithfield, for which Gaunt provided minstrels and where his son, Henry Bolingbroke, had the opportunity to exhibit his burgeoning talent in the lists.[7]

Henry Bolingbroke was still an infant when Blanche of Lancaster died and was subsequently raised – like his sisters – by Katherine Swynford. Three months younger than his cousin Richard, Henry was knighted, alongside Richard, in 1377 shortly before Edward III's death. Henry was also given the title Earl of Derby – at the age of ten, he was already a wealthy landowner and high-ranking member of the nobility. After Richard's ascension to the throne, Henry Bolingbroke existed in Richard's shadow at court, a loyal courtier, cousin and friend. But by 1382, and Richard's marriage to Anne, Henry had settled into his Earldom and had his own household of around twenty loyal servants. He enjoyed sport – falconry and hunting – and fashionable clothes, but above all, he loved to joust, gaining attention as a rising star in the lists.

After the tournament, Anne was installed as Queen and Parliament resumed. The summer's Rising came under analysis, as did the defence of the realm – despite the purpose of the crippling poll tax, coastal towns continued to be raided by foreign insurgents. Commons Speaker Sir Hugh Seagrave, a steward in the household of the King, pointed out 'they are still no better defended against the enemies of the Kingdom . . . but are burned, robbed and pillaged every year'.[8] The Commons called for the King's advisors to be removed, yet John of Gaunt was directed to manage Richard's government. Perhaps he escaped blame due to his position as the senior royal uncle, but it is also likely that he was a highly valued figure who the King needed onside for his diplomacy and his wealth.

Despite the domestic stability of the country being the main concern, John of Gaunt ambitiously floated the idea of a campaign to Castile to relieve his brother Edmund of Langley, Earl of Cambridge, who urgently needed support. Gaunt asked for a vast loan of £60,000 to fund the campaign, including the wages of 4,000 soldiers and archers.[9] He promised to repay the loan within three years and pledged Castile as an ally, claiming the country would help to protect the English coastline, which was under constant threat. Gaunt's plea for funds was either highly optimistic or he woefully misread the current state of domestic affairs.

The country was still recovering from the Rising. To leave the realm without a defensive army could invite further rebellion, or even a French invasion. Gaunt's proposition would also require another tax – following the one that resulted in near-revolution. Despite the tentative backing of some of the lords, Gaunt's proposal was unsurprisingly rejected. Richard did not defend his uncle's plan; instead he gave him the responsibility of keeping peace with the Scots following a period of constant harassment of the borderlands. This appointment would remove Gaunt from London politics – where he always found trouble – and allow Richard to exert his authority as King without being over-shadowed by Gaunt and his unpopularity. Two Kings in the realm was an uncomfortable dynamic and, as Richard grew in age, the awkward power-balance became a point of contention.

Shortly after Anne's coronation, a large party of around 600 Londoners from various merchant crafts, led by Nicholas Brembre, sought an audience with Richard at Kennington. They requested that they 'might have only one King', implying that Gaunt's power was not only too great, but it was also unwelcome – an echo of the same issue raised during the Peasants' Revolt. In fear of another uprising, Gaunt fled London. With the Savoy burnt to ashes, he had no powerbase near the City and was aware that a false move could result in more than the loss of his property. It is also clear, by his swift departure, that Gaunt felt that he could not rely on the protection of his nephew.

The mutual bad feeling between John of Gaunt and the Londoners continued; he despised the leverage that the merchants had over the government, but was more circumspect than in previous years at keeping his involvement in mercantile politics in the City to a minimum. The Duke spent the next six months away from London. He took his household to Kenilworth, Leicester, Yorkshire and visited Rothwell to hunt whenever the opportunity arose. However, Gaunt was not content exercising his self-proclaimed kingship so far away from the country he claimed to rule. His key ambition was still to take Castile, but with-out royal consent and Parliamentary backing he had little choice other than to remain in England and do the King's bidding. From 1382, much of Gaunt's time was begrudgingly spent on diplomatic missions on behalf of his nephew, whose personal interests began to align with a new circle of close friends, ambitious characters capitalising on royal favour, who would cause massive upheaval amongst the nobility for the duration of Richard's reign.

As a young man, Richard was naturally influenced by his friends and he became particularly close to Robert de Vere, the debonair and quick-witted Earl of Oxford. De Vere was ambitious and persuasive. His relationship with Richard was reminiscent of the bond between Edward II and Piers Gaveston, which ended in rebellion and the scaffold. Robert de Vere's pursuit of personal power did not go unremarked. Froissart describes de Vere as a man who 'did everything in his power to make a breach between the King and his uncles' and the Earl deliberately steered Richard against John of Gaunt.[10] Richard II was generous to de Vere, prompting Thomas Walsingham to later speculate that they had an 'impure', possibly homosexual, relationship. Any attempt to specify the exact nature of their relationship must remain purely speculative; however, Robert de Vere was clearly Richard's favourite. In July 1382, the first public dispute over this blatant favouritism came to a head when the Chancellor, Richard Scrope, questioned Richard's decision to gift extortionate Crown funds to de Vere. Lord Scrope carefully tried to make his case to Richard that the money he proposed to give to Robert de Vere came at a cost to the realm. Instead of acknowledging Lord Scrope's sage advice, Richard flared up in a rage and immediately dismissed him as chancellor – the first in a series of furious backlashes against anyone who dared criticise the young King's judgement.

Despite Richard's developing self-assurance and Parliament's rejection of a Castilian campaign, Gaunt had cause for hope. The Portuguese Ambassador, Lourenço Fogaça, arrived in England to try to muster further support for the Anglo-Portuguese alliance. Fogaça and Gaunt spent significant time together trying to cultivate a plan for a force great enough to oust the Castilian King. The hours spent in deep conversation about strategy and government support proved fruitless, for almost as soon as Fogaça had set sail from Portugal, the Earl of Cambridge's campaign began to fall apart.

Edmund of Langley, Earl of Cambridge, had led an expedition to Portugal which finally set sail in June 1381 in the immediate aftermath of the Peasants' Revolt. Cambridge commanded a force of around

3,000 men and, due to his lack of military experience or success, he was accompanied by the veteran of Crécy, Poitiers and Sluys, Sir Matthew Gournay, who despite being seventy years old was determined to continue his military career. Also on board one of the Portuguese galleys – ships loaned to the English for the crossing – were Sir William Beauchamp, a retainer of Gaunt's who had fought at Nájera and was familiar with the territory, and the Castilian secretary, Juan Gutierrez, who had loyally served the Duke of Lancaster over the previous decade. John of Gaunt had equipped his brother and representative to the best of his ability, and as the forty-one Portuguese ships drew out of the harbour at Portsmouth, the campaign for Castile looked promising.

The Earl of Cambridge doggedly supported John of Gaunt's political pursuits. He was dependable, genial and easily led. With the support of more seasoned military leaders, it is possible that Gaunt saw Edmund as the natural choice to lead the expedition. Edmund also had a legitimate dynastic connection to Castile; he was married to Constance's younger sister, Isabella. Subsequently, Cambridge sailed to Portugal with his own dynastic bargaining chip, his eight-year-old son Edward, who was to be betrothed to Beatrice, the daughter of Fernando of Portugal and his Queen, Leonora Teles.

By mid-July, the Earl of Cambridge's fleet had anchored at Lisbon and the English and Portuguese engaged in a prolonged series of feasts and talks. Gaunt had pushed for the campaign to be considered a crusade – a branding he would engage in more heavily in the coming years. However, this proved problematic for the Portuguese. In 1380, Fernando had pledged his support to Clement VII, the Pope in Avignon. In order to legitimise his alliance with the English, he was now forced to switch to the Pope in Rome, who had sanctioned Gaunt's 'crusade'. Following a letter of support from Pope Urban VI, preparations for war were underway, including the English army trying to round up wild horses from the Portuguese countryside to serve as mounts. Cambridge had expected Fernando to provide for the army and was disappointed at the lacklustre attitude of the Portuguese King. As their relationship fell apart, so did the army: it soon became clear that Cambridge could not control his men. By autumn, the army that was camped outside the city walls began to raid local villages. The English quickly became an unwelcome presence in Lisbon and, as winter drew closer, it was clear that the King of Portugal showed little interest in war, despite his promises. The Earl of Cambridge wrote to his brother to warn him about the situation – unless Gaunt could provide another 4,000 men, the campaign would likely fail.

At the end of July, there was a moment of hope when the English and Portuguese army united near the Castilian town of Badajoz. There, they confronted Juan Trastámara in the early hours of the morning, on an expanse of flat, dry land free of the olive groves that grew liberally in the area. Aligned for battle, knighthoods were duly proffered and the usual ceremonial prerequisite of war took place as John of Gaunt's banner was unrolled and released to fly high in the hot air. The English lined up, taking the vanguard with their Portuguese allies behind. As they prepared for battle, there was a great cry, 'Castile and León, for King John, son of Edward of England!' The Castilians watched the chivalrous preliminaries unfold from across the battlefield . . . before unceremoniously dispersing.

Eventually, Juan Trastámara offered Fernando terms of peace and a treaty was signed at Badajoz. The marriage agreement between Edmund's young son and the Infanta was revoked and her hand was instead offered to Juan of Castile. The English army was now depleted, a third of its original size, and a humiliated Edmund of Cambridge was forced to return to England on ships leant to him by Juan Trastámara in a pointed act of generosity.

John of Gaunt was busy dealing with local affairs in Yorkshire when he received Portuguese Ambassador Lourenço Fogaça, who broke the news of the failed campaign. Desperate not to concede defeat, or give up on his ambition, the Duke simply refused to face the truth and threw his weight behind redeeming a situation that seemed to most, for now, unsalvageable.

*   *   *

The Lords and Commons were quickly ushered out of Westminster, as the walls of the palace shook and bricks fell through the air. People ran, screaming in fear, as the earth shifted. Buildings crumbled and crashed and barges bobbed on the unsettled waters of the Thames. A great earthquake had struck England, so severe that 'pinnacles of temples' crashed to the ground.[11]

Before the earthquake struck and Parliament was abruptly dissolved, it had been embroiled in a discussion over the way of war. John of Gaunt continued to promote his campaign in Castile, which was languishing in the absence of reinforcements. However, an opportunity had also arisen out of the civil war raging in Flanders. The people of Ghent continued to resist the Count of Flanders, Louis de Male, and were led by Philip van Artevelde, the son of the politician and brewer Jacob van Artevelde. As a result of the ongoing war, trade with Flanders was badly damaged, threatening England's historic and wealth-creating wool exports. In February 1382, Philip van Artevelde sent envoys to Westminster to ask Richard II for his support against the Count of Flanders. He pledged to recognise Richard as Count of Flanders and King of France if he supplied an army to help liberate Ghent. Although government had previously stipulated that the priority was peace, this offer – should it prove successful – promised to restore the dwindling wool trade and reforge the alliance with Flanders which had historically proven beneficial. The van Artevelde family were formerly on good terms with the English crown – Philip was named after Queen Philippa and his father, the murdered Jacob, was Gaunt's godfather. At the next Parliament held in October, Gaunt prepared to push hard for an expedition into Castile, but he was faced with competition.

As the Lords and Commons entered Westminster on a brisk October day, the question heavy in the air was 'the way of Flanders' or 'the way of Castile'. Desperately pushing his case, John of Gaunt ambitiously promised that he could conquer Castile with 4,000 men and £40,000.[12] He added that he would also manage to complete the campaign and secure the country within six months as well as repay the debt. This seemed too good to be true . . . and Parliament agreed that it probably was. Gaunt's plan was yet again sidelined and, with mercantile support, Parliament considered the 'way of Flanders' the better option.[13]

A campaign into Flanders to help liberate Ghent was given an injection of energy by one of the most flamboyant and egocentric characters of the period. Henry Despenser, the Bishop of Norwich, hailed from one of the old noble families of England – his grandfather was the hated Hugh Despenser the Younger, a favourite of Edward II. Although a cleric by title, he was better suited to war, and during the Peasants' Revolt he took it upon himself to round up rebels and personally punish them without trial. When hunting down insurgents, Walsingham describes the Bishop cutting an intimidating figure: 'armed as a knight, accoutred with a metal helmet and a strong hauberk impregnable to arrows and wielding a substantial two edged sword . . . gnashing his teeth like a great boar'.[14]

Bishop Henry Despenser had managed to gain support from Pope Urban VI for a crusade against Clementists – supporters of the Pope in Avignon, Clement VII. The Pope in Rome issued a Papal Bull to the Bishop and permitted him to grant indulgences to those supporting the crusade – as the Count of Flanders was loyal to the Clementist French, this was considered a legitimate cause. Before Parliament had reached a decision over which war to support, the Bishop had already begun to make plans for his crusade. Despenser had Pope Urban VI's Papal Bull publicly announced – even had it nailed to church doors – and began requesting financial donations from around the country. According to Knighton, 'women in particular were keen to donate to the bishop, one woman even gave him one hundred pounds'.[15] As gold, silver, jewels and plate were collected, Despenser liberally granted indulgences. People gladly relinquished their worldly goods so 'they might secure absolution for their friends who had died, as well as for their own sins' for they would be granted 'the same indulgence as is given to those who go on Pilgrimage to the Holy Land'. It was people buying their way out of hell that filled Despenser's war chest.

John of Gaunt was furious about the Bishop's intervention, which forced a wedge between his Castilian invasion plans and the Parliamentary support he needed in order to enact them. In February, Parliament quickly agreed to the Flanders crusade and the Bishop's preparations were fully endorsed. It was briefly suggested that the Duke lead the campaign rather than the Bishop, but the Commons – still mistrustful of Gaunt and allied with the merchants – argued that Despenser was the best candidate. It was agreed that John of Gaunt would be best placed at home, managing the defence of the realm. This was the right decision for England, and not necessarily made out of mistrust for the Duke of Lancaster; he was yet to prove he could lead a successful military campaign, but he was certainly able to diffuse tension on the borderlands with Scottish rebels.

Theatrically, Bishop Despenser carried a cross from Westminster to St Paul's Cathedral before departing for his crusade. He had more than enough gold to pay for the expedition.[16] John of Gaunt was humiliatingly thrust to the sidelines; jaded and frustrated, he recklessly began to pick fights in London by making spiteful remarks about the Bishop's supporters in Parliament. His words became public knowledge and the unpopular Duke was forced, yet again, to make an embarrassing escape from the City. He fled on horseback with just a few of his men for company.

John of Gaunt spent significantly less time in Westminster during this period. Richard, now fifteen and married, was becoming increasingly independent and belligerent. Gaunt was also so unpopular in London he could not even sleep soundly, out of fear for his life. He was duly sent north to Scotland to make terms yet again with Carrick in response to a Scottish attack on Wark-on-Tweed. By the end of the summer of 1383, John of Gaunt was in no better position than the year before. Richard's close and influential circle worked against him, including Robert de Vere and Thomas Mowbray, but also some older advisors such as his former tutor Simon Burley. The clique that had formed around the King noticeably alienated the royal uncles, particularly John of Gaunt who found his position steadily weakened.

As Gaunt tried to bargain with the Scots, Henry Despenser's crusade in Flanders was falling apart. With Ghent allies, he besieged Ypres – which contrary to the point of the crusade was a largely Urbanist town – but had been forced to break off the siege when the French reached the River Lys with an army. The Bishop wanted to meet the French King, Charles VI, in battle, but the leaders of the Ghent rebels wanted to continue the siege. Overnight the army broke up in disagreement and Despenser made his way to Gravelines. In Paris, Charles VI was handed the Oriflame – the war flag of France – by the Abbot of Saint-Denis and gained the support of the Pope in Avignon, who offered the French generous indulgences that matched Urban VI's offers to the English. As Despenser laid siege to Gravelines, news spread that the French army was prepared to invade Flanders with a force greater than had been seen for a generation.[17]

John of Gaunt was at Pontefract Castle when he heard the news that Despenser's crusade was in trouble. Gaunt could not trust Richard to act fast and deliver orders. He decisively summoned his men, rode south and took passage to Flanders from the Isle of Thanet in Kent, intent on rescuing the crusaders before Bishop Despenser dragged them into French hands and the situation became unsalvageable.

Remarkably, despite being in a position of strength, the French proposed a truce and Despenser was able to negotiate safe passage for his men to Calais. As the humiliated Bishop set sail back to England, John of Gaunt met with Philip of Burgundy, the uncle of the French King. With permission from Richard to negotiate as Lieutenant in Flanders and France, John of Gaunt worked to repair the damage caused by the Bishop of Norwich. The disastrous situation in Flanders brought John of Gaunt no closer to the throne of Castile, but his actions in France served as a reminder of his importance as a figure of diplomacy and authority, perhaps inspiring Richard II to utilise him further. The situation gave Gaunt a morale boost, even if domestic politics remained set against him in the long term.

The Bishop of Norwich did not escape criticism for his failed campaign. He was pulled up before the King and Parliament in October and put on trial, accused of bribery and surrender to the French on appalling terms. Despenser shifted the blame wherever he could but it didn't work. The Bishop was stripped of his secular assets, fined the cost of the expedition and forced to abandon his hopes of military glory and return to his Norwich diocese.

Almost as soon as John of Gaunt had returned from Calais, he was deployed to manage another Scottish incursion against an English-held garrison. The Earls of Douglas and March had taken Lochmaben Castle, a singularly important and strategic outpost for the English in Annandale. The long truce that had been agreed with Scotland in 1370 was coming to an end in 1384; the recurrent border raids and antagonism managed by Gaunt previously were only a prequel to the potential threat of a Scottish attack at the end of the long truce.

By spring, John of Gaunt and his brothers – Thomas, Earl of Buckingham, and Edmund, Earl of Cambridge – marched towards Edinburgh with an army of over 4,000 men. They passed Melrose Abbey, where Gaunt had previously been given protection by the Earl of Douglas – it is for this reason he forbade his men to burn the abbey to the ground in the manner of conventional warfare. However, the army chopped down and burnt woodland – Henry Knighton records 'the sound of eighty-thousand axes at work, chopping down trees which were then fed to flames'.[18] Passing through towns and villages and destroying them, the army pushed on to Edinburgh where the town's residents fled, and the English army occupied the fortress. Despite taking the castle, Gaunt was unable to draw the Scottish leaders into battle as they fled over the Firth of Forth estuary. Eventually the royal brothers were forced to abandon the campaign. To his frustration and humiliation, Gaunt was forced to rely on his old adversary Henry Percy to maintain the borders in his absence. John of Gaunt left Scotland without any resolution, giving the Scots free rein to return and to continue to attack the last of the English-held garrisons in their country.[19]

*   *   *

The court travelled to Salisbury for the spring Parliament in 1384 which was held in the great hall of the Bishop's palace. During a break from proceedings, the King took mass in the chamber of Robert de Vere, the Earl of Oxford. After the liturgy was complete and Richard made ready to leave, the Carmelite friar who conducted the mass requested the attention of the King in person and Richard allowed him to speak. The nervous friar warned Richard that he was in grave danger, revealing a plot to kill him – a plot hatched by his uncle, the Duke of Lancaster.

Richard was now seventeen and increasingly volatile and impulsive. After years of growing tension between the King and John of Gaunt, he did not question the truth of the accusation; spitting with rage, he ordered the immediate execution of his uncle, without trial. This was not Richard's first outburst during the Salisbury Parliament. John of Gaunt had already diffused Richard's attack on the abrasive Earl of Arundel after the Earl accused the government of mismanagement. Richard retaliated with threats and cursed the Earl to 'go to the devil'.[20]

The lords present when Richard ordered Gaunt's execution panicked and tried to reason with the King. Such an order could not be enacted without trial; to do so would be against the law. Finally, Richard calmed down and was persuaded to hear John of Gaunt's side of the argument. The friar, a Carmelite called John Latimer, was ordered to put his charges against the Duke of Lancaster in writing. Faced with the sudden pressure of the task, Latimer feigned madness, stripping off and throwing his shoes out the window.[21]

When Gaunt was informed of the claims made against him, he was exasperated rather than afraid. Thomas Walsingham's account of the exchange is that Gaunt was summoned to a public meeting before the King. Gaunt apparently sighed and replied to his nephew, 'Oh why, my Lord, do you trust such informers? Am I not your uncle? Am I not your protector? Am I not the chief man in the realm after you? What could influence me to betray or even kill you, when I would gain nothing from your death?'[22] He then went on to defend his honour in the chivalric manner he was accustomed to, challenging any man who accused him of treason. After the Peasants' Revolt, Thomas Walsingham took a favourable turn in his portrayal of John of Gaunt and his description of Gaunt's indifference towards the claim of attempted regicide is believable. Over his lifetime, John had endured a variety of rumours and slanders against his name and, as he was well aware of the position many of Richard's close advisors took against him, it is likely that he knew the origins of the accusation. It is no coincidence that Gaunt made his challenge aloud and that Richard was informed of the alleged plot in the company of Robert de Vere, who had probably invited Richard to participate in a mass conducted by a priest of his choosing. As for the priest, John Latimer, he became a tragic scapegoat for this short period of political backstabbing.

As Parliament proceeded, Latimer was incarcerated at Salisbury Castle under the care of a gaoler and, after a few days imprisonment, the priest was tortured to death. John of Gaunt blamed the gaoler for his death and flatly denied any involvement in the man's murder. The ill-fated priest had undergone a period of brutal questioning, led by Sir John Holland, the King's half-brother. Under duress, the priest admitted that Lord la Zouche knew of the plot against Richard. Following this accusation, William, Third Baron Zouche – incapacitated with gout – was brought before the King on a litter, to swear an oath that he had no knowledge of a plot, before he was allowed to return home to continue his recovery.[23] Under agonising physical duress ('they lit a fire beneath him, choking and burning him and hung a heavy stone from his genitals'), Latimer begged to speak with Lord Zouche but as he appeared to have no knowledge of the plot, the conversation came to nothing. In order to turn attention away from Latimer's murder, it was spun that he should suffer the same fate as he attempted to inflict on the man he falsely accused. His corpse was placed on a hurdle and dragged through the streets of Salisbury before he was buried at the church of St Martin. Some claimed that green foliage sprouted from the pallet and flowers grew, and even that as the pallet was dragged past woeful onlookers, they were touched by miracles.[24]

As the Salisbury Parliament continued, Gaunt's authority seemed to have survived the Latimer scandal. The Commons raised the issue of retainers abusing their power through their connection to powerful vassals. According to the *Westminster Chronicle*, the Commons complained that livery badges – visible attributes which demonstrate that one is in the service of a particular lord – were handed out too readily and those who held them over-exercised their authority. The Commons requested that the giving of livery badges should be prohibited, to which Gaunt argued that the complaint was too general and that lords were able to punish the crimes of their men. Gaunt's stamp of authority on the subject was evident and the issue was put to rest.

John of Gaunt's busy period of diplomacy and military activity – both successful and not – proved that he was still a linchpin in the management of the realm. It was his steady authority that kept Richard from overexerting his power and causing internal contention. However, Richard resented his uncle's authoritative presence, his smooth diplomacy and his vast wealth and power. This resentment came to a head when John of Gaunt suggested that Richard was old enough and able enough to cut his teeth in a military campaign and lead an army in the manner of the Kings before him.

In January 1384, Louis de Male, Count of Flanders, died in Lille, leaving his daughter Margaret to inherit Flanders, Brabant, Artois and Burgundy. As Margaret was married to Philip, Duke of Burgundy, otherwise known as Philip the Bold, he became the new Count of Flanders. As the French King's uncle, it was inevitable that Flanders would fall under Charles's jurisdiction. To protect English interests in Flanders, John of Gaunt, with the support of his brothers the Earls of Cambridge and Buckingham, pushed Richard to invade France before the French could invade England. During an intimate council in February 1385, the issue was raised with furious consequences. Richard argued that the realm needed to be defended, not abandoned by an army sailing across the Channel. Furious at Richard's stubborn decision to remain safely in England, John of Gaunt stormed out of the council chamber 'in high dudgeon'. In a foul temper, he left the King's presence shouting that he would not offer his support or any of his men to the King, unless he resolved to invade France.[25]

On Valentine's Day, Richard held a two-day jousting tournament inside Westminster Hall. As chargers raced towards each other, the clattering of hooves and heavy armour rang out through the hall and the crowd surrounding the lists cheered loudly. The King was accompanied by his close friends and advisors, including Robert de Vere, Earl of Oxford, and Thomas Mowbray, Earl of Nottingham. After John of Gaunt's furious outburst against Richard at the previous council, de Vere and Mowbray had no trouble convincing the King that his uncle should be silenced. Aware that they would never be able to unseat Gaunt via traditional politics, de Vere and Mowbray worked covertly, planning on 'removing him by underhand means'.[26] As the crowd cheered and lances cracked and splintered through Westminster Hall, whispers circulated between de Vere, Mowbray and even the King himself, to have the Duke of Lancaster assassinated. The plot against John of Gaunt did not get very far; on hearing a rumour of the conspiracy against him, he was understandably furious. Gaunt was a prince who vigorously upheld the code of chivalry; the murder of one's family was the ultimate betrayal. Decisively and bravely he went to confront the King, alone.

The river was quiet at the dead of night as a small barge rowed upstream towards Richmond. On board were armed guards dressed in Lancastrian livery, led by John of Gaunt who was also armed and wore a breastplate. As the boat silently moored at the side of the Thames, Gaunt disembarked and made his way towards the Palace of Sheen, where the King was staying. Gaunt entered the palace, telling his men to wait outside and not allow entry to anybody until he returned. He found the King, surrounded by the men who likely orchestrated the plot against him, and strode forward into Richard's presence where he bowed graciously before publicly scolding with 'harshness and severity' the surprised Richard for his deeply 'shameful' behaviour.[27] The King crumbled and desperately apologised to his uncle, swearing that he would reform his inner circle. However, Gaunt was unconvinced.

He loudly scorned those who wished him dead and left Richard's presence instantly. He was rowed back over the river and away from London to his castle in Hertford. John of Gaunt's intrusion at Sheen was impulsive and theatrical, but in that one decisive action he reasserted his position over his enemies at court and even over the King.

Word quickly got out about the plot against the Duke of Lancaster. Archbishop Courtenay, who had historically been Gaunt's adversary, was exasperated with the King's fecklessness and complained about his actions against Gaunt during a council at Westminster. The humiliated Richard leapt to his feet and spat 'a volley of threats against him' and later even drew his sword against the Archbishop. Princess Joan was appalled at Richard's behaviour and, unlike his reaction to the Archbishop, Richard glumly accepted her anger and promised to reconcile with his uncle. Princess Joan had always been a reliable and constant support to John of Gaunt and, as a popular princess amongst the people, she had – on multiple occasions – tidied up his disputes. This occasion was no different and Thomas Walsingham stipulates that Joan went to great lengths to repair the rift between Richard and Gaunt: 'though not strong and used to luxury and hardly able to move about, because she was so fat, nevertheless neglected her own tranquil way of life and gladly took upon herself the troublesome journey first to the King and then to the Duke, until she achieved her desire to restore peace and concord between the two men'.[28] At her request, John of Gaunt met Richard II at Westminster in early March and forgave him.

As Gaunt and Richard reconciled their differences, a natural opportunity arose for them to spend time together on campaign. An army of 1,000 men at arms and 600 bowmen had landed in Scotland led by the French general, Jean de Vienne.[29] They had allied with the Scots to push the English from Scotland and attack the North of England.

John of Gaunt was present at a war council that met at Reading Abbey in early June. What had initially been concern over the situation in Scotland grew into panic, as it was clear that the French were intending to invade from Scotland, as well as taking Ghent in a separate attack. At Reading, the leading magnates of the realm were forced to make solid strategic decisions to protect England from what was potentially an enormous invasion. It was agreed that seventeen-year-old Richard would lead the army in his first military campaign and that they would muster at Newcastle before entering Scotland in mid-July. John of Gaunt would meet them at Durham, after preparing his men and supplies from Pontefract.

By early July, Richard had set off on the expedition, leaving a council in Westminster to manage the defence of the coastline to the south. Around the same time, the King of France took up the Oriflamme and moved towards Arras. Jean de Vienne reached Edinburgh where he pushed for an attack on the borderlands and English northern castles; however, the Scots resisted, insisting on avoiding siege warfare. Eventually, a treaty between the old allies was signed in Edinburgh stipulating that the army would follow the French course of action and, after weeks of discussion and conflict over strategy, the campaign was set to start near the end of the month – almost ten days after the Anglo-Scottish peace treaty had expired. However, the French army had already grown agitated. According to Froissart, they were distinctly unimpressed with Scotland and its 'savage race'. They hated the food and the poor quality of the wine, and Jean de Vienne complained that Scotland had nothing but 'wild beasts, forests and mountains'. After the army captured Wark Castle, murdering all inside its walls, the tension between the Scots and the French became unresolvable and the Scottish army turned back. Jean de Vienne's French army continued south towards Berwick-upon-Tweed, with only the Earl of Douglas remaining out of the Scottish nobles. However, when they received news that a massive English army was on the march, they turned and fled to avoid defeat.

Richard's move against the recent Franco-Scottish alliance stirred the country into action and the largest army of Englishmen since Crécy banded together to march north.[30] John of Gaunt led the largest division, marching at the head of the vanguard with his brother, Thomas, Earl of Buckingham, and Thomas Mowbray, the Earl Marshal. Even the humiliated Bishop of Norwich took part in the expedition, carrying the banner of St Cuthbert.

The campaign to Scotland came at a time when the English lords needed uniting. After the plot against Gaunt came to the fore, tension was rife amongst the nobility. When they arrived at Durham, Richard sought to repair the feud and insisted that Gaunt, Robert de Vere and Thomas Mowbray put aside their differences and form a united front. After the army entered Scotland in early August, Richard knighted his men and elevated his uncles Buckingham and Cambridge to the Dukes of Gloucester and York. It was this traditional display of kingship that John of Gaunt expected of his nephew and he was pleased by the performance, more so when his son, Henry Bolingbroke, was given the title Earl of Derby. However, Richard could not honour his uncles without satisfying the intensely ambitious expectations of his dear friend, Robert de Vere. In extraordinarily preferential treatment, Richard made de Vere Marquis of Dublin. This was the first ever use of this noble title and the royal uncles were highly unlikely to have approved.

Shortly afterwards, the army marched towards Edinburgh and were faced with a familiar scenario when trying to lure the French and Scots into battle. The Scots would not meet the English in open combat, but picked away at their flanks, resulting in minor skirmishes and no real result. The Scottish people fled at the familiar sight of an imposing English army, taking their supplies with them, leaving nothing for the men to plunder or feed themselves. The army took prisoners where they could and burned the landscape, sparing Melrose Abbey – perhaps again at Gaunt's request – and stationing men there to protect it from pillagers. The army camped in the forest of Ettrick on their march towards Edinburgh and the prisoners they had gathered on their way were put to death – Richard's first campaign was merciless. When they reached Edinburgh, the town itself was deserted except for some Scots garrisoned inside the castle; they watched from its high walls as English soldiers ignited the town below. Out of respect to those who protected him from his own countrymen in 1381, Gaunt persuaded Richard to spare Holyrood Abbey the same fate.

Shortly before the army reached Edinburgh, news came from the south that would crush Richard. His mother, Joan of Kent, had died. Joan had grown increasingly overweight and immobile, but nonetheless was a calming influence on Richard and a consistent ally to John of Gaunt. This sad news may have contributed to the squabbling between uncle and nephew that soon followed.

The Scots were careful to remove any food from the path of the English, and as the army had been put into the field without sufficient time to organise the necessary logistics to ensure steady supplies, the men grew hungry in Edinburgh. Without being able to engage the French and Scottish forces, the English were heading for the same problem they had faced in Gaunt's earlier campaign: the enemy had once again retreated across the Firth of Forth. John of Gaunt was keen to push on and hunt them down to secure victory; however, Richard disagreed. With a famished army, he was adamant that it was time to retreat. Such concern for the welfare of his men was uncharacteristic; it is more likely that Richard had had enough of Scotland and enough of war. In a rage, the King turned on his uncle and accused him of treason, screaming 'you have been the ruin of me because of your bad leadership, your advice, the bad terrain and because of hunger, thirst and poverty. Always concerned for your purse, you are totally unconcerned for me. And now, it is typical of you to want to force me to cross the Scottish sea, so that I may perish with my men'.[31] Gaunt was quick to point out his loyalty to Richard, plainly stating, 'but I am also your man!' However, Richard was now determined to see his uncle as a traitor and a threat, disputing that Gaunt had ever demonstrated loyalty to the King. It was in Walsingham's later interest to force his narrative against Richard, but if there is any truth in his account of the argument, Richard appears more concerned over Gaunt's acknowledgement and servitude than the welfare of the army. Angry and frustrated, Richard ordered a retreat.

As the army moved through the wreckage, they returned to Melrose Abbey, to find the English soldiers left on guard there had been slaughtered. Out of spite, Richard had the beautiful Cistercian abbey burnt to ashes. The lacklustre army continued to Newcastle, where they disbanded, and Richard returned to Westminster. John of Gaunt did not accompany him, but stayed in the north. As expected, the Scots came out of hiding and followed the army, attacking stragglers before raiding the border towns that were once again left in the care of Henry Percy, Earl of Northumberland. Meanwhile, the French finally managed to take Ghent and any hope of English sovereignty in Flanders was lost.

As the King and Gaunt bickered over strategy in Scotland, another decisive battle was under way in the region of Aljubarrota in Portugal. After the death of King Ferdinand in 1383, Portugal was plunged into a period of interregnum after a rebellion out of Lisbon ended the possibility of Portugal being ruled by Castile. Instead, the Grand Master of the crusading Order of Aviz took the position of Defender of the Realm and was later made King of Portugal. Juan, the King of Castile, was furious that his wife's birthright had been stripped from her – and therefore from him – and duly invaded his neighbour. The monarchical contest came to a head on a field at Aljubarrota on 14 August 1385.[32]

The Portuguese held a strong defensive position at the top of the hill, forcing the Castilians to attack from below. After a brutal melée, during which the Castilian standard-bearer fell, the Portuguese pursued the Castilian army down the hill, slaughtering them as they fled. Throughout the night and the next day, Castilian soldiers were hunted down and killed; a popular legend claims that a six-fingered woman who ran a bakery in the nearby town killed six Castilians with her bare hands when she found them hiding in her bread oven.

When the news reached John of Gaunt of the victory at Aljubarrota, he had only recently returned from Scotland after Richard's failed campaign. The information elated him and he was desperate to convince Parliament to sanction a Castilian expedition. Like Bishop Despenser, John of Gaunt had sought the approval of Pope Urban VI to travel to Castile as a crusade against the Clementist schismatics. He was granted a Papal Bull which sanctioned his crusade, but it was not until 1386 that he was finally able to enact it.[33]

At the October Parliament held at Westminster, John of Gaunt – electrified by the new opportunity – stood to argue his case to the Lords and Commons. He made an address, promising that he would establish peace in perpetuity between England and Spain.[34] He requested funding for the crusade and anticipated further aid with the promise of indulgences. Parliament finally granted his wish and he spent the next five months preparing for his invasion. However, the people did not appear to be as supportive of Gaunt's crusade as of Bishop Despenser's, for he did not accumulate nearly the same sum by the sale of indulgences. It was perhaps too clear that this was not a crusade against schismatics, but the Duke of Lancaster's dynastic and territorial conquest.

On Easter Day 1386, John of Gaunt, along with Constance, came to say goodbye to the King and Queen. Aside from the necessary formalities, there was no familial love that endured between Gaunt and Richard. The King had likely sanctioned his uncle's crusade to be rid of him, allowing him finally to exercise his incessant desire for kingship away from England, ending a long and painful power-struggle between uncle and nephew. Richard declared him the true heir of Castile and Leon, and gifted him a golden crown.[35] Finally, Gaunt was ready to leave Westminster for Castile. He set off through the West Country, stopping at various shrines before reaching Plymouth, where he would set sail with a fleet of galleys sent by King Joao of Portugal. John of Gaunt took with him his three daughters, Philippa, Elizabeth – who was by now married to the King's half-brother John Holland – and Catherine, as well as his wife Constance, through whom he could claim Castile. Significantly, Henry Bolingbroke would not accompany his father to abet his lifelong dream of the Spanish throne. Gaunt was close to his son, they often toured Lancastrian lands together and, as Gaunt fell out of favour with the King, Richard had grown increasingly hostile to Henry. As father and son were so frequently in each other's company, it is telling that Henry did not go to Spain. The night before the fleet set sail, John of Gaunt and Bolingbroke dined together on board one of the Portuguese galleys. Gaunt appears to have wished his son to remain in England, to protect the vast Lancastrian fortune that would be his inheritance. On board the ship that night, Gaunt made Henry 'lieutenant of all that he had in England' for Gaunt did not trust Richard or those who advised him.[36][37]

As darkness fell over Plymouth, the fleet carrying John of Gaunt and his family – as well as the army that would fight for his throne that summer – set sail for Spain. Gaunt was convinced that he would finally take Castile and establish himself at the head of a powerful continental dynasty, as intended by his father, King Edward III.

TEN

KING OF CASTILE AND LEON

'Then they shook out the bridle rein further to ride afar.
They had the crow on their right hand as they issued from Bivar;
And as they entered Burgos upon their left it sped.
And the Cid shrugged his shoulders, and the Cid shook his head:
"Good tidings Alvar Fanez We are banished from our weal,
But on a day with honor shall we come unto Castile." '

Cantar del Mio Cid

AN IMPOSING FLEET OF SHIPS HOVERED ON THE EDGE OF THE horizon as the sun rose off the coast of Galicia, a mountainous terrain in the north-west of Spain. Corunna was the main coastal port, usually quiet except for fishing vessels and local traffic. The only foreign vessels that regularly docked in the harbour were those carrying pilgrims, intent on visiting nearby Santiago de Compostela – the jewel of Spain and holy resting place of the Apostle St James. As the fleet approached, it became clear that the ships floating closer to the port were not domestic galleys, but belonged to the enemies of Spain: Portugal and England. On board was the pretender to the Castilian throne, the Duke of Lancaster.

Galicia was, strategically, a reasonable choice of landing-place. Portugal – Gaunt's promised ally – was to the south and Castile and

Leon lay to the east. Equally, the Galicians were traditionally loyal to the late King Pedro's cause and were more likely to support Gaunt with Pedro's daughter Constance at his side. The fleet dropped anchor on 25 July and began the massive task of disembarking Gaunt's army, retinue, horses and supplies. The date of landing was no coincidence. Galicians were celebrating the feast of St James, leaving the port unguarded and allowing the English to land without having to face a hostile reception. Equally, Gaunt's landing, neatly coinciding with the holy day, was meant as a sign – *he* was the rightful King of Castile.

Corunna's port was soon overrun with Englishmen. Goldsmiths, painters, embroiderers, cooks, minstrels and chaplains all disembarked, as well as Gaunt's wife, three daughters and their ladies. Men and boys who had sought opportunity in Gaunt's venture eagerly took stock of the expansive mountainous landscape. These boys had been granted an early chance to cut their teeth at war, likely as squires. Three young men – probably in their teens or younger – stepped from the galleys that day. Ralph Bulmere, a young man who was just old enough to receive his inheritance at home, Baldwin Saint George from Essex and Thomas Chaucer, the son of writer and diplomat Geoffrey Chaucer.[1] Gaunt was also accompanied by some of his most trusted men, Juan Gutierrez and Richard Burley, who had fought alongside him at Nájera and who he appointed marshal of this army. Thomas Morieux, a Norfolk landowner and Gaunt's son-in-law by his first (illegitimate) daughter, Blanche, accompanied him to Spain, as did Sir Thomas Percy, the keeper of Roxburgh Castle, who brought with him over 200 men.[2]

John of Gaunt commanded loyalty. He cared for his men and rewarded those who served him well. From the outset, he was careful with the financial management of the campaign, forfeiting his own benefits to secure the fidelity of his men. In a letter to Thomas Percy during the preparations for the voyage to Castile, Gaunt requested that Percy pay his own expenses, and those of his men. In return for this awkward request, Gaunt would relinquish any profit from the war – such as loot, or prisoners – which had the potential to amount to a significant sum.[3] This was all he could offer, but Percy dutifully agreed to the Duke's request.

In light of the Earl of Cambridge's experience in Castile in 1381 – having relied on the Portuguese to supply horses only to be woefully let down – Gaunt prepared mounts from England, ensuring his men would not be left stranded or at the whim of an ally. Gaunt had an impressive army of around 7,000 men at arms, who before long were arrayed outside the weakly defended crenelated fortress of Corunna.[4] Citizens cowering behind the walls had not prepared for an attack. Apart from a few competent soldiers, they were defenceless and had no choice other than to surrender quickly. John of Gaunt was consistently courteous to the locals, and at no stage during his invasion of Castile did he intend to launch a ruthless attack on civilians. His men were ordered to show clemency and Gaunt took the town with the agreement that, if he could conquer all Spain, the citizens of Corunna would welcome him as their King. Shortly after Gaunt's army occupied the town, his flags were hoisted above the turrets, emblazoned with the castles and lions of Castile and quartered with the arms of England and France, marking his first victory.

Relations between the soldiers and the inhabitants were initially amicable. Gaunt allowed his men to purchase goods from the town's people, expressly forbidding them to pay a lower-than-asking price or use force to guarantee a better deal. Raiding, rape and any other form of violence was expressly forbidden on pain of severe punishment.

Gaunt's stay at Corunna was short. The town was small and was useful only as a temporary base to disembark and rest before marching forward. He left behind a small contingent of troops as a garrison and assembled his army to move south, to the sacred town of Santiago de Compostela. At around forty miles inland from Corunna, the march would take less than two days. The army and its retinue, including Constance and her ladies, embarked on the hot journey to Santiago, which may have been particularly uncomfortable for the Duchess, as the chronicler of St Denys suggests that she was pregnant during the invasion of Castile. By 1386, John and Constance had only one surviving child, Catherine of Lancaster, who accompanied them on this expedition, aged fourteen. It was certainly in the couple's interest to produce another heir for the throne of Castile – preferably a boy – so it is possible that Constance was pregnant, but there is no further suggestion of her condition and no baby born in Spain subsequently survived.

Santiago de Compostela was a small, walled city, with the cathedral at its centre. Largely unfortified and unprotected, the clergy and the citizens of the town had little choice other than to accept the English army on the same terms as Corunna – that Gaunt, in turn, would protect the city and its people. Crowds gathered as John of Gaunt and Constance were ceremonially handed the keys to the city and accompanied through the vast doors of the imposing cathedral – the beating heart of the town. By conquering Santiago de Compostela, Gaunt made a clear and powerful statement that he was the rightful King of Castile, which his father Edward III had tried, and failed, to do when besieging France's holy city of Reims in 1360. Gaunt was aware of the potential weight of such an achievement, for if he could be accepted as King in Spain's holy city, then the rest of the country was more likely to accede to his claim. In Galicia, this proved to be the case and people from surrounding towns and villages flocked to Santiago de Compostela to kiss the ringed fingers of the true King of Castile. Gaunt demonstrated his crusading intentions to the Pope in Rome by ousting the Clementist Bishop of Santiago de Compostela and installing an Urbanist in his place. This action would have stung the Castilian royalty even more as the deposed Bishop was also Juan Trastámara's Chancellor.

Despite the religious prestige of Santiago de Compostela, Gaunt needed a suitable fortress to contain his army and serve as a base for further conquest. A natural choice for such a garrison was Orense, a well-fortified city only a day's march away, surrounded by the River Miño and conveniently close to the Portuguese border. The high walls that made it appealing to Gaunt had to be breached for it to come under English occupation. The resistance from the Galicians was brave, but Gaunt incentivised his men to fight hard against the defenders of the town, promising generous rewards. Against the might of Gaunt's besieging army, the citizens of Orense could not hold out for long and the English invaders were admitted into the town. Orense was quickly established as Gaunt's powerbase in Galicia and he set about forging the fundamentals of monarchical administration, such as his own chancery. In an attempt to solidify his position as King through both money and propaganda, Gaunt had his own coins minted at Orense, fashioned from bullion he had carried across the sea from Plymouth.[5]

As John of Gaunt established himself in Orense, Juan Trastámara held court in Zamora, a large city at the centre of Castile and Leon. The invasion from Galicia caught Juan completely off guard, for he was expecting Gaunt to invade through Portugal rather than launching his own attack from the north. Following the Battle of Aljubarrota, Juan Trastámara had a depleted army of only around 2,000 fighting men, half of whom were French soldiers led by Olivier de Clisson, the now Constable of France, following the death of Bertrand du Guesclin in 1380. After a desperate plea to Charles VI, he was also promised another 2,000 men at arms, who would be assembled and led by the Duke of Bourbon. In the meantime, after a war council with Olivier de Clisson, Juan was persuaded to stay within the confines of the fortress whilst he waited for the French reinforcements. De Clisson likely warned Juan of the dangers of pitched battle, for the strong horses and longbows of the powerful English army were the cause of his father's defeat at Nájera.

Initially, Juan Trastámara sent four emissaries to John of Gaunt, offering terms of peace if Gaunt would relinquish his claim to Castile and return to England. One of the terms was the offer of marriage between his son Enrique, the Prince of Asturias, to Catherine of Lancaster, thereby making Gaunt's daughter Castile's future Queen. The offer was tempting, but not enough for Gaunt to make terms and end his campaign. In hindsight, this was a chance at peace that he would have done well to accept.

With Gaunt's rejection of his terms, Juan was forced to employ the same strategy frequently used by the French when under attack from the English. He ordered that all possible supplies be removed from the lands, crops burned, grain and livestock brought inside walled or garrisoned towns, and that all villages and towns be stripped bare, denying any opportunity for plunder. All Juan Trastámara had to do was wait for Gaunt's campaign to unravel.

Much like previous expeditions in France, the lack of supplies became seriously problematic, as the English army needed to feed itself off the land. Orense continued to serve as a base for the army and for the Duke's household; Constance and her ladies remained in the town whilst Gaunt continued his campaign. However, after an initially promising start to the invasion – conquering Galicia – the English were growing agitated at the lack of food and plunder.

The intense heat of the Spanish sun became unbearable for English soldiers who were not used to the climate. According to Jean Froissart, 'the days grew hotter and hotter, until no one dared to go out riding after nine o'clock unless he wanted to be scorched by the sun'.[6] When soldiers consistently began to return to the camp empty-handed, Froissart describes the complaints that began to circulate. Frustrated soldiers groaned, 'this campaign is shaping badly, we stay too long in the same place' for one of the main issues of contention was Gaunt's insistence on bringing his wife and daughters with him, slowing down the march. Equally, the army knew that 'they will defeat us without giving battle. They don't need to fight us'. The men were so at odds with the terrain that they reminisced about France with its 'big villages . . . cool rivers, lakes and pools, mild and palatable wines to give new strength to fighting men and that temperate climate . . . everything is different here'.[7]

Jean Froissart describes a sudden change in the mood of the camp. Frustrated soldiers became fearful as, only two months into the campaign, their comrades began to die from an unknown sickness. The epidemic spread during the hottest months of the year, killing the first few men in August. John Hawlay who came from Utterby in Lincolnshire was amongst the first wave of Gaunt's men to die.[8] In

September it would claim another valued knight and brother-in-arms, Lord Walter Fitzwalter, who died at Orense.

Trapped in Galicia with no food and his men rapidly sickening, Gaunt was faced with two options: to sue for peace with Juan Trastámara, or to formally ally himself with the Portuguese. The Portuguese King, Joao of Avis, was eager for such an alliance. Sir William Par, an English knight, had been dispatched to Portugal to announce Gaunt's intention to invade Castile, laying the groundwork for an alliance. Accompanied by a squire, Hugo de Hayward, William Par had successfully persuaded Joao of Avis to send six Portuguese galleys to carry Gaunt's army over to Castile. In return, he wanted land, should Gaunt be successful.

Having already won a great victory against the Castilians at Aljubarrota, Joao had little to lose by allying himself with Gaunt, and a lot to gain. Through a dual attack on Castile, he could secure the borders of Portugal and extend its territory, as well as forge an alliance with an influential neighbour – should Gaunt be successful in taking the throne. In early November, the Duke led his already depleted army over a small bridge on the outskirts of a village called Ponte de Mouro on the Castilian-Portuguese border. He had arrived for the long-anticipated meeting with Joao of Avis to discuss the terms of an alliance against the Castilian King. The council was possibly all part of Gaunt's grand invasion plan; his consistent proximity to Portugal throughout the duration of his campaign suggests as much, and may also account for his daughters' presence in Spain – to secure loyalty through marriage.

Joao awaited the arrival of the Duke of Lancaster on top of a hill overlooking Ponte do Mouro, beneath an impressive canopy tent that he had claimed from the Castilian King following the Battle of Aljubarrota. He was accompanied by Constable Nun'Alvares, the leader of his army, and an impressive retinue of 500 men at arms. His intention was clearly to demonstrate his military ability. John of Gaunt was equally keen to maximise the show of power in front of the Portuguese King, bringing a large retinue carefully compiled of English and

Castilian knights to present an image of the scale and variety of territory he controlled.

Underneath the grand Castilian canopy, John of Gaunt and Joao of
Avis formalised their alliance and planned a major Anglo-Portuguese
dual invasion of Castile. Joao promised Gaunt 5,000 men at arms that
he would lead himself. In return, Gaunt would extend Portuguese
territory by granting Joao land along the Castilian-Portuguese border.
He also offered his daughter, Philippa, in marriage to Joao, uniting
both countries in kinship as well as politics. After a bleak few months
of trying to appease hungry and agitated soldiers, this alliance promised a great opportunity for John of Gaunt to resuscitate the campaign.
It was decided that the second wave of his grand invasion would begin
in January, and both sides celebrated the new treaty of Ponte do Mouro
into the night with feasting and drinking. The New Year brought the
prospect of a long-awaited victory.

Philippa of Lancaster was around twenty-six at the time of her
father's invasion of Castile. She was the daughter of John of Gaunt and
his first wife, Blanche, and had grown up in the care of Katherine
Swynford who was employed as her 'maistresse' – a governess who
taught her courtly manners and prepared her for a noble marriage and
the expectations that came with it. In early December, she was accompanied by her brother-in-law John Holland and her father's most
trusted knights, Thomas Percy, Richard Burley and Juan Gutierrez, to
meet her future spouse in the city of Oporto, south of Ponte do Mouro.

The marriage between Philippa and Joao was a natural diplomatic
arrangement that tied the two houses together in perpetuity. However,
John of Gaunt had not considered his future son-in-law's previous
role as a Grand Master in the House of Avis – a holy order that required
a vow of chastity. Joao had been initiated into the Order at the age of
six, precipitating years of military and religious education. The
Portuguese King had spent his life so far in martial commitment to
God: he was bound to the authority of the Church. As John of Gaunt
proffered his campaign as an Urbanist crusade, he was forced to
comply with Church regulations and formalities and appeal for an

urgent dispensation to formalise the agreement. Gaunt anxiously waited in Oporto for news from the Pope in Rome, sanctioning the marriage. It is surprising that he had not expected the delay, considering that the King's holy vows were no secret, but it sent him into a rage; it is possible that Joao had not relayed the crucial celibacy detail before tempting Gaunt into an alliance at Ponte do Mouro with no marriage to bind it. The delay over the dispensation dragged on for two months before the wedding finally took place. With his plans for a swift attack on Castile thwarted due to Joao's vow of chastity, John of Gaunt remained in a furious mood.

As the army waited in Oporto they grew restless, upsetting the townspeople, looting and causing anarchy in the locality. Relations had started cordially, but over the winter months they soured, resulting in the vengeful murder of some English soldiers. As the local people turned on them, infection also rapidly spread through the camp as soldiers remained sedentary, waiting to move into Castile. The Papal dispensation had still failed to arrive, and cold and damp spread through the camp carrying a sickness with it – possibly plague.

Finally, after weeks of antagonism, the marriage between Philippa of Lancaster and Joao of Avis took place in February, probably at Gaunt's insistence, even though the pair had not received an official sanction from the Pope. Notably, John of Gaunt did not attend the wedding. Gaunt's absence was either due to his own sickness – contracted in the infectious camp – or anger over the delay to the invasion, having placed his bets on the Portuguese King to achieve his greatest ambition.

By the end of February, Philippa of Lancaster – the new Queen of Portugal – and her ladies were on the road with King Joao, John of Gaunt, and the Anglo-Portuguese army, eagerly pushing forward into Castile. However keen Gaunt was for the invasion, it soon became clear that his influence and standing did not extend beyond his own men. In an awkward exchange between Joao, Gaunt and the Constable of the Portuguese army – Nun'Alvarez – Gaunt was informed that he had been demoted. Prior to the expedition, Gaunt had assumed that he would lead the vanguard, as he had at the Battle of Nájera. However, Nun'Alvarez would not allow it and demanded the position for himself, leading his own troops. Joao – uncomfortably placed in the middle of two leaders at loggerheads – respectfully apologised to his father-in-law but did little to alter the situation. This slight was a clear indication that control of the invasion lay in the hands of Joao and his Portuguese army, not with the English. Gaunt's promising alliance had in fact compromised his own influence.

In Castile, people and supplies were still locked behind the fortresses peppered throughout the country. French reinforcements had not arrived, and Juan Trastámara faced an intimidating Anglo-Portuguese fighting force. Nervous that John of Gaunt was a potentially acceptable candidate for King, Juan panicked. He spread lies around the country, pushing for national resistance against the invasion. He insisted that John of Gaunt was a dangerous usurper who would destroy Castile and had already sacrificed the country by offering a portion of it to the Moors of Grenada, if they would fight for his cause. In case this did not provide sufficient deterrent, Juan also turned on his people, threatening punishment should they support the Duke of Lancaster. Personal letters were opened and read in case they contained seditious content and he threatened torture for those who spoke out against the existing government. Even if Castilians had warmed to the idea of an English King, they were likely too scared to surrender their towns for fear of the consequences. As the Anglo-Portuguese troops moved into Castile, Juan imposed a tax on his people to pay for emergency mercenary troops and waited for the promised French army to arrive. With an inferior force to hand, Juan Trastámara again employed French tactics: he went to ground.

Garrisons heaved with Spanish and French troops, who were stationed in Castile to support Juan. They were ordered to avoid battle and secure their defences. The challenging objective for the invading army was to reach Leon, forcing them almost 300 miles across Castile, past a series of garrisons that were opportune targets for conquest and plunder. Benevente, a Castilian garrison which lay on the south approach to Leon, was one of the first that the army attempted to besiege. Its approach was slow, hindered by the train of women that accompanied the army, including both Gaunt and Joao's respective wives, Constance and Philippa, and their multiple ladies.

With no siege engines, an attack on the walls of the Benevente garrison – the largest in Castile – was ambitious. Gaunt and Joao made camp outside the town, out of range of the bowmen who lurked on top of the high walls, scanning for targets below. However, Benevente was also occupied by French soldiers and it was here that the English and French began to fraternise for the first – but not the last – time during the invasion. Many who served Gaunt in Spain were seasoned soldiers, having experienced campaigns in France. When they appeared outside the walls of Benevente, some of the French soldiers recognised the men and called out to them. In a display of traditional chivalrous sport, French and English troops arranged jousts and tilts, leaving the Portuguese to look on in disbelief, and initiating a wave of scepticism over the loyalty of Gaunt's men and even Gaunt's intentions in Castile, insulting the loyalty of the Portuguese.

The army was unable to take Benevente and moved on to try its luck in smaller towns such as Valderas, where the townspeople manned the defences. Under pressure from the huge Anglo-Castilian force, they soon surrendered, but not before destroying the town's supplies. Joao – probably aware of Gaunt's bruised ego and dwindling respect amongst the Portuguese troops – suggested that the Duke's banners be flown over the town, marking it as his possession. Despite the Valderans' attempt to thwart the pillaging of their town, there were still ample pickings for hungry soldiers, which caused a rift between the men so furious that it caught the attention of both Gaunt and Joao. As the army entered the town, Portuguese and English began to fight over the potential booty, until it was ordered that the English could plunder for the first half of the day, and the Portuguese for the second. After a few hours, Portuguese soldiers grew restless and stormed the town anyway, leading to further skirmishes between the men, until Joao galloped into the town and drew his sword against his disobedient soldiers, ordering them to desist.

The good relationship between the English and the Portuguese had, by now, completely disintegrated. There was more friction between Gaunt and Joao's men than there was action against the Castilian enemy, and the animosity was jeopardising the campaign. The French and Castilians remained garrisoned, and as Olivier de Clisson had predicted, and Juan Trastámara had hoped, the enemy army began to unravel. In a bold attempt to draw the Castilian forces from behind their walls, Nun'Alvarez led a large contingent of troops to Villalpando, a garrison directly south of Leon that was controlled by Olivier de Clisson and his men. According to Jean Froissart the French were impatient for action and, despite their orders, took their mounts outside the castle to face the enemy. Nun'Alvares led his men into battle formation outside the castle, waiting for the French to retaliate. Froissart describes a charge between the two sides resulting in injured men, but it had to cease due to the amount of dust stirred up from the dry Spanish ground under the horses' hooves. However, Ayala suggests otherwise, that the French saw the size of the army that stood before them, arrayed for battle, and immediately retreated. This minor skirmish was the closest that the Anglo-Portuguese force came to pitched battle against the Castilian-French army.

The sun burned the earth in Spain at the hottest part of the day and the horses – weak and parched – mauled the hard, dry ground for want of grass. As spring moved towards summer at the camp in Villalpando, the men suffered in the growing sticky heat. Sweating and lethargic, soldiers picked grapes for moisture and drank heavy Portuguese wine out of desperate thirst. The more they drank, the drunker and more dehydrated they became, stripping off their clothes to try to stay cool. Froissart describes the temperature dropping dramatically overnight and the hot, drunken soldiers freezing in the cold night air, for 'the more they drank, the hotter they became, for the wine burnt their livers and lungs and all the entrails of the stomachs ... then came the morning chill which struck through their whole bodies, giving them sickness and fever and afflicting them with flux [dysentery]'. Such fluctuations of temperature, the malnourishment and dehydration – both from the wine and the agonising bouts of dysentery – led to more deaths in the camp and the spread of further disease.

It was in this wave of crushing deaths that John of Gaunt lost some of his best men and with them, his morale. By the end of May, he had lost Lord Scales, Lord Poynings, Thomas Morieux (his son-in-law), his chamberlain John Marmion and, most painfully, his dearest friend and loyal marshal of his army, Simon Burley, who died at Villalpando. It was after Burley's death that Gaunt retreated into his own company 'weighed down with anxiety' and took to his bed out of 'weariness' and 'lay in his bed without moving'.[9] It is very possible that the terrible outcome of Gaunt's greatest ambition, the loss of good and loyal men, and the crushing of his morale and self-esteem sent him into a deep depression as his army made plans to desert him.

John Holland came to Gaunt as he remained in his tent during this bout of melancholy. As the Constable of Gaunt's army, he had received numerous complaints from scared, exhausted troops who were furious with the Duke of Lancaster and desperate to go home. Having watched the men sicken and die, Holland informed Gaunt that his men had decided to request permission from Juan Trastámara to travel through Spain to reach Gascony and then home. Joao of Avis counselled his morose father-in-law that he had no chance of winning the war. Over the next few days, English soldiers began to desert the disease-infested camp at Villalpando, where Gaunt waited to receive word from Juan Trastámara. He was forced to come to terms not only with his failure to take Castile, but also with the massive loss of life. As soldiers packed up and left the camp, Joao angrily called them traitors and Gaunt bowed his head and wept into his horse's mane. Disease had followed Gaunt through Spain ever since he established his camp in Galicia, and over 800 squires, archers, knights and barons perished at Villalpando. A knight named Thomas Quinebery escaped Spain and met Jean Froissart on his way home to England, depleted but grateful for his life. He informed the chronicler that Gaunt lost at least half of his army in Spain.[10] Did the young squires – Ralph and Baldwin – who eagerly accompanied Gaunt to Corunna the previous summer survive the sickness? If Thomas Quinebery's estimation is correct, then statistically it was unlikely that both returned home. Thomas Chaucer, however, made it back to England.

The remaining army withdrew, retreating to Salamanca en route to Portugal, and camping outside the city walls. Salamanca was occupied by French soldiers and, witnessing the sorry state of the English, they had cartloads of supplies delivered to the camp to feed the ravenous men. This generous offering was reciprocated with a courteous invitation to join the camp for jousting and feasting, and Renaud de Roye, an esteemed knight, brought fifty knights and squires to participate in a joust for around five days, arranged by the English.[11] The Portuguese were, by now, hated by both the French and the English. Although English and Portuguese soldiers fought on the same side, for the same cause, hungry Portuguese men were left out of the feasting and forced to scavenge in birds' nests on the sides of the roads for meagre sustenance.

Salamanca was a natural base for the time being. Gaunt was determined to remain on Castilian soil while he negotiated peace terms with Juan Trastámara, but the city was close enough to Portugal to then make a relatively swift exit. John Holland had already escorted Elizabeth and her ladies, clutching letters of safe conduct from Juan Trastámara, out of Castile via the Roncevalles Pass into Gascony. They must have been relieved to be escaping from a camp that reeked of death and from Gaunt, who showed little promise of redeeming the situation.

After initially greeting the ambassadors of Juan Trastámara at the Castle of Transcoso in early June, John of Gaunt appointed Sir Thomas Percy, who had survived the sickness, and Sir John Trailly to conduct negotiations. It is notable that Gaunt was not present, perhaps out of humiliation that Juan Trastámara was equally absent, or perhaps – considering his state of mind – he was unable to conduct himself accordingly. After two days of talks the previous proposition of marriage between Asturias and Catherine of Lancaster was agreed. The couple would be granted a large endowment as well as a guarantee that they would succeed to the throne of Castile, grafting Gaunt's bloodline onto the dynastic family tree of Spain. The wedding was agreed for the following year and would take place in the incomplete but impressive Palencia Cathedral. Gaunt was given enough gold to make him extremely wealthy for the rest of his life, doubling his current income and securing his position as the richest man in England. After Gaunt left Castile, forty-seven mules were laden with crates of gold and 'immense riches' were sent to Gaunt in payment for relinquishing his claim.[12] Constance's birthright was also acknowledged and she was granted the revenues of three major Castilian cities – Medina del Campo, Guadalajara and Olmedo – as well as a generous annuity for life.[13]

Gaunt and his loyal stragglers left Salamanca for Bayonne, where they determined to stay for a period to ensure that Juan Trastámara kept his side of the agreement. Gaunt was now wealthy beyond imagination and had secured an impressive position for his youngest daughter. However, twenty years after the victory at Nájera, the glorious battle that had propelled him towards Castile, John of Gaunt wearily left Spain never to return. As a parting gesture he had a personal gift delivered to Juan Trastámara: the gleaming golden crown Gaunt had been given by Richard as he left England the year before, full of ambition and hope.

ELEVEN

PEACEMAKER

'And high above, depicted in a tower,
Sat Conquest, robed in majesty and power,
Under a sword that swung above his head,
Sharp-edged and hanging by a subtle thread'.

Geoffrey Chaucer, *Canterbury Tales*

Westminster Hall was undergoing elaborate re-development. Along with a new delicately carved roof, a new floor and wide, fashionable windows, Richard II commissioned thirteen statues of the formidable line of Kings that came before him: from Edward the Confessor to Richard himself. The deceased monarchs' likenesses were chiselled carefully from the finest Reigate stone and were ensconced along the south wall. Their crowns were gilded with the finest shining gold leaf, and red and green robes flowed over their stony forms. As work continued in the hall around them, the statues gazed down intently on the scene unfurling beneath them: three Lords Appellant prostrated on the polished Purbeck marble floor, their heads at the King's feet.

The King's uncle, the Duke of Gloucester, the Earl of Arundel and the Earl of Warwick had rebelled against him and instigated a coup to remove his most loyal and trusted advisors, including his beloved friend Robert de Vere. It was November and a cold wind whistled outside the gaping windows of Westminster Hall. Richard stifled his violent temper and reluctantly agreed to hear the lords' terms. Although they bowed deferentially to the King, they also controlled 300 horsemen who circled Westminster in support of their uprising. Richard had little choice other than to listen, squirming on his high throne and carrying his sceptre, ensconced in fine ermine and velvet robes.

Gloucester, Arundel and Warwick did not address the King themselves but were represented by Sir Richard Scrope, who had been sent to parley with the lords three days before, along with the Archbishop of Canterbury, the Bishops of Winchester and Ely and the knights John Cobham and John Devereux. The lords had gained a dangerously large following and even mustered an armed retinue at Hornsey Park, north of London. With the threat of a noble uprising, Richard was forced into talks and sent an invitation for a meeting at Westminster Hall.[1]

Richard was accompanied by his usual loyal favourites – the friends and advisors who were the focus of the lords' contention – including Robert de Vere, Mayor Nicholas Brembre and Richard's former tutor Richard Burley. Lord Scrope announced that the lords had 'appealed of treason' against 'both King and Kingdom'. The men specifically accused were the Archbishop of York, the Earl of Suffolk, Robert Tresilian – the Chief Justice of the King's Bench – and Robert de Vere. All were requested to answer for their crimes and, begrudgingly, Richard agreed to the petition, setting a date for the next Parliament to formalise an impeachment process.

Almost as soon as John of Gaunt set sail from Plymouth to claim the Castilian throne in 1386, bubbling political tension in England had risen to the fore. Richard, at twenty, had grown closer to a cluster of noblemen headed by Robert de Vere (now Duke of Ireland) and became ever more hostile to those critical of his friends – particularly Gaunt's youngest brother the Duke of Gloucester. Gloucester had an uncomfortable relationship with his difficult nephew, and, of all the royal uncles, trod a fine line between treason and scrutiny. In a particularly tense moment, Gloucester responded to a bout of Richard's petulance in Parliament by boldly stating: 'If a King, through any evil counsel, or foolish contumacy or out of scorn, or some singular petulant will of his own, or by any other irregular means, shall alienate himself from his people and shall refuse to be governed and guided by laws of the realm ... then it shall be lawful ... to depose that same King from his regal throne, and set up some other of the royal blood in his room'.[2] By naming an 'evil counsel', Gloucester directly attacked de Vere, going as far to suggest another Plantagenet should take Richard's place.

The hostility between Gloucester and Richard's close circle came to the fore in 1387 when Robert de Vere, having become too comfortable under the King's protection, gravely insulted the royal family. De Vere was married to Philippa, the King's cousin and the daughter of Gaunt's eldest sister, Isabella, Countess of Bedford, and her French husband, Enguerrand de Coucy. The marriage – for Robert de Vere – was a good one, for it bonded him to the King through a familial alliance, yet he was unsatisfied with his wife and appealed to the Pope in Rome for a divorce, bringing enormous embarrassment to Philippa de Coucy and her royal uncles. The *Westminster Chronicle* states that the divorce was granted but through 'false witnesses', and when de Vere subsequently illicitly married a Bohemian woman from the Queen's bedchamber named Agnes de Lancercrona, the situation became a 'scandal' that 'shamed and infuriated the royal princes'.[3] Thomas Walsingham was not as gracious about the situation. He stated that de Vere was so 'puffed up by all the honours which the King loaded upon him, promptly reputed his young and beautiful wife', going on to marry Agnes who he called 'a saddler's daughter certainly not noble – and ugly too'.[4] Robert de Vere's recklessness in divorcing – possibly illegally – a member of the royal family demonstrates his egotism and the protection and power he believed he enjoyed in John of Gaunt's absence. Without the mediating presence of the Duke of Lancaster, the Duke of Gloucester staged an intervention.

Gloucester, Arundel and Warwick were the first of five noblemen who would become known as the Lords Appellant.

Soon after the appeal at Westminster, Robert de Vere raised an army, with the support of the King. De Vere had rallied the support of the Constable of Chester, Thomas Molyneux, 'a wealthy, ambitious man and the whole of that region [Cheshire] waited upon his command'.[5] An army of 4,000 men from Chester rode overnight to Oxford, where it was intended that they would cross Radcot Bridge over a narrow part of the River Thames. News had reached the Lords Appellant that de Vere was moving towards London with a substantial following and their response was swift. On 12 December Gloucester, Arundel and Warwick were joined by Thomas Mowbray, the Earl of Nottingham, at Huntingdon to formulate a battle plan. The lords were also joined by Henry Bolingbroke, who commanded the Lancastrian men at arms and archers.

It is likely that Henry Bolingbroke – already infuriated by Robert de Vere's treatment of his cousin Philippa – was responding to the call to arms of his uncle, Gloucester. It is uncertain what instructions John of Gaunt delivered to his son that evening in 1386 as they dined together aboard his ship. But considering Gaunt's determination to oversee Richard's kingship, promise to his brother and consistent demonstration of loyalty to the Crown, it is certain that Gaunt would have stopped Bolingbroke from taking up arms against Robert de Vere. It was this decision to stand against the King's friend – and by proxy, the King – at Radcot Bridge, teetering dangerously close to treason, that laid the foundations of Richard's future distrust of his cousin.

Frost blanketed the ground beneath the feet of Henry Bolingbroke as he waited at the foot of Radcot Bridge on 19 December for Robert de Vere's army to arrive. As the Duke of Ireland approached the narrow pass with his men, it became clear he was unable to cross as intended without a fight. According to Henry Knighton – who was given an eyewitness account – de Vere raised the King's standard 'which he had there all ready to be unfurled' and prepared for engagement.[6] He rode on, intending to cross the bridge to where Bolingbroke waited with his army, only to find that Bolingbroke's men had torn up the paving stones, leaving the bridge impossible to cross. As soon as Robert de Vere realised he had been trapped, Gloucester and his army moved in. The Duke of Ireland, too afraid to fight, embarrassingly stripped off his gauntlets and hurled himself into the River Thames, swimming to safety. He managed to escape capture and possible death, but his ally Thomas Molyneux met a brutal end, for the Constable of Cheshire found himself trapped.

Stood beneath the bridge, having attempted to escape downriver, he was given an ultimatum: die in the water, or die fighting. Gloucester and Bolingbroke's men closed in around the bridge and the helpless Molyneux was accosted by Sir Thomas Mortimer, who 'urged him to climb out or without doubt he would pierce him with arrows'. Thomas Walsingham accounts for the exchange between the two men: 'If I climb out', said Thomas, 'will you spare my life?' to which Mortimer replied, 'I'm making no promises . . . but you must either climb out or else soon be killed'. Bravely, Molyneux requested 'if that is so, permit me to climb out so that I can fight with you or one of your men so that I can die like a man'. However, as the Constable emerged from the water, Mortimer grabbed him by his helmet and, pulling it off his head, 'drew his dagger and split his brain'.[7]

Having successfully defeated Robert de Vere at Radcot Bridge, the Duke of Gloucester and Henry Bolingbroke searched his wagons and found letters from Richard – he had ordered de Vere to assemble an army.

The lords' appeal at Westminster had been peaceful, yet Richard responded with tyranny. The King's actions were unnervingly reminiscent of Edward II and his war against the nobility who questioned his judgement and his chosen favourites.

The King spent a dismal Christmas in the Tower of London where he was confronted by the Lords Appellant for raising an army against them. During the interrogation, he burst into tears. Robert de Vere was now in exile and Richard was forced to face the inevitable impeachment of his favourite councillors. In the bloodiest and most dramatic

Parliament of his reign, the 'Merciless Parliament' which took place in early February, the five Lords Appellant[8] – Gloucester, Arundel, Warwick, Mowbray and Bolingbroke – condemned two of Richard's advisors to a brutal death by hanging, drawing and quartering and the other three to exile. Those who met the executioner were Nicholas Brembre, an adversary of John of Gaunt and former Mayor of London, and Simon Burley, Richard's boyhood tutor – who eventually avoided bloody quartering and was beheaded. Robert de Vere, Michael de la Pole and the Archbishop of York were permanently exiled. This outcome was crushing for Richard. He was left powerless without the zealous de Vere to direct his interests, but most importantly, without Simon Burley. For Richard, Burley's execution was the most distressing outcome of the Merciless Parliament. Simon Burley had practically raised him and cared for Richard as a young boy and young King: it was he who had tenderly carried the exhausted ten-year-old to bed on the night of his coronation. Richard's sadness over Burley's execution was acknowledged by John of Gaunt four years later. Empathetic for Richard's loss – and perhaps to mitigate the tension between the King and the lords – Gaunt contributed the generous sum of ten pounds to the cost of Burley's tomb.[9]

Grieving for his friends, Richard was forced to swear that from now on he would obey the law and not adhere to 'flatterers' but to 'Parliament and the Lords'.[10] The rising was over and the lords had won; however, it was clear that the events of these two years – the years that Gaunt was away in Spain – were imprinted on Richard's consciousness, for 'he always felt these things very deeply, and the Lords said about themselves that all three should never gather in his presence at the same time'. The England that John of Gaunt returned to the following year was permeated with Richard's dormant rage.

After three years abroad, John of Gaunt arrived in Plymouth in November 1389, laden with Castilian gold and barrels of Gascon wine – gifts for the King and family who had remained in England. Gaunt had spent the previous year in Bayonne finalising the agreements made at Trancoso until they were eventually ratified in a formal treaty concluded in July 1388. He had endured months of constant, humiliating delays as Juan Trastámara accumulated his immense payoff. In the meantime, from Bayonne, he made efforts to forge an alliance with Castile – even if he could not take the throne of Castile for himself, he was still heavily invested in furthering the interests of the Plantagenet dynasty.

After Gaunt returned to England from Spain, his interests lay wholly in the establishment of peace. His change of heart, from war and conquest to peace and alliance, was initiated at Bayonne where he attempted to create a lasting peace with Castile, but was rejected by Juan Trastámara. Although Gaunt failed to achieve lasting peace in 1388, his vision of a successful alliance was eventually realised in 1467 – the centenary year of the Battle of Nájera.

Returning home with news of a Castilian alliance had been John of Gaunt's best hope of mitigating the disaster of his campaign. However, the political unrest that hung over England in his absence had turned the spotlight away from the Duke of Lancaster. After Gaunt disembarked, he made his way to a council at Reading where he would face Richard and take on his new royal and political position of peacemaker.

John of Gaunt approached Reading in the first week of December.[11] He had travelled from Plymouth, through the changing wintery landscape of England; a stark contrast to the heat and dust he had endured in Spain. Before he could reach the town, the King's men rode out to meet him and Gaunt was surprised to find Richard amongst them, for his very presence extended Gaunt a great honour. Uncle and nephew embraced warmly and an uncharacteristically pleasant Richard escorted Gaunt into Reading where, at the council, he showered him with flattery. The King intended to demonstrate to Gaunt that his influence was – for the first time – appreciated, having spent Gaunt's absence at constant loggerheads with his conspiring uncle, Gloucester. The Duke of Lancaster's return to England turned out to be an elaborate affair. He arrived at Westminster to find Londoners – who had formerly closed the City gates to him – welcoming and gracious. He was formally received by the mayor and aldermen, and was awarded a ceremonial procession into the Abbey accompanied by chanting.

Remarkably, Gaunt had returned to find himself in a position of increased influence. Richard needed his skilful diplomacy and smooth politics, particularly as a new round of negotiations with France came to the fore. Despite his previous enthusiasm for extending the window for war with France, John of Gaunt was tired of fighting and returned to England intent on peace. With his youngest daughter, Catherine of Lancaster, in Spain as its future Queen, war with France – Castile's ally – would jeopardise her position, as well as Gaunt's Spanish income that had only recently been ratified. It was not long before Richard dispatched Gaunt, along with the reluctant Duke of Gloucester, to negotiate new terms for a truce between England and France, which was agreed at Leulingham, a town near Calais, in June 1389. This was to last three years, with the intention of then drawing up terms for a lasting peace.

In the interests of such peace, nearing the end of Parliament, Richard made Gaunt Duke of Aquitaine in March 1390.[12] Aquitaine was a historically contentious territory; the French would not allow England to rule it exclusively – without acknowledging the French King as a feudal overlord – and the English refused to do so as their government would then be subjugated to the French. The territorial situation, that had been a relatively simple problem during war, proved a nightmare when brokering peace. In 1390, another option was considered: that Gaunt rule Aquitaine as an independent English lord, but be expected to give homage to the King of France. Richard and the English government would therefore be independent from French rule.

Having been away so long, Gaunt briefly visited Aquitaine to oversee its administration.[13] However, his main focus was touring his estates at home and settling himself back into court politics. He also eagerly dedicated time to his only legitimate son, Henry Bolingbroke, particularly in overseeing his future security; Gaunt clearly suspected that Bolingbroke's part in the Lords Appellant uprising would have consequences.

After Gaunt's return to England, it was apparent that the Lancastrian lands were his immediate concern and in February – shortly before he was granted Aquitaine – Richard generously bestowed on Gaunt the Duchy of Lancaster as a palatinate entailed on his male heir. This meant that the entire Duchy would be passed to Henry by right, after Gaunt's death. This boded well for Bolingbroke's future, but it was unusual for Richard, who harboured animosity against anyone who had previously acted against him. It is possible that he was still unsettled after his feud with the Lords Appellant and knew he needed the powerful support of Gaunt in order to keep his throne. Equally, after Gaunt's return, Henry Bolingbroke was careful to avoid the King, grateful for his father's interest in keeping the peace.

Despite John of Gaunt's recent return and keen interest in his son's future, Henry Bolingbroke was unsurprisingly eager to leave England himself, to chase adventure overseas – a desire for action and sport that was typical of his character. Henry Bolingbroke certainly cut the figure of a chivalrous knight. He was skilled in the lists – even travelling to St Inglevert in France to learn from the jousting master, Boucicaut, in 1389 – and was a rising star in domestic tournaments. Bolingbroke was also – despite appearances as a Lord Appellant – keen to avoid meddling in domestic politics. During peace, he sought further military opportunity and, in the summer of 1390, John of Gaunt gave his son permission to cut his teeth as a crusader.

On 19 July, Henry Bolingbroke set sail from the port town of Boston in Lincolnshire. His ship was bound for Prussia, which was where the Teutonic Knights waged a holy war against the Lithuanians in order to convert the native Slavic people to Christianity. The Order was formed of loyal warriors drawn to the Teutonic continuation of the early crusades in Jerusalem – the Christianization of non-believers – and in *The Knight's Tale,* Chaucer nods to the Order as the most esteemed crusaders in the world, describing his Knight to be fighting alongside its members in 'Lettow', now Lithuania. It is possible that Chaucer drew on the notoriety of the Teutonic Knights – who in the later part of the fourteenth century were at the height of their formidable powers – because they controlled a large part of eastern Europe. All of this probably appealed to the intrepid Henry Bolingbroke.

Much like Chaucer's Knight, some of his contemporaries also went on crusade – with no war to fight in, it was a glamorous opportunity for chivalric and religious virtue. Sir Peter de Bukton, to whom Chaucer had previously dedicated a poem, left England alongside Bolingbroke in 1390.[14] As his friends turned towards knightly ambition and away from a King soured by domestic politics, Chaucer – unlike his Knight – looked inwards, involving himself in his new position as clerk of the King's works at Westminster Abbey. Like Gaunt, he had no interest in participating in further war.

John of Gaunt was supportive of Bolingbroke's desire to crusade and funded his son's travels (which continued into 1392 from Eastern Europe to Jerusalem). Gaunt was also supportive of his son's companions: when two of Bolingbroke's men – Sir Thomas Renston and Sir John Clifton – were captured in Lithuania, Gaunt personally bailed them out, beseeching King Vladyslav II of Poland-Lithuania to free them from imprisonment.[15]

Whilst his son was involved in warring in Eastern Europe, Gaunt was wholly focused on maintaining peace and spent much of his time poring over possible options. John Gower, a London poet, condemned the continuation of the war with France as a vain pursuit in a long Latin poem, *Vox Clamantis*, stating: 'If a King is vain, greedy, and haughty, the land subject to him suffers'. Christine de Pisan, who lived and worked out of the French court, counselled the Dauphin, Louis, Duke of Guyenne – the son of Charles VI – against conflict in her *Book of Peace*: 'Troy, Rome and others that I leave out for brevity, which were once so powerful that the whole world in concert could do them no harm – but they were undone by discord'. Following Gaunt's return to England, he was seemingly deterred from such discord; it seems likely that the failure of the Castilian campaign had a similar, but more lasting, effect on Gaunt as the Peasants' Revolt. Having experienced the trauma of losing so many men in Spain, failing at his greatest ambition, and suffering possible depression, Gaunt chose to adopt a peaceful and more pious perspective on the world. This would echo the traditionally pacifist ideals of Lollardy, Wycliffe's movement that had previously inspired him. In 1391, whilst in hiding following charges of heresy, the Lollard preacher William Swinderby wrote to the Bishop of Hereford, attacking Catholic doctrine by stating: 'Christ's law bids us to love our enemies, the Pope's law gives us leave to hate and kill them'.

Gaunt's desire for peace was also reflective of the general mood of England's nobility at the end of the fourteenth century. Even Chaucer, who had fought in France, remembered the ugly side of war when he wrote in the *Tale of Melibee* 'Lordynges', quod he, 'ther is ful many a man that crieth "Werre, werre!" that woot ful litel what werre amounteth . . . that shal sterve yong by cause of thilke werre, or elles lyve in sorwe and dye in wrecchednesse'. Certainly those who were aware of what war 'amounteth' to wished not to live in 'sorwe' and die in 'wrecchednesse'. Even the mercenary warrior Sir Robert Knolles, who had fought on campaign with Gaunt and spent a lifetime at war, ended his life in pious contemplation. In a period where war was often a part of life, there was an inevitable paradox between sin (during war) and penitence. Crusades, indulgences, benefactions and prayer were all efforts to mitigate sins committed in one's lifetime. It was, perhaps, a natural course to reach a penitential phase of life.

Whilst final proposals for peace were being considered in England, the French covertly planned an invasion of Italy. Charles VI, having recently supported his cousin, Louis of Anjou, to succeed the throne of Naples, hatched a master plot to invade Italy from the south, with the support of the Pope in Avignon. This was an extraordinary problem for the English, who could not allow their relationship with Italy – and indeed, the Papacy – to come under the control of the French whilst peace was still highly precarious. Equally, the French were hamstrung in peace talks with the English. With such historic rivalry between the two countries, Charles VI would never leave France undefended whilst waging war in Italy. With such a complex political stalemate, the situation required a creative and more intimate style of diplomacy.

In spring 1390, Richard dispatched heralds throughout 'England, Scotland, Germany, Flanders and France', inviting the finest nobility of Europe to participate in a tournament. Sir William de Hainault, Count d'Ostrevant, 'engaged many knights and squires to accompany him' and Waleran de Luxembourg, the Count of Saint Pol – a French noble – assembled knights and squires to accompany him to England. When the invitation to the tournament at Smithfield arrived at the French court, the Count of Saint Pol was nominated as the natural contender. Not only was he already involved in peace talks with the English, but he was also a famous jouster. His trip to England also became a diplomatic mission on behalf of Charles VI; he was charged with delivering a letter to Richard, suggesting a meeting between the two Kings near Calais.[16] The tournament was, above all, an opportunity for European nobility to peacock against one another in the guise of diplomacy.

At around three o'clock on 10 October 1390, there was a deafening clattering of hooves within the courtyard of the Tower of London as a team of sixty warhorses stamped nervously, waiting for the heavy gates to open. Onlookers watched and waited for an inevitable spectacle as trumpeters sounded and flags were raised. The horses 'ornamented for the tournament' were ridden out of the Tower by squires, followed by 'sixty high ranking ladies, mounted on palfreys [a ladies' saddle horse], most elegantly and richly dressed, each leading by a silver chain, a knight armed for tilting'.[17] The theatrical procession moved towards Smithfield, where the King had organised the largest social spectacle of his entire reign.

Celebrations began with a feast, hosted at the Bishop of London's palace – a grand building near St Paul's church. Nobility from across Europe were received at the first feast by King Richard and Queen Anne. In a shrewd diplomatic move, the Count of Saint Pol was given the great honour of judging the prize for the challengers, for he was regarded as 'the best knight at this tournament' and the Earl of Huntingdon, John Holland, as the defenders' judge (the home team). This was meant to represent the historic rivalry between France and England, played out in a tournament setting.

Despite the political undertones of the occasion, the jousts were a success. Richard behaved like a King, enjoying the attention, finery and theatre of the tournament, and knights jousted into the evening. The Count of Saint Pol 'eclipsed all who tilted' and those who took part were 'courageous', despite many being unhorsed or losing their helmets in the dramatic clash of lance and armour. According to the *Westminster Chronicle*, Richard also participated in the jousting on the first day of the tournament and was awarded a prize.[18] The nights were spent feasting and dancing, with guests lavishly entertained by fine food laced with spices – pepper, cardamom and cloves – and minstrels who played into the small hours. On Friday, the penultimate night of the tournament, John of Gaunt hosted the grand finale. Given his experience of tournaments – a regular feature at the court of Edward III – along with his knack for politics and expert diplomatic skills, it seems plausible that John of Gaunt was the brains behind the success of the event. After the Smithfield tournament, the stalemate was resolved; the French – who could not defeat the English just as the English could not defeat the French – abandoned all plans for their invasion of Italy, paving the way for promising talks at Calais.

The sudden change of heart on the part of the French King was probably due to the astute Thomas Percy, who was sent to Paris to contest the planned invasion. As Percy was John of Gaunt's man and had loyally served him through the disastrous campaign in Castile, it is likely that his mission to Paris had come at Gaunt's request. It is unsurprising then, that when the time came for the meeting on the march of Calais, it was the Duke of Lancaster who represented the King, rather than Richard attending himself, despite the French King's personal request. Gaunt was now a consistent advocate for peace; however, the lords in Parliament had to agree to the final settlement – and many were sceptical of the French terms, including the Duke of Gloucester, who argued for a continuation of war.

A Great Council was held at Reading in 1391, during which Richard expressed his desire to 'see the King of France and have conversations with him about the means of establishing a definitive peace between them'.[19] This course of action was delayed and picked up again at Westminster, where the lords were concerned about the meeting with Charles VI. Questions were floated; would he come with 'an armed force' or in 'peace time fashion, in company with a few knights'? As Richard planned to negotiate with the French King with only a few advisors at his side, the lords considered the size of each retinue an important matter.

Thomas Percy was one of four envoys who were batted back and forth across the Channel in an attempt to broker a suitable meeting place, time and party size, all at enormous cost. Richard – ever the aesthete – funnelled money into suitably accoutring his royal party and himself for the encounter with Charles VI, yet the meeting never went ahead. As the period of truce was drawing to a close and the proposed conference date approaching, a raucous council was held at Westminster with Richard and all three of his uncles present. Over five days, the lords shouted over one another demanding aggressive terms for the peace treaty, with the Duke of Gloucester leading the charge, arguing his case against a lasting peace with the old enemy. Eventually it was decided that John of Gaunt would travel in place of Richard, who was the trump card in negotiations, to Amiens, seventy miles north of Paris, where a peace conference was arranged for March. The English requirements for peace were the return of all land in France allocated to the English at Brétigny – except Ponthieu – and the outstanding balance of John II's ransom which, all these years later, was in serious arrears.

John of Gaunt was getting old. Now fifty-one, constant trips across the Channel had doubtless taken their toll. However, duty-bound, he set off from the port of London on board the *Seinte Marie of Calais* to France where he would act diplomatically and regally, with only seventeen days to negotiate a peace.[20] As Gaunt arrived at the gates of Amiens, accompanied by the Dukes of Berry, Burgundy and Bourbon, he insisted on paying his respects to Charles VI before settling in to his fine lodgings. Gaunt and his men – his brother Edmund, Duke of York, John Holland and the Bishop of Durham, Walter Skirlaw, who was a retired diplomat, all visited the French King shortly after their arrival still dressed in their travelling clothes. The finest nobility of the French court peered at Gaunt and his companions as they stamped through the Bishop's palace for an audience with the King, ill-attired for a royal meeting. Nonetheless, Gaunt knew how to provide a show and knelt before Charles VI three times as a matter of chivalry and great courtesy.

Despite the pomp, ceremony and expense of the conference, its only outcome was an extension of the truce to 29 September 1393. John of Gaunt returned to England having achieved little, for the only option again proposed was that he hold Aquitaine as part of the French crown. This was a suggestion that the Gascon nobility would never entertain, for Aquitaine had always been held by the English King, or his heir. Even if an agreement could have been reached, the health of Charles VI led to further postponement of any decisions on the matter.

On a boiling hot August day in 1393, Charles VI left Le Mans where he had been attending a multitude of councils. Whilst at Le Mans, the King had become unwell. He was not eating or drinking, and became afflicted with a fever and a fluctuating temperature almost daily. The King was travelling to Brittany with members of his court and the Dukes of Berry and Burgundy, who rode confidently ahead. Under the midday sun the King's horse was sweating and the sand underfoot felt hot to the touch. It was 'the hottest day that had ever been known' and the King was sweltering under a 'black velvet jerkin.'[21] As they were riding, a loud noise – the dropping of a lance – caused Charles to jump in fright which immediately sent him into a panicked frenzy. Charles drew and brandished his sword, attacking anyone in his proximity, shouting 'Attack! Attack the traitors!' Eventually, the King was restrained – having already injured some of the travelling party – and his three uncles and brother rushed to his side; however, 'he had lost all recollection of them and gave no sign of affection or recognition. His eyes were rolling very strangely, nor did he speak to anyone'.[22] This episode of nonsensical fury was the first occasion of the madness of Charles VI, which would threaten the stability of France into the next century.

Peace talks with France inevitably abated with the King's illness, and the domestic focus turned to Gaunt's potential – and unpopular – position in Aquitaine, which had become public knowledge. Meanwhile, in the early summer of 1393, Henry Bolingbroke's ship landed at Dover. He had returned from his crusades in Prussia and Jerusalem.

Henry Bolingbroke by now had distinguished himself amongst the nobility of England. He had a wife, Mary de Bohun, and four sons and a daughter, including the future Henry V.[23] Mary de Bohun was the child of a wealthy landowner, Humphrey de Bohun, a great patron of the arts and in particular of illuminated manuscripts. Humphrey de Bohun even patronised a manuscript workshop in Essex where some of the most intricate and beautiful illuminations made in England in the fourteenth century were produced. One stunning illuminated psalter depicts the arms of Bohun and Lancaster intertwining, referencing the union of two great houses on the marriage between Henry and Mary, which had been carefully arranged by John of Gaunt.

The Duke of Gloucester was married to Mary's elder sister, Eleanor, but it was Gaunt who personally saw to Mary's welfare until she was old enough to be a wife to his son. Henry Bolingbroke and Mary de Bohun were married at Arundel Castle in February 1381, when Henry was thirteen and Mary eleven. The marriage – like most elite marriages of the period – was purely contractual, a political union between powerful families. Despite Henry's already vast Lancastrian inheritance, his marriage was also lucrative, echoing Gaunt's first marriage to heiress Blanche. Bolingbroke was close to his siblings, including his illegitimate half-siblings, particularly Thomas Beaufort. It is likely that the Christmas of 1393, held at Hertford Castle, was a joyful one; Gaunt was with his family, and his sons Henry Bolingbroke and Thomas Beaufort arranged a joust to celebrate the festivities. Mary de Bohun was also pregnant with her sixth child. But as the House of Lancaster looked forward to the promise of new life in the following year, it was met with a series of tragic deaths.

At the end of March 1394, Constance of Castile, Duchess of Lancaster, was administered the last rites, surrounded by her loyal ladies in waiting. It is likely that she fell sick and deteriorated swiftly, as Gaunt was absent in France on the King's business, and would have dutifully returned to his Duchess's side had he known of her illness in time.

Gaunt gave his wife a magnificent funeral that July, and she was buried at Newark in Leicester. Constance's final resting place was far from Gaunt's future tomb, planned at St Paul's Cathedral; the separation between them that had existed for the duration of their loveless marriage had become an eternal one. Where Gaunt seemed pragmatic about the death of his wife, he was certainly saddened when his young daughter-in-law Mary, whom he had keenly protected, died giving birth to her sixth child, a girl named Philippa. Mary died at only twenty-five, leaving her children motherless, much as her mother-in-law Blanche, at a similar age, had left Henry and his sisters. Mary's children did not forget her and she appears to have remained in the heart of her son, Henry V, who, soon after becoming King, commissioned a copper effigy of his late mother to lie over her tomb and immortalise her likeness for the ages.

Almost two years after the death of Constance, the King granted John of Gaunt leave from court and from Westminster. He left immediately and rode hard for Lincoln, where on 13 January 1396 he married his long-term mistress Katherine Swynford. After the couple's separation in 1381, and Gaunt's period in Spain, their relationship had endured although – judging by the lack of any further children during this time – it was probably not sexual again until their marriage. On 14 February 1382 – the first Valentine's Day after the Peasants' Revolt and their separation – John of Gaunt had granted Katherine full ownership of the property she inhabited. This was a sign of the love and respect that endured for the fifteen years until they were finally able to marry. The wedding between John of Gaunt and Katherine Swynford caused as much controversy as their infidelity had. John of Gaunt took his new Duchess north, to tour his estates where they stayed at Pontefract and Rothwell – likely to avoid court gossip. This was the same journey that Gaunt had made with Blanche in the months after their wedding, so it is possible that he was repeating the process with Katherine as a way of formally presenting the new Duchess of Lancaster to her people. It is also likely that John of Gaunt was eager to delay her reception at court, which proved to be as cold and unwelcoming as predicted. According to Froissart, who visited England a year after the marriage, high-born ladies of the court, such as Eleanor de Bohun, the Duke of Gloucester's wife, and the Countess of Arundel snubbed Katherine, stating that Gaunt had 'disgraced himself by thus marrying his concubine'; in truth they were more appalled by her low birth than her morals. The Duke and Duchess of Gloucester allegedly considered Gaunt to be a 'doating fool' whilst Froissart comments on Katherine's 'base extraction compared to his two former duchesses' and seems unable to grasp the concept of a love match. The only practical reason for the marriage – he concluded – was because 'the Duke fondly loved the children he had by her'. As Gaunt aged, he became keen to settle his personal matters honourably, so it's likely that a leading motive for the marriage was to eventually legitimise the Beaufort children, whom he publicly acknowledged and provided for. But in marrying Katherine Swynford, it appears that John of Gaunt was committed to consolidating his affection for his long-term mistress, at the risk of public affront.

A year after Gaunt and Katherine were married, he approached the King about the legitimisation of their four children, John, Henry, Thomas and Joan. Richard accepted his request and it was eventually granted by Pope Boniface IX. However, Richard was sullen and subdued, and received his uncle 'without love', for he was consumed with grief and anger over his own recent loss: that of his beloved Queen, Anne of Bohemia.

At only twenty-eight, shortly after the deaths of Constance and Mary de Bohun, Queen Anne died at Sheen. In his grief, Richard began to attack those around him in fits and furious outbursts, most publicly at Anne's elaborate funeral in Westminster Abbey. At the beginning of proceedings – according to Thomas Walsingham – Richard became irritated with the Earl of Arundel, for 'some trivial reason'. Snatching the cane of his attendant, Richard beat the Earl over the head which such force that Arundel collapsed, 'spreading blood all over the pavement'. The funeral had to be delayed whilst the priests forced a reconciliation. It was nightfall before the service ended and Anne was finally interred.

One year after Anne's death, Richard sent a payment of over £2,000 to masons, bricklayers, craftsmen and labourers, directed by John Gedney, the clerk of the King's works, to pull down and raze to the ground 'all the houses and buildings of the manor of Sheen'.[24] He intended to destroy the building that he had shared with his beloved wife, where Anne had drawn her final breath. As Sheen was torn apart, Richard sank into a continued period of violent and tyrannical behaviour pre-empting his final downfall. Those around him became vulnerable to his whims, and John of Gaunt was unable to exercise the same influence that had previously cooled Richard's fury.

Since his return from Spain, Gaunt had worked tirelessly on the King's behalf as a peacemaker. He managed to calm Richard's temper in domestic politics and steer him towards a peaceful outcome with France, paving the way for a peaceful reign following Gaunt's death. In doing so, he had also secured a stable inheritance for his eldest son and the legitimacy of his Beaufort children.

John of Gaunt had carefully and meticulously been laying the groundwork for the dynasty that would follow him, protecting its interests and the interests of the country. The death of Queen Anne unleashed a tyranny in Richard that his uncle had been careful to avoid, as if treading softly over a pane of glass. The despotism of Richard II would swallow the final years of Gaunt's life and throw the future of the country into peril.

TWELVE

TIME HONOUR'D LANCASTER

'My body to be buried in the Cathedral Church of St. Paul, of London, near the principal altar, beside my most dear late wife Blanch, who is there interred'.

The Last Will and Testament of John of Gaunt, 1340–99

ON 24 APRIL 1385, TWO FLORENTINE MERCHANTS NAMED Peter Mark and James Monald, 'of the Society of Albertini', received their expenses for a long trip from London to Florence on behalf of the King of England.[1] The six pounds that they received in recompense for their journey covered the cost of their passage, their stay at inns and guesthouses for pilgrims and travellers, and the inevitable cost of feeding and shoeing their horses. The King had charged the two men with a personal errand: to carry a gift to Pope Urban, of a 'gold cup and a gold ring set with a ruby', and also a 'Book of Miracles of Edward late King of England, whose body was buried at the town of Gloucester'.[2] As Edward III and Edward I were buried in Westminster Abbey, there can be no doubt who Richard was referring to: his great-grandfather, Edward II, who was deposed by Isabella and Mortimer in the political coup of 1327. The decorous gift that Peter Mark and James Monald were charged with carrying was Richard's second attempt to have his ancestor canonised, thanks to his firm belief that Edward II was a martyr. In the latter part of his reign, Richard was known to have visited his great-grandfather's tomb at Gloucester. Richard's interest in Edward II meant he was familiar with the historic feud between the late King and his cousin Thomas of Lancaster; the feud that ended in revenge and bloodshed. Thomas of Lancaster's rebellion may have stewed in Richard's mind in the late 1390s, as tension between the Crown and the House of Lancaster bubbled to the surface. Richard's resentment of the power and potential of John of Gaunt and Henry Bolingbroke became increasingly clear as he began to alienate them from his inner circle of advisors and courtiers. Richard's pursuit of sainthood for his great-grandfather was likely an identification of his own fears: usurpation and murder at the hands of those closest to him.

By the end of the 1390s, John of Gaunt became concerned over the future of his family and his estate and began to put his affairs in order, writing his will in 1398. Around this time – after his marriage to Katherine – Gaunt's grip on domestic politics began to slacken as Richard leant on other members of the nobility, particularly his cousin Henry Rutland, son of Edmund, Duke of York. During the 1390s, Richard promoted Rutland to Constable of England, Constable of the Tower and Dover Castle, Admiral of England and Warden of the Cinque Ports – coastal towns in Kent, Essex and Sussex – and bestowed on him the Lordship of the Isle of Wight. Richard also promoted his half-brother John Holland, who became Chamberlain of England. A former Lord Appellant, Thomas Mowbray, captained Calais. John of Gaunt and Henry Bolingbroke were notably absent from Richard's inner circle.

Henry Bolingbroke deliberately avoided court and politics and, in 1396, stated his intention to leave England to chase adventure in Friesland, to aid the Counts of Hainault and Ostrevant in crushing a rebellion that had spiralled out of control in the region. Bolingbroke was invited by 'his cousins of Hainault and Ostrevant' who sent an emissary to England to recruit men and archers for their war. On a diplomatic trip to England, the Duke of Guelders advised Gaunt against his son's trip, suggesting 'the expedition would be attended with much danger'. Henry Bolingbroke was eager to leave, whereas after Guelders' intervention, Gaunt was firmly against the journey. The dispute caused a rift between father and son, yet the journey to Friesland was no more perilous than Bolingbroke's years fighting alongside the Teutonic Knights. It is more likely that John of Gaunt wished to keep his son close, due to Richard's volatility. With the House of Lancaster already treading water with the Crown, Gaunt could not risk losing his heir.

Despite Richard's melancholy, hope emerged after the death of Anne of Bohemia, for a truce with France was finally decided. It was agreed that England and France would be at peace for twenty-eight years, and Richard was betrothed to the daughter of Charles VI, Isabella – she was only seven years old. The settlement of the King's new marriage suggests that, by this time, John of Gaunt had been elbowed out of Anglo-French politics as, surprisingly, he was not involved in the negotiations; instead, they were managed by Thomas Mowbray and the Earl of Rutland. However, it is possible that it was ill-health that prevented Gaunt from travelling to France. In a letter to the King, he referred to an illness that often left him incapacitated.[3] Nonetheless, the Duke of Lancaster oversaw the finalisation of the marriage agreement with the Duke of Burgundy and was part of a grand spectacle at Ardres. The town was a short distance from Calais – the same site of the Field of Cloth of Gold, held 120 years later. In early October, at Ardres, surrounded by sumptuous courtly splendour, the monarchs of England and France attended four days of talks, before the marriage between Richard and Isabella was settled to take place at the Church of St Nicholas in Calais five days later. John of Gaunt loyally – and possibly in pain from whatever malady afflicted him – attended the second wedding of his nephew to his child bride, having sworn to oversee the safe return of the French Princess to Paris should Richard die. The marriage – despite the large age gap – promised a new beginning for England and France. However, with a secure truce, Richard turned his attentions inward and began to pick away at the underlying resentment that he had harboured against his critics for a decade.

Around the time of Richard's marriage to Isabella, he began to heavily invest in his self-image. One of the most striking examples of this is the *Wilton Diptych*, a dual-panelled altarpiece commissioned by Richard around 1396 that is steeped in symbolism. On the left panel, Richard kneels, his hands clasped together in prayer. Although Richard was an adult by the time the *Diptych* was painted, he is pictured here as a boy – around the same age as his great triumph against the rebels at Smithfield. Behind him stands Saint Edmund, Edward the Confessor and John the Baptist and facing him, gazing down at his youthful face, is the Virgin Mary and Christ Child. Richard is innocent, saintly, blessed by the Holy family, yet elsewhere in the painting lies a symbol of personal power and vanity. Behind the Virgin and Child are a line of Angels, all wearing Richard's personal emblem, his badge of authority – the white hart. A seated white stag with a golden collar around its neck was a symbol used by Richard continuously in the latter years of his reign. As Richard developed Westminster Hall, his domain, he was sure to include the emblem of the white hart along the stringcourse, the horizontal band on the exterior wall. The emblem was not only used in art and architecture, but as a military insignia. The army that fought for Richard, from Cheshire, wore the white hart to demonstrate that they were in the King's service. Richard's emblem littered Westminster, but the most powerful representation of his kingship is in the beyond life-sized Westminster Portrait painted in the 1390s. Unlike the *Wilton Diptych*, Richard is shown as an adult, bearded, crowned and enthroned and stares directly at the viewer with a penetrating, almost chilling gaze. Although portraits of monarchs and nobility became fashionable from the fifteenth century, such a picture was uncommon and no parallel to the Westminster Portrait survives. By investing in the projection of his image and his emblem, Richard was trying to forge his identity as a King, an icon, whose authority was supreme.

Lords and Commons congregated at Westminster Abbey clothed in furs and wool capes for protection against the bitter cold, prepared to endure a long winter Parliament. In November, shortly after the royal wedding at Calais, the King dispatched summons to Parliament which would be held in the refectory of Westminster Abbey, as Westminster Hall was undergoing renovation. The King's most pressing issue was an ambitious promise he had made to the King of France during the negotiations at Ardres. In pursuit of an end to the Papal Schism, Richard had promised to assist Charles VI in a joint expedition against the Duke of Milan. All of this was an attempt to earn the respect of the French King. However, the Commons were visibly against the proposal and flatly rejected the request for a subsidy. Smelling a rat, they suggested that if Richard wanted to play into the hands of the French King, he would have to pay for the cost of the expedition himself. Eventually, the Milanese proposal was abandoned, for Charles VI suffered another period of psychosis – having most famously believed he was made of glass – and was unfit to campaign, but the Commons' response to the request lingered with Richard, eating away at his self-importance.

After the King had eaten on a cold February day, he summoned the lords into his presence. The nervous audience of clergymen and the nobility shuffled into the King's chamber and waited to hear what he had to say. Richard complained that the Commons had acted contrary to his regality, nodding to a statement that he had received, noting that the expenditure of the King's household was excessive. Richard's response was theatrical, taking 'great grief and offence' at the accusation. Spitting with rage, he ordered John of Gaunt to command the Speaker of the House, a knight from Lincolnshire named John Bussey, to find out who had included the criticism of his expenses on the bill.[4] Eventually, a name was delivered to the King; a clerk called Thomas Haxey had produced the offending bill. A terrified Haxey was arrested and gave a grovelling, tearful apology, and it seemed – for a short while – that the matter was laid to rest. Five days later the clerk was summoned to the White Chamber at Westminster where he was questioned by John of Gaunt and subsequently condemned to death as a traitor. This act of injustice suggests that Gaunt was eager to remain in the King's favour, even at the cost of the life of a clerk.

The day before John of Gaunt questioned the clerk for treason, Richard had granted his wish to have his Beaufort children legitimised. As the 'undoubted emperor in our realm of England', Richard declared all four of Gaunt's children, 'by the plenitude of our royal power, and with the assent of Parliament', to be fully legitimate and able to inherit 'whatsoever honours, dignities, pre-eminencies, status, ranks and offices, public and private, perpetual and temporal, feudal and noble there may be . . . as fully, freely and lawfully as if you had been born in lawful wedlock'.[5] For Gaunt, this was a crucial part of securing his dynastic future. It was also through this declaration that the course of English history was altered, with the Beaufort's Tudor descendants usurping the Plantagenets a century later. Although John of Gaunt had previously contended the Commons' reproach on royal lifestyle choices, it is unlikely that he considered Thomas Haxey to be a traitor to the Crown. His uncharacteristic support of Richard's drastic treatment of the clerk was surely to avoid antagonising the King after one of his greatest requests had been so recently granted.

Prior to Haxey's sentence being carried out, the condemned man was under the supervision of Archbishop of Canterbury Thomas Arundel – the brother of Richard Arundel, a Lord Appellant. The Archbishop approached Richard asking him to pardon Haxey, rather than deliver such a cruel fate. Remarkably, the King agreed. These whiplash actions were an unsettling demonstration of power and manipulation that would become Richard's hallmark in the final years of his reign. Shortly after the January Parliament and the Haxey affair, Richard was invigorated with power, knowing that he made men fear him. Before long, he made his first move against the enemies he had quietly observed over the previous decade.

On 10 July 1397 the Earl of Warwick climbed on board a barge destined for Coldharbour House, situated on the northern banks of the River Thames within the heart of the City. He had been invited to a banquet in the King's honour at the mansion home of John Holland, the Earl of

Huntingdon. The King had also invited the Duke of Gloucester and the Earl of Arundel, who had rejected the invitation and cautiously remained at his castle in Surrey. Unfortunately for Richard – who was eager for dramatic vengeance – the Duke of Gloucester was also unable to attend, for he was bedridden with sickness at his home in Pleshey, Essex. Only the Earl of Warwick came that night to dine with the King, where he ate well and was lavishly entertained.

At the end of the banquet, the unassuming Earl was arrested and immediately imprisoned at the Tower of London. As Warwick was bustled out of Coldharbour House, an army was already on its way, marching through the night towards Gloucester's residence. As the army stamped across the countryside, Thomas Arundel, the Archbishop of Canterbury, rode hard to his brother's home in Reigate where he arrived by nightfall, breathless from his journey. Thomas Arundel beseeched his brother, the Earl, to give himself up. Arundel had the option to run and hide, or give himself up as an innocent and hope for a fair trial. He was soon arrested and dispatched to Carisbrooke Castle, whose Lord was Richard's cousin, the Earl of Rutland.

With a deep, personal interest in vengeance against his uncle, Richard accompanied the force that rode through the darkness to arrest him. Judging by the events ten years earlier, he assumed that Gloucester would already have assembled an army. When the horses clattered closer to the Duke's home, the household was woken and a disorientated Gloucester stumbled from his bed, accompanied by his scared and tearful wife. In an eagerly anticipated moment, Richard personally arrested the stunned Duke of Gloucester, and swore to his uncle that he would receive the same treatment as Simon Burley.

The Duke of Gloucester was already a contentious political figure and showed himself to be consistently hostile to peace negotiations with France; it is unlikely his arrest came out of the blue. Froissart's account of the situation is probably exaggerated, but he does accuse Gloucester of plotting against the King, providing ample opportunity for Richard to legitimately enact his revenge. Allegedly, Gloucester had been attempting to rally the Londoners into rebellion and, with the

Earl of Arundel, 'plotted to seize his person [the King] and that of the Queen and carry them to a strong castle where they should be confined under proper guards', and then 'four regents should be appointed over the Kingdom of whom the Dukes of Lancaster and York were to be the chief, and have under them the government of all the northern parts . . . the Duke of Gloucester was to have for his government, London and Essex and that part of the country to the mouth of the Humber . . . the Earl of Arundel was to have Sussex, Kent, Surrey, Berkshire and all the country from the Thames to Bristol.'[6]

Gaunt and his brother, the Duke of York, had wanted nothing to do with Gloucester's alleged coup and, according to Froissart, they absented themselves from the tumultuous situation to go north on a hunting trip. Less than a week later, Gaunt was nonetheless expected to publicly announce that he had given his assent to the arrests. Katherine Swynford went with Gaunt – possibly at his request, for her safety – despite her active role caring for and educating the young French Queen. With Katherine's background as a governess for Gaunt's two daughters, it is likely that her affections as well as her duties were engaged with the child bride. The Lancastrian party went north and Gaunt left the King to handle the situation, an action that Froissart supposed he came to regret, for he lost the opportunity to mitigate Richard's drastic revenge.

Despite Gaunt's absence, the Lancastrian force was fully behind the King, committed to guarding his person. Henry Bolingbroke loyally commanded a force of men at arms and archers to protect the King whilst he stayed at Nottingham. Richard worked tirelessly to uncover proof of Gloucester's plot against him before holding a council to decide the fate of his prisoners. Without Gaunt present to reason with the King, the outcome was inevitable and Richard was as heavy-handed as he wished. Warwick and Arundel were to be tried for treason, but the fate of the Duke of Gloucester was more complicated. If Gloucester were put on trial, John of Gaunt would naturally preside, as Lord High Steward of England. It was rightly assumed that Gaunt would not send his brother to the executioner, so a covert operation was necessary for

Richard to be rid of his meddling uncle. After his arrest at Pleshey, the Duke of Gloucester had been spirited away to the garrison at Calais. With the Channel between the prisoner and his followers, an angry uprising from his supporters was less of a threat.

Thomas Mowbray was the Captain of Calais where the Duke of Gloucester was held prisoner. At the end of August 1397, Mowbray was given his second command to murder the Duke – having initially not been able to carry out the deed. Under pain of torture – and likely the promise of mercy – Gloucester admitted that he had acted treasonously and 'wickedly' against the King and his 'regality'.[7] He admitted to plots against Richard and to threatening to depose him, and begged for the King's mercy. All of this was recorded in a document by Sir William Rickhill, a judge on the Common Bench. After his confession and Rickhill's departure from Calais, the Duke of Gloucester was taken from the castle dungeon to an inn in the town. He was smuggled into a back room where a priest was waiting to hear his last confession. The Duke was then pinned to the ground and smothered to death with a feather mattress.

Members of Parliament were quiet as the breeze whipped through the open-sided tent and strained to hear the new Chancellor, Bishop Stafford of Exeter, open proceedings. He took Ezekiel 37:22 as his theme: 'There shall be one King over them all . . . for the realm to be well governed, three things were needed: first the King should be powerful enough to govern; secondly, his laws should be properly executed; and thirdly, his subjects should be duly obedient'. The Chancellor went on to add that the King – in order to govern sufficiently – must be permitted 'his regalities, prerogatives and other rights'. Amongst the lords present at the outdoor Parliament, watching the Chancellor make his address, were John of Gaunt and his son Henry Bolingbroke. They had both been permitted by the King to bring armed retinues to Westminster and both were anxiously prepared to play their part in keeping the peace. It is certain that by this stage both Gaunt and Bolingbroke were aware of the death of Gloucester, for the King had ordered a proclamation to be released at the end of August announcing it – from natural causes.

Richard had largely remained at Westminster prior to the trial of the Earls of Warwick and Arundel. He was protected by a private army, mostly made up of Cheshire archers, who were an unwelcome bullish presence in London. Parliament met on the feast of St Lambert, on 17 September, in a large tent in Palace Yard as renovations to Westminster Hall were still underway, providing a hammering din throughout the proceedings. The tent was surrounded by soldiers, adding to an already tense atmosphere. According to Thomas Walsingham, the nobles of the kingdom attended nervously, 'by their fear of the King', and were allowed to bring their retinues only if they held a licence. The Commons was made up of a very different crowd to the previous Parliament and was wholly compliant; almost half the Members had never previously stood in the Commons, and the Speaker, Sir John Bushy, was one of Richard's most trusted men. It appeared as though the King had heavily rigged proceedings in his favour.

The main cause of the Parliamentary summons was the trial of Warwick and Arundel, who had been charged with an 'Appeal of Treason', echoing the same appeal presented to the King in 1387. On the feast of St Matthew, four days after the opening of Parliament, the King's cousin the Duke of Rutland, along with Thomas Holland and the Earls of Nottingham, Somerset and Salisbury, Lord Despenser and William Scrope, walked into Parliament all dressed in red silk robes, banded with white silk and powdered with letters of gold. They then ceremoniously handed the King the appeal against the traitors, which they had prepared at Nottingham. They accused Thomas, Duke of Gloucester; Richard, Earl of Arundel; Thomas, Earl of Warwick; and Thomas de Mortimer of 'having traitorously risen in armed insurrection against the King at Harringay Park'.[8] This accusation was in reference to the original uprising against Richard in 1387.

After the court was seated, the first of the accused – the Earl of Arundel – was brought forward wearing a scarlet hood and was ushered before John of Gaunt, who as Steward of England was expected to conduct the trial. Gaunt gestured to the prisoner and asked him to 'remove your belt and his hood' before loudly reading the charges against the Earl who adamantly denied his guilt.[9] Arundel stuck fast by the pardon he received from the King after the 1387 uprising, which had later been revoked, and continued to deny his treachery. The court quietly watched as John of Gaunt sharply rejected the accused Earl's bold defence. Despite his best attempts at redemption, Arundel had been cornered, for it is likely that he had suggested forcible removal of the King. As the Earl insisted his innocence, Henry Bolingbroke angrily rose to his feet and reminded Arundel of his former intention to 'seize the King'. With this, Richard ordered his uncle to speak the inevitable sentence: 'I, John, steward of England, adjudge you a traitor, and sentence you to be drawn, hanged, beheaded and quartered, and the lands descending from your person, both entailed and unentailed, to be forfeited forever by you and your heirs'. The condemned Earl was then manhandled through Cheapside to Tower Hill, followed by 'a great crowd of citizens' who were eager to witness the bloody dispatch of a noble. In a final act of mercy, or honour for Arundel as a noble-man, Richard spared him the agony of being hung and drawn. Instead, he was forced to his knees and his head was severed from his body. According to Thomas Walsingham, 'the colour in his face remained the same the whole time'. The Earl, who bravely stood up to a tyranni-cal King, never paled at the imminence of his death.

Three days after Arundel's execution, his brother Thomas was removed from his position as archbishop and banished. Warwick was brought to trial, 'sobbing and whining' as he desperately begged for mercy. After initially receiving the same sentence as Arundel, he was granted some clemency and was banished to the Isle of Man. Thomas Mortimer was also banished, and the Duke of Gloucester was posthu-mously tried and declared a traitor.

It is highly unlikely that John of Gaunt condoned the sentence, or truly believed that the Duke of Gloucester was a traitor. Gaunt vigor-ously upheld royal authority, yet he was also unbendingly loyal to his immediate family above all. The only reason that Gaunt could possibly have to remain silent whilst Gloucester met a sorry end was to protect his heir, who stood perilously close to the block himself: it smacks of the probability that Gaunt chose to save his son, rather than his brother. As Gloucester was condemned as a traitor against the Crown, a devastated John of Gaunt quietly wept.

It was pitch black in the graveyard of Austin Friars on the night of 1 October. The silence was pierced by a handful of men who clumsily carried torches to aid the Duke's path towards the fresh grave of the Earl of Arundel. After Parliament was adjourned until the New Year, Richard quietly ordered Gaunt to conduct a covert and macabre mission.

Damp soil, glazed with dew, was piled to the side of the grave as men dug deep into the earth. A heavy corpse was exhumed, which Gaunt identified as the stinking body of the Earl of Arundel. The Earl's lifeless form was carefully raised from its resting place and placed on a cart, which was duly wheeled off into the night.

The body of the Earl – who had fought his hardest against condemnation in Parliament – had attracted interest as a political martyr. London had historically been loyal to Gloucester and, without his body to mourn, the mob's attention was turned to the other executed Lord Appellant. With no respect for the dead, Richard demanded Arundel's body be moved to another location before any cult around him could gain momentum. In compensation for overseeing the morbid deed, Richard granted John of Gaunt a portion of Arundel's land in Norfolk.

At the end of a politically turbulent year, Henry Bolingbroke rode towards London from Woodstock, where he had just spent two nights with the King. For Henry – although cautious – all appeared well. He had recently received the Dukedom of Hereford and was, seemingly, in the King's favour with little cause for concern. As he rode through Brentford, he crossed paths with the former Appellant and Captain of Calais, Thomas Mowbray, who had also been elevated in status, to the position of Duke of Norfolk. On seeing Bolingbroke, Mowbray veered his horse over to the newly appointed Duke and began to offer him secret information. According to Henry, Thomas Mowbray anxiously revealed his suspicions, stating 'the King has ordered you and me to be killed, because we rode with the Duke of Gloucester'. Henry did not believe Mowbray's assertion, and argued that the King had already pardoned both of them. However, Mowbray was adamant that the King planned to undo his pardon, and 'annul that record', revealing a plot that never gained ground: to kill Bolingbroke and Gaunt earlier in October. Mowbray accused Richard's loyal supporters of hatching the plot: the Earls of Surrey and Wiltshire, Thomas Holland, Lord Scrope, Lord Despenser – now the Earl of Gloucester – and John Montagu, Earl of Salisbury. He believed that the men intended to murder him and six others, including Gaunt's son by Katherine Swynford, Thomas Beaufort.[10] Crucially, Thomas Mowbray also accused the lords of plotting 'to reverse the judgment of Earl Thomas of Lancaster, and that would be to our disinheritance, and of many others'.[11] Mowbray had identified a conspiracy that would destroy the House of Lancaster. With little choice, Henry Bolingbroke went straight to his father.

The possibility of war between the nobility and the Crown had presented itself, and John of Gaunt was desperate to maintain peace and familial harmony. He advised that the best option, on the back of Mowbray's rumour, was to go to Richard and tell him the truth. In January 1398, Henry Bolingbroke duly recounted to the King what was said in his meeting with Thomas Mowbray on the road at Brentford. Bolingbroke was evidently terrified, for shortly before he came to Richard in Shrewsbury, he visited the shrine of John Bridlington, where he prayed for safety, and as he faced the King, he may have been wearing a necklace he had recently commissioned, containing a medicinal stone, known for protection against poison.[12]

Richard carefully listened to Henry Bolingbroke's account of his meeting with Mowbray and asked him to write it down, before issuing an order for Mowbray's arrest. Henry met with the King at his lodgings in Great Haywood in Staffordshire, whilst John of Gaunt prepared to ride west to meet his son and attend the resumption of Parliament, which was to be held at Shrewsbury. By this point, Thomas Mowbray had been made aware of Henry's report to the King. It is possible that he had attempted to manipulate both Gaunt and Bolingbroke into a conspiracy against Richard, but was thwarted by Gaunt's loyalty – a crucial misjudgement on Mowbray's part, but one that emphasises the continuing tension between Richard and his uncle. Furious that he had backed the wrong horse, Mowbray allegedly planned the assassination of Gaunt as he made his way to Shrewsbury. It has never been definitely decided whether Mowbray did indeed orchestrate such a plan, but in any case Gaunt survived. The Duke was warned of the threat and travelled to Shrewsbury via an alternative route.

Thomas Mowbray eventually gave himself up and was imprisoned in the Tower. He was stripped of office and title and was forced to await his fate in a cold, dark cell. Henry Bolingbroke cut a humble figure, apologising profusely to Richard for his role with the original Lords Appellant and begging further pardon. After a brief and agonisingly anxious period in the Tower, he was granted his freedom. Under the strain of the outcome of the Shrewsbury Parliament and his honourable advice to his son to be honest with the King, John of Gaunt fell ill. Struck with a fever, he was forced to spend his recovery at Lilleshall Abbey in Shropshire, where his worried wife Katherine stayed by his side until he recovered. The pressure of Richard's unpredictable behaviour and concern for the safety of his son had an inevitable impact on the ageing Duke's health.

On 31 January a commission gathered at Bristol, having received an order to handle the Mowbray conspiracy. It was led by John of Gaunt and was peppered with enemies of Thomas Mowbray; Henry Bolingbroke immediately had the upper hand. Both Mowbray and Bolingbroke were permitted to speak as John of Gaunt presided, and before the entire committee, Henry Bolingbroke revealed his anger with Thomas Mowbray, accusing him of neglecting his office as Captain of Calais, stealing Crown funds and even murdering the Duke of Gloucester. Mowbray denied all charges laid before him and it was ordered that, if the matter could not be resolved, it would have to be decided 'by the laws of chivalry'. During a following meeting at Windsor, Mowbray admitted plotting to kill John of Gaunt, and the King offered both men the chance to reconcile their differences.[13] Furious that his honesty had put him on the back foot, Henry Bolingbroke refused to make amends with Thomas Mowbray, and Mowbray likewise. Both men had played into Richard's hands, and it was decided that the two great Lords of England would fight it out in a duel.

It is surprising that John of Gaunt was willing to accept this outcome to the dispute and it is highly unlikely that it was his decision. Having previously rejected Bolingbroke's wish to fight in Friesland for fear that it would be too dangerous, Gaunt would hardly be willing to risk the life of his firstborn son and heir in a duel – even in adherence to the code of chivalry. It seems that the decision was Richard's, in the guise of a diplomatic solution. Whatever the outcome of the duel, it would suit the King. If Mowbray were defeated, he was rid of a probable traitor and the dutiful killer of Gloucester. If Bolingbroke were defeated, he was rid of a threat, for upon the death of Gaunt – as Richard was well aware – Bolingbroke was set to inherit unfathomable wealth and power. And so the most famous duel in history – later dramatised by Shakespeare – was set to take place at Coventry on 16 September – almost exactly one year after the Parliament that rid the King of Arundel, Warwick and Gloucester. With the two remaining Lords Appellant about to fight one another, Richard had seemingly managed to play an impeccable political game.

In the five months between the announcement of the duel and it taking place, Henry Bolingbroke anxiously moved around the Lancastrian lands. John of Gaunt accompanied his son to Yorkshire where they probably hunted together and discussed the impending event. Bolingbroke was known for his skill in the lists. He was a trained knight, excellent jouster and seasoned warrior, which may have eased Gaunt's concern for his wellbeing. However, as a nobleman, Thomas Mowbray had also received such training. News of the duel spread throughout the country, for it was going to be the spectacle of the year. Rumours even travelled overseas, as members of the French nobility wrote to Bolingbroke during the summer hiatus and Gian Galeazzo Visconti, the Duke of Milan, sent him a brand-new suit of armour, with four Milanese armourers to enable him to correctly assemble it.[14]

After a final, dutiful attempt to reconcile Henry Bolingbroke and Thomas Mowbray, Richard dispatched invitations to the duel. Bolingbroke's immediate family were evidently concerned for his well-being. In the weeks leading up to the duel, Henry was at Kenilworth Castle – Gaunt's favourite home – and his half-brother, Henry Beaufort, who was now the Bishop of Lincoln, ensured that the diocese prayed for his cause.[15]

Early on the morning of 16 September, eager spectators began to arrive at Coventry, grappling for a good view of the lists. Representatives from Scotland, France and Germany attended; the French were led by the Count of Saint Pol, who had been present at the Smithfield joust. John of Gaunt was also present, but according to Froissart, 'seldom saw his son' and also 'never went near the King'. Shortly before nine o'clock, Henry Bolingbroke emerged, wearing the Milanese armour he had been gifted, with seven magnificent horses that were suitably adorned. Bolingbroke addressed the crowd – an audience of hundreds – who had come to witness a theatre of chivalry and politics: 'I am Henry of Lancaster, Duke of Hereford . . . and I have come here to do my duty in combat with Thomas Mowbray, Duke of Norfolk, a false and disloyal traitor to God, the King, his Kingdom and myself'. He then raised his silver shield which bore the arms of Saint George – a red cross – and made his way to his decorated pavilion.

As part of a fashionable display of authority at such a tense event, the King was the next to arrive and, as he made himself comfortable, Thomas Mowbray was permitted to enter – dressed in German armour – and rode towards his pavilion. Following strict sporting rules, both men had their lances measured before the pavilions were removed from the arena and the horses were unrestrained. At the highest moment of tension, just as Henry Bolingbroke made ready for the advance, the King abruptly stood and loudly ordered the duel to stop. Bolingbroke and Mowbray backed down, shocked. The crowd – who had been denied a show – whispered and grumbled as Richard left the stand and waltzed away into a two-hour discussion over the next course of action.

His loyal man – Speaker of the Commons, John Bushy – finally returned to deliver the King's verdict. He announced that both Bolingbroke and Mowbray were to be exiled; Henry Bolingbroke for ten years and Thomas Mowbray, eternally. John of Gaunt had been anxiously watching events unfurl. It is unknown whether he was with Richard as he came to his decision, but Gaunt quickly pleaded with the King to reduce the years of his son's exile. Richard hesitantly ordered Bolingbroke's sentence to be reduced, but by only four years. It is uncertain why Richard chose exile as the course of action, but it reeks of indecision. It is likely that he had been looking for an opportunity to remove Henry Bolingbroke as a political threat. Exile was a better option for the King than allowing Bolingbroke to triumph – as he probably would have – in an exhibition of knightly prowess.

John of Gaunt and Henry Bolingbroke had a month to say their goodbyes and, for Gaunt, it was a time to give welcome advice to his hot-headed son. In the immediate aftermath of the duel that never was, Bolingbroke stayed with Gaunt at Leicester and made arrangements for the welfare of his children, who were in the care of Sir Hugh Waterton at Eaton and their tutor, Thomas Rothwell. Bolingbroke suggested he might go to the Count of Ostrevant in Hainault, as he had previously hoped, but John of Gaunt instead advised that he go straight to the Valois princes in Paris to seek their support. John of Gaunt was popular in Paris, respected by the royal circle and throughout his life had conducted himself well in their presence. His suggestion for Bolingbroke to seek their help was shrewd. Richard had previously sought to impress the French King and was dependent on their truce, making it plausible that, with French intervention, he might reduce or even relinquish Bolingbroke's sentence. Financially and logistically prepared for his exile, Henry Bolingbroke left Dover for Calais on 13

October 1398. He most likely said his final farewell to his father at Eltham Palace in Kent, where he also took leave of the King. Considering John of Gaunt's decision to write his will the previous year, the recurring illness that had prevented him travelling and a fever that left him at the mercy of the monks in Shropshire, it is likely that he felt the gravity of his son's possibly final goodbye deeply.

Around Christmas, two months after Bolingbroke's departure, John of Gaunt's health began to deteriorate and he wrote to Henry, urging him to visit his sisters, Philippa in Portugal and Catherine in Castile. It was also around this time that – according to Froissart – Henry Bolingbroke received news from Gaunt's physicians that his father 'laboured under so dangerous a disease, it must soon cause his death'.

From January 1399 Gaunt remained exclusively at Leicester Castle and, it appears, anticipated his approaching death, for he made amendments to his will. According to a chronicle written around twenty years later, his languor was 'suddane', which would account for Gaunt's inability to attend a diplomatic conference in Scotland that year; with his Scots experience, his presence would have certainly been expected. The chronicle also reveals that Richard visited Gaunt on his deathbed, offering him words of comfort. However, such words were unlikely to allay Gaunt's fears for the inheritance of his family, soon to be at the whim of a volatile and ruthless King. Shortly after Richard's visit, John of Gaunt died in his bed at Leicester Castle on 3 February 1399, with his beloved Duchess Katherine at his side. He died anxious and distressed over the future of his son, Henry, and the Lancastrian dynasty he had fought tirelessly to strengthen and develop.

The chroniclers at the time paid little attention to the death of the King's uncle, despite his influential role in European and domestic politics over the previous half-century. This means the exact cause of Gaunt's death remains a mystery. Thomas Gascoigne, a fifteenth-century chronicler, blamed the Duke's vigorous sex life for his demise. He claimed that when Gaunt was visited by Richard, he exposed himself to the King, to show him how his genitals had become rancid, rotting from venereal disease.[16] This is unlikely, playing on earlier outraged morality over his extramarital relationship with Katherine Swynford.

John of Gaunt's will makes no clear reference to the cause of his death, but demonstrates the great concern he had for his loved ones and the preservation of his estate. In a final act of loyalty and duty to Richard, Gaunt bequeathed him his favourite gold cup, which had been a gift from Katherine, and a gold salt cellar with a garter motif and a jewel. To Katherine he gave his most precious personal jewels, all kept together in a 'little box of cypress wood, to which, I carry the key myself'. He carefully allocated his remaining possessions and ensured the obits that he had secured in his lifetime for the souls of his former Duchesses would continue. As Gaunt died in Leicester, a large cortège was necessary to accompany his body south. It travelled through St Albans, the home of Thomas Walsingham, who had been scornful of Gaunt in his lifetime, but may also have been one of the monks who humbly prayed over his corpse as it was laid out in the abbey for one night. As his will requested, Gaunt's body was then transported to the Carmelite church in Fleet Street, in recognition of his lifelong commitment to the Carmelite Order.

The strangest stipulation in his will was that his body be laid out for 'forty days' – ten times the usual period – and that there may be 'no cering or embalming', before finally being buried. The longevity of the allocated period may suggest Gaunt's repentance, humility and piety. He acknowledged his negligence of the commandments and requested three candles be burned in reference to the Holy Trinity, 'to whom I submit for all the evils I have done'. So in a wash of candlelight, John of Gaunt posthumously hoped to be absolved of the many offences he believed he had caused God.

Nonetheless, his funeral was a magnificent affair and was attended, dutifully, by Richard, who – according to Froissart – was darkly pleased over the death of his uncle, writing to the King of France with the news 'with a sort of joy' but neglecting to tell Henry Bolingbroke.[17] Devastated, Bolingbroke clothed himself as a mourner and held a requiem mass for his father. The King of France and the Dukes of

Orleans, Berry and Burgundy attended, as they had all greatly respected the Duke of Lancaster.

Finally, as he wished, John of Gaunt was interred in 'the Cathedral Church of St Paul, of London, near the principal altar, beside my most dear late wife Blanch, who is there interred', around the Passion (16 March). Choosing to be buried next to his first wife, the mother of his heir, was John of Gaunt's final honourable act. His third wife, however, loyally and mournfully followed his body on its journey from Leicester to London.

What should have been a smooth transition of status, wealth and land from father to son, became an irresistible opportunity for the King. Before Gaunt was even buried, Richard ordered Henry Bolingbroke's exile to be extended for life. He stripped Henry of his lands and took possession of the Duchy of Lancaster himself.

As Henry waited in Paris, mourning his father, a messenger arrived with news from William Bagot, a knight who was present for Richard's decision. Bagot took it upon himself to write to the exiled Duke, urging him to 'help himself with manhood'.[18] Henry Bolingbroke was faced with a crucial, life-changing decision: to fight an anointed King, his own cousin, for the dynastic rights and responsibilities his father had carefully accumulated and protected, or surrender all to the will of a tyrant, thus adhering to the code of chivalry, law and familial loyalty his father had sworn to protect.

A century after Gaunt's death, Niccolò Machiavelli wrote: '[a] new ruler must determine all the injuries that he will need to inflict. He must inflict them once and for all'.

Around 4 July 1399, a small vessel bobbed about off the Yorkshire coast, finally landing at Ravenspur.[19] Henry, Duke of Lancaster, leapt from the boat accompanied by around sixty men. In the North of England, he was warmly welcomed and soon began reclaiming the castles that had belonged to his father: the rebellion had begun. As Henry arrived at Pontefract Castle – his father's favourite northern residence – 'crowds of gentlemen, knights and esquires from Yorkshire and Lancashire flocked to join him' and by the time he had reached Doncaster, he had 30,000 men under his command, fighting for the House of Lancaster.

The King was in Ireland at the time of Bolingbroke's invasion and promptly returned with a force that dwindled under the realisation that Richard could not defeat his cousin. The King fled into hiding disguised as a 'poor priest', but eventually Henry captured him at Flint Castle and transported him to the Tower of London under 'close guard'.[20] As Richard was imprisoned, Henry processed through the streets of London, lauded as a hero. His first action was to visit the tomb of his father, where he knelt by candlelight and wept. His tears were likely for his father, but also, possibly, for what Henry was about to do. At the feast of Michaelmas, an incensed Richard resigned his kingship to his cousin; in one last display of petulance he refused to hand over his crown to Henry, and instead laid it on the ground at his cousin's feet.

'The Lord Richard, late King, after his deposition, was carried away on the Thames in the silence of dark midnight, weeping and loudly lamenting he had ever been born'. According to the Welsh chronicler, Adam Usk, who served the Archbishop of Canterbury at the start of the fifteenth century, Richard was transported to Pontefract Castle, where he lay in chains, cold and damp and slowly starving to death.[21] Henry IV had won his crown, but the Lancastrian royal dynasty, that Gaunt wished to be defined by honour, began in blood.

EPILOGUE

'Thus lay in ashes that most venerable Church, one of the most ancient pieces of early piety in the Christian world'.

John Evelyn, 7 September 1666

THE LID OF THE ALABASTER TOMB, IMMACULATELY DESIGNED and constructed by Henry Yevele, depicted likenesses of Blanche of Lancaster and John of Gaunt with their eyes peacefully closed, their left hands raised as if in prayer and their right hands lovingly clasped together. After forty days, Gaunt's body was laid to rest in the tomb he had commissioned after the death of his first wife. The tomb, of such emotional significance to John of Gaunt, has been lost to eternity. In 1666, almost 300 years after his death, the Great Fire of London began only one mile away, in Pudding Lane, and swept through St Paul's Cathedral. Today, the dome of the cathedral pierces the skyline of London, replacing the edifice Gaunt knew and loved, one of many great buildings that stood in his lifetime and are now vanished or crumbling around the country: emblems of an age of war, chivalry and innovation. Stone speaks of longevity, but over centuries of fires, revolutions and storms, it too can be lost.

As John of Gaunt lay on his deathbed at Leicester Castle in 1399, he was in agony at the thought of his life's work – the cultivation of his father's dream alongside his own vision of a great European dynasty – crumbling into history, to be forgotten. However, it was after his death that his vision was finally realised and etched into eternity. His youngest daughter, Catherine, became Queen Consort and then Regent of Castile, and through her came the most famous alliance of the sixteenth century: the marriage between her great-granddaughter, Catherine of Aragon, and the King of England, Henry VIII. This union brought the dynasty full circle, for in 1485 Henry VIII's father, Henry VII, landed on the coast of Pembrokeshire and took the throne in the name of Tudor, through his mother, Margaret Beaufort. His victory at Bosworth and marriage to Elizabeth of York ended the War of the Roses between York and Lancaster, resolving the bloodshed between cousins that had begun with Bolingbroke's seizure of a throne he was not next in line to. Through the dynasty and European alliance he worked tirelessly to create, John of Gaunt became the father of a long line of famous monarchs, who dust the pages of history books to this day.

John of Gaunt's legacy: a family tree

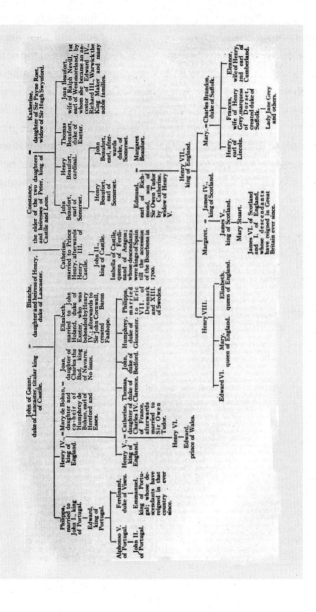

A Note on Sources

THERE HAVE BEEN TWO SCHOLARLY BIOGRAPHIES OF JOHN OF GAUNT. The first, written by Sydney Armitage-Smith in 1904, and the second, by Anthony Goodman in 1992. Armitage-Smith led the vanguard in unearthing the body of documents relating to John of Gaunt. He transcribed, translated and published John of Gaunt's Register – his roster of accounts: a crucial source on his life and movements as the Duke of Lancaster. Anthony Goodman provides a thorough analysis of John of Gaunt's life, looking meticulously at his movements, politics and ambitions in impeccable detail – a crucial starting-point for this book. W. Mark Ormrod's work on Edward III and the political landscape of the fourteenth century has also been essential reading. Professor Ormrod has offered smooth explanations on complex medieval politics, for which I am grateful. Equally, Michael Jones's excellent biography of the Black Prince has shed new light on the life and times of the world-famous Prince. I am indebted to Dr Jones's new research on the siege of Limoges, which I discuss in the book. In unpacking the complexities and nuances around the war in France, I have relied on the excellent series on the Hundred Years War by Jonathan Sumption. The colour, detail and even humour that leaps off the pages of his books enabled me to unpack how the ongoing war with France might have affected John of Gaunt.

Of the original sources available for Gaunt, his Register is the most insightful. It is preserved in the National Archives as part of the Records of the Duchy of Lancaster, PRO 30/14. Two hundred and thirty-five folios (pages) of original manuscript are bound in vellum in a large volume, around thirty centimetres in length and twenty centimetres wide. Inside the two volumes that make up the complete register are a series of documents with names and dates listed in the margins, that

were copied by Lancastrian clerks and passed under John of Gaunt's
Privy Seal – his personal seal, akin to a signature. The Register is a
crucial piece of evidence in understanding Gaunt's movements, the
management of his land and property, and his relationships. There is
information concerning the most senior members of his household –
his council – which included a chancellor, a steward, a chamberlain, a
controller and a receiver. There is also information on his treasurer,
castle constables, grooms, cooks, carpenters, minstrels, falconer,
gardener and armourers. The Register discloses information about
Gaunt's personal life in the gifts and grants he gave to family, loyal
retainers, the church and his wives and mistress, and provides the
greatest source of information on Lancastrian administration. The
Register sheds more light on John of Gaunt's personal activity and
decision-making than any other source available.

Other administrative records that have been crucial in my research
are the Parliamentary Rolls, the Calendar of Close Rolls and the
Calendar of Patent Rolls and the Inquisitions Post Mortem in
the reigns of Edward III and Richard II, amongst others. All of these
are helpful in analysing the political landscape of the fourteenth
century that John of Gaunt spent the majority of his life – successfully,
and unsuccessfully – navigating. At the National Archives in Kew are
the Duchy of Lancaster records which I have rifled through – resulting
in black fingertips and a sneeze. John of Gaunt's personal seals, also
held at the National Archives, provide a visual representation of his
rise to power – notably in the change of his seal to include the arms of
Castile and Leon.

The most colourful description of Gaunt's world comes from the
chronicle accounts of the period. Chroniclers were historians – often
clerical – who described events in chronological order. The archetypal
image of a chronicler is a monk or scribe clutching a quill and inking
colourful manuscripts but, by the fourteenth century, a chronicler
could also be secular and attached to a great household as a clerk.

The chronicles covering John of Gaunt's early years were largely
focused on the war with France and give detailed accounts of the battles

and campaigns that took place. Jean le Bel was a French soldier from Liege and one of the early chroniclers to write in French rather than in Latin. Of all the chronicle accounts, his was largely reliable. As a soldier, he travelled to England and Scotland and often wrote from personal experience. When he was not present, he did acquire good eyewitness accounts. Le Bel was a canon at Liege Cathedral, whose clergy were heavily involved in the practice and preparation of war, where he gathered much of his information.

Jean Froissart, writing from the 1360s, was heavily influenced by Jean le Bel and even repurposed sections of Le Bel's chronicle in his own. Froissart came to the English court under the patronage of Queen Philippa of Hainault – consort of Edward III – around 1361, until her death. The Queen employed Froissart as a court poet and story-teller. After the Queen's death, Froissart found employment in France with the Duke and Duchess of Brabant, and later as a chaplain to the Count of Blois. Around this time, his accounts of the Hundred Years War, particularly the siege of Limoges, became less favourable to the English. Through his prolific account of the period, Jean Froissart has become one of the best-known medieval writers.

The leading chronicles for the second part of the fourteenth century covered – amongst many things – the Black Death, war with France, the Good Parliament, the death of Edward III and ascension of Richard II, Wycliffe and Lollardy, unrest on the Scottish Borders and the Peasants' Revolt.

Thomas Walsingham's Chronicle is a polemic against John of Gaunt and anyone else Walsingham considered to be in breach of the Christian order of things – a large part of the Edwardian and Ricardian court. Thomas Walsingham was a Benedictine monk, based at St Albans Abbey – one the greatest monasteries of medieval England. Non-secular chroniclers of the fourteenth century were, like Walsingham, based in monasteries and dedicated to recording history as it was made. Thomas Walsingham was responsible for the scriptorium – the writing room – in which scribes, illuminators and binders worked tirelessly to produce manuscripts. Thomas Walsingham's chronicle was not from first-hand experience, but he seems to have had a network of informants – particularly for the Good Parliament in 1376. Walsingham has been a crucial source, for he was also one of the only English chroniclers to record events in Europe, such as the Papal Schism of 1378. This allows a glimpse into English reactions to major events overseas as well as domestic ones. In 1399, when John of Gaunt's son Henry IV ascended the throne, Walsingham's polemic was replaced with a less hostile version of events.

A stark alternative source to Thomas Walsingham is Henry Knighton. An Augustinian canon from St Mary of the Meadows in Leicester, Knighton was an advocate of John of Gaunt, and always offered a favourable representation of the Duke. Although Knighton shared Thomas Walsingham's views on Lollardy and infidelity, he blamed those around John of Gaunt, rather than the man himself. Knighton gathered his information from abbey documents and discussion with the Abbot. Otherwise, his knowledge was from informants in London and rumour. However, at Leicester, Knighton would have seen and possibly met John of Gaunt so had some level of authority regarding his character. His description of Gaunt's popularity in Leicester and the citizens' protection of his assets during the Peasants' Revolt is likely correct.

From the North of England, the *Anonimalle Chronicle* is the best source, compiled at St Mary's Abbey in York. It is considered to be one of the best accounts of the Good Parliament of 1376, and although the scribe was in York, he had a reliable informer. Equally, the chronicle gives a detailed account of the Peasants' Revolt and the destruction of John of Gaunt's property. The chronicler may have used the same London informer, but it is also possible that the account was copied from an unknown London chronicle. Nonetheless the *Anonimalle Chronicle* is a valuable source.

The best and least polemical source for the period, particularly the political scene in London, is the *Westminster Chronicle*. This covers 1381 to 1394 – five years before Gaunt's death. It is unknown exactly who wrote the chronicle and its author is often nicknamed the 'Monk of Westminster'. Of all of the medieval records, the *Westminster Chronicle* is the best narrative source of the reign of Richard II and is immaculately chronologically ordered, making it easy to follow events as they happened. Where other chroniclers were forced to rely on London informants, it is likely that the Monk of Westminster did witness much of his account. The information regarding fractious internal politics, particularly between John of Gaunt and Richard II, is invaluable.

Chroniclers were not usually present for the events they describe and many had an external motivation behind their accounts. Documents that survive were usually written by clerks and are largely administrative; however, many have been lost, or are barely legible. Together they build an understanding of John of Gaunt's world, but we can never know what it was truly like.

John of Gaunt, and the reigns of the Plantagenets, cannot be studied without examining their extensive castle-building. On inheriting the Dukedom of Lancaster, Gaunt assumed an impressive roster of properties, including some iconic castles that still stand today. Kenilworth Castle in Warwickshire was a particularly important building project and I have spent time walking within its grounds and inspecting its stones. Pontefract Castle's ruins rest in Yorkshire, Gaunt's powerhouse in the north where he rested or mustered his army before and after marching to Scotland. It was at this castle that Henry IV ruthlessly incarcerated and murdered his cousin, Richard II, shortly after Gaunt's death. The area around the Savoy is particularly atmospheric. The palace, or 'fair manor', symbolised John of Gaunt's inheritance as the Duke of Lancaster, a title and duty he hugely respected. The destruction of the Savoy Palace was cataclysmic for Gaunt and I believe that the year 1381 was pivotal in his life thereafter. The Savoy represented power, kingship, wealth, grandeur and, most importantly, the Lancastrian legacy. When the palace was reduced to ashes, he never recovered the loss, and today only the foundations of the chapel remain.

Acknowledgements

It is often said it takes a village to raise a child, I think the same applies to writing a book.

Thank you first and foremost to my wonderful editor, Sam Carter, and the team at Oneworld for taking a chance on John of Gaunt and on me, as an author in my infancy. Over the last three years you have nurtured me, steered me in the right direction and been enormously kind and patient. I couldn't have asked for a better publisher. Thank you to Rachel Mills, the best agent I could ask for, who has been with me throughout the whole journey. You listened to me wax lyrical about John of Gaunt and medieval history and you have waved my flag thereafter – thank you, always. Dan Jones, thank you for coffee in Battersea, telling me to write this book, for generally being at the end of the phone or email when I need your advice, and for your abundant kindness and encouragement to myself and others.

Thank you to everyone who has – at some point over the last three years – offered me a few days or a few hours of childcare in order to write. Imogen, Julia, Sarah and Sam, Tom, Carys, Dad and Debbie, thank you for that crucial help – even if it was just pushing the pram around the park whilst I scribbled.

Thank you to Jan Cooper, for taking the time to show me around Kenilworth Castle and for your expertise. It was a highlight in my research and enormously helpful to bring colour to John of Gaunt's world. Thank you especially to Sean Cunningham, Head of Medieval Records at the National Archives, for helping me dig and for brilliant conversation as we got our hands dirty. Thank you Laura Tompkins for sharing your extensive research on Alice Perrers, I am so grateful for your generosity and time. Thank you to Holy Trinity Church in Rothwell, the convenors of the Institute of Historical Research

Medieval Seminar and the staff at the London Library, the British Library, the Park Theatre and Hot Numbers, for keeping me well supplied with conversation, books, wine and coffee.

To the amazing community of historians who have been an enormous support along the way. There are too many of you to name all, but in particular; Joanne Paul, Estelle Paranque, Rebecca Rideal, Emma Wells, Dan Snow, Suzannah Lipscomb and Sophie Ambler.

I must acknowledge the memory of my dearest grandparents who passed away during the writing of this book and who would have been so proud to hold it: thank you for being constant and kind. In memory of Patricia Fickling; may you, inimitable lady, rest in peace. Finally, in memory of Professor W. Mark Ormrod, whose expertise on Edward III shaped much of my understanding of the fourteenth century: I am so grateful.

Thank you to my siblings; Hayley, Tom and Imogen for your endless support. To my daughter, Effie, for being the light of my life. And to my darling husband, Henry, whose unbending kindness, love, encouragement, lion's share of dishwashing and bed-time routine, plus well-timed offers of sustenance, enabled me to complete this book – I couldn't be more grateful for you, nor could I have done it without you. Thank you so much to my Mum, who has always taught me that anything is possible, because, why not? Lastly, thank you to my Pa, for trudging around castles, museums and mounds with me over the last three decades. This book could not have been conceived without those ramblings and your enduring support thereafter. It is only appropriate that this is dedicated to you.

Helen Carr, November 2020

Further Reading

This note is for anybody interested in learning more about the fourteenth century – war, revolt, plague and politics – or more about John of Gaunt and his family. The best place to start when researching the period is the ODNB (Oxford Dictionary of National Biography) available online in most good libraries or through a university portal. For the lives of Edward III, Richard II and Henry IV, I would recommend starting with the Yale English Monarchs Series for the most comprehensive biographies.

For primary reading material I would suggest looking at BHO (British History Online). Founded by the Institute of Historical Research and the History of Parliament Trust in 2003, this is an invaluable source of records from the fourteenth century. The Parliamentary Rolls are transcribed and there is an introduction to each Parliament held.

For those wanting to dig a little deeper, the National Archives is a treasure trove. It is open to anybody with a reader's card – you do not have to be a scholar or professional researcher. I would highly recommend this as an experience.

For John of Gaunt's surviving properties, some are owned by English Heritage and others are private. I would recommend Kenilworth Castle as the best example of Gaunt's investment in architecture. Kenilworth also provides an extensive visitor guidebook which has an abundance of information on Gaunt and fourteenth-century architecture.

For general reading on the fourteenth century, a good start is McKisack, May, *The Fourteenth Century 1307–1399* (Oxford: Clarendon Press, 1959) and Keen, Maurice H., *England in the Later Middle Ages: A Political History*, 2nd ed. (London: Routledge, 2003). On the social landscape of the fourteenth century, Scott, A.F., *Everyone* a Witness: *The Plantagenet Age*, Commentaries of an Era (New York: Thomas Y. Crowell Co., 1975) and more the more recent Picard, Liza, *Chaucer's People* (London: Weidenfeld & Nicolson, 2017). Another entertaining read that helps shed light on the religious and devotional history of the fourteenth century is the contemporary account of Margery Kempe. This is the first memoir known to have ever been written by a woman in the English language: Kempe, Margery, *The Book of Margery Kempe*, trans. Anthony Bale (Oxford: Oxford University Press, 2015).

On the wool trade – a crucial part of fourteenth-century infrastructure – see Power, Eileen, *The Wool Trade in English Medieval History: Being the Ford Lectures* (London: Oxford University Press, 1941). Also, the more recent study, Lloyd, T.H., *The English Wool Trade in the Middle Ages* (Cambridge: Cambridge University Press, 2005).

The original comprehensive biography of John of Gaunt was written by Sydney Armitage-Smith, who also transcribed and printed John of Gaunt's registers, *John of Gaunt* (s.l.: Constable, 1904). This is best read in conjunction with the best – and most detailed – scholarly take on Gaunt, Goodman, Anthony, *John of Gaunt: The Exercise of Princely Power in Fourteenth-Century Europe* (Harlow: Longman, 1992).

For the Black Prince, there are three excellent biographies. Barber, Richard, *Edward, Prince of Wales and Aquitaine* (Woodbridge: Boydell Press: 1996) also Green, David, *Edward, the Black Prince* (Harlow: Longman, 2007). And most recently, and with new research into the siege of Limoges, Jones, Michael, *The Black Prince* (London: Head of Zeus, 2017). For a contemporary account of the Black Prince's life, the best is Chandos Herald, *Life of the Black Prince by the Herald of Sir John Chandos*, ed. Mildred K. Pope and Eleanor C. Lodge (Oxford: Clarendon Press, 1910).

There are several good biographies of Edward III available, but the best is by the leading expert on Edward III, Mark Ormrod. His Yale biography has been invaluable: Ormrod, W. Mark, *Edward III* (New Haven: Yale University Press, 2013). I would also recommend other readings by Mark Ormrod on the fourteenth century, particularly the royal household: Ormrod, W. Mark, 'The Trials of Alice Perrers', *Speculum*, 83 no. 2, 2008, pp. 366–96. And Ormrod, W. Mark., 'The Royal Nursery: A Household for the Younger Children of Edward III', *English Historical Review*, 120 no. 486, 2005, pp. 398–415. Of his consort, Philippa, I used Hardy, B.C., *Philippa of Hainault and Her Times* (London: John Long, 1910).

Of Edward III's contemporaries Henry, Duke of Lancaster, is the most discussed in the book. His best biography is Fowler, Kenneth, *The King's Lieutenant: Henry of Grosmont, First Duke of Lancaster, 1310–1361* (London: Elek, 1969). This sheds light not only on Henry but on the life of a wealthy magnate in the fourteenth century, outside of royalty.

For an understanding of the history of the House of Lancaster, the best start is Somerville, Robert, *History of the Duchy of Lancaster* (London: Chancellor and Council of the Duchy of Lancaster, 1953). For information on the establishment of Leicester as the main Lancastrian seat see Bothwell, J.S., 'The Making of the Lancastrian Capital at Leicester: The Battle of Boroughbridge, Civic Diplomacy and Seigneurial Building Projects in Fourteenth Century England', *Journal of Medieval History*, 38 no. 3, 2012, pp. 335–57. The best scholarly study of Lancastrian power is this detailed analysis of the Lancastrian retinue, under John of Gaunt. This is crucial to understand the bulwark of land, properties and people John of Gaunt controlled. Walker, Simon, *The Lancastrian Affinity 1361–1399* (Oxford: Clarendon, 1990). The most information I could find on the Savoy Palace is here: Loftie, W.J., and White, H., *Memorials of the Savoy, the Palace, the Hospital, the Chapel* (London: Macmillan and Co., 1878).

There is a variety of reading material on the Black Death. I have relied on Green, Monica H., ed., *Pandemic Disease in the Medieval World: Rethinking the Black Death* (Kalamazoo, MI: Arc Medieval Press, 2015) for a detailed medical explanation of the effects of *Yersinia pestis*. I have also read Cantor, Norman F., *In the Wake of the Plague: The Black Death and the World it Made* (New York: Simon & Schuster, 2001) which discusses the impact the Black Death had on English society. Another useful study on the effect of the plague is Hays, J.N., *Epidemics and Pandemics: Their Impacts on Human History* (Santa Barbara, Calif.; Oxford: ABC-CLIO, 2005). For a study of the Black Death in London see Porter, Stephen, *Black Death: A New History of the Bubonic Plagues of London* (Stroud: Amberley Publishing, 2018).

On the Hundred Years War, the best starting point is the first three volumes of Jonathan Sumption's series. The first three cover the war under Edward III and Richard II: Sumption, Jonathan, *The Hundred Years War, Volume 1: Trial by Battle* (London: Faber & Faber, 1990); Sumption, Jonathan, *The Hundred Years War, Volume 2: Trial by Fire* (London: Faber & Faber, 1999); and Sumption, Jonathan, *The Hundred Years War, Volume 3: Divided Houses* (London: Faber & Faber, 2009). I would also suggest, Taylor, Craig, *Chivalry and the Ideals of Knighthood in France During the Hundred Years War* (Cambridge: Cambridge University Press, 2013).

For war at sea, and the organisation of Edward's navy, see Cushway, Graham, *Edward III and the War at Sea: The English Navy, 1327–1377* (Woodbridge: Boydell Press, 2011). For information on Calais as an English outpost, the most informative text I found was Grummitt, David, *The Calais Garrison: War and Military Service in England, 1436–1558* (Woodbridge: Boydell Press, 2008). On the organisation of the army see Bell, Adrian R. and Curry, Anne, *The Soldier in Later Medieval England* (Oxford: Oxford University Press, 2013). Another useful article on London's effort to support the war is Konieczny, Peter Michael, 'London's War Effort during the early Years of the Reign of Edward III', in *The Hundred Years War; a Wider Focus*, ed. L.J. Andrew Villalon and Donald Kagay (Leiden: Brill, 2005). An invaluable book which compiles chronicle accounts of the war, with introductions, is Rogers, Clifford J., *The Wars of Edward III, Sources and Interpretations* (Woodbridge: Boydell Press, 1999). The best and most up to date biography on Bertrand du Guesclin is Vernier, Richard, *The Flower of Chivalry: Bertrand du Guesclin and the Hundred Years War* (Woodbridge: Boydell Press, 2003). On the human impact of war, I have relied on Green, David, *The Hundred Years War: A People's History*

(New Haven: Yale University Press, 2014) alongside Wright, Nicholas, *Knights and Peasants: The Hundred Years War in the French Countryside* (Woodbridge: Boydell Press, 1998). For an understanding of the confusing culture around war, battle, the taking of prisoners and securing ransom, see Ambühl, Rémy, *Prisoners of War in the Hundred Years War: Ransom Culture in the Late Middle Ages* (Cambridge: Cambridge University Press, 2013).

On Spain and Castile, the most detailed analysis is in Russell, P.E., *The English Intervention in Spain and Portugal in the Age of Edward III and Richard II* (Oxford: Clarendon Press, 1955). On Pedro the Cruel, the biography I have used is Estow, Clara, *Pedro the Cruel of Castile: 1350–1369* (Leiden: Brill, 1995). For the military campaign leading up the Battle of Nájera, see Villalon, L.J. Andrew, 'Spanish Involvement in the Hundred Years War and the Battle of Nájera', in *The Hundred Years War: A Wider Focus*, Part 1, ed. L.J. Andrew Villalon and Donald J. Kagay (Leiden: Brill, 2005).

On the ongoing conflict with Scotland, a broad and informative study is Nicholson, Ranald, *Scotland: The Later Middle Ages* (Edinburgh: Oliver & Boyd, 1974). This can be read alongside Holinshed, Raphael, *The Scottish Chronicle: Or, A Complete History & Description of Scotland; Being an Accurate Narration of the Beginning, Increase, Proceedings, Wars, Acts and Government of the Scottish Nation, from the Original Thereof, Unto the Year 1585*, Volume 2 (J. Findlay, Scotland, 1805).

For more information on the Good Parliament, see Holmes, George, *The Good Parliament* (Oxford: Clarendon Press, 1975), for a clear analysis of the cause, action and effect of the Parliament. On the accusations against John of Gaunt following the Good Parliament see Wedgewood, Josiah C., 'John of Gaunt and the Packing of Parliament', *The English Historical Review*, 45 no. 180, 1930, pp. 623–25. I think it is useful to read William Langland's poem which references Gaunt as 'the cat of the court' – Langland, William, *Piers Plowman*, https://chaucer.fas.harvard.edu/pages/william-langland-c1332-c1400, which should be read alongside Dodd, Gwilym, 'A Parliament full of rats? *Piers*

Plowman and the Good Parliament of 1376', *Historical Research*, 79 no. 203, 2006, pp. 21–49.

For more on the literature of the period – Chaucer in particular – the best start is the most recent, excellent biography on Geoffrey Chaucer which brings an extraordinary amount of colour and detail to his world. Turner, Marion, *Chaucer: a European Life* (Princeton, New Jersey: Princeton University Press, 2019). For a broad understanding of the development of the English language, see Rigg, A.G., *A History of Anglo-Latin Literature, 1066–1422* (Cambridge: Cambridge University Press, 1992).

For the Peasants' Revolt, the most useful study is this compilation of edited sources. This has been invaluable and contains – at length – the most information on the uprising, from contemporary accounts. Dobson, R.B., ed., *The Peasants' Revolt of 1381* (London: Macmillan, 1970). For a gripping narrative account of the Revolt, I would recommend Jones, Dan, *Summer of Blood: The Peasants' Revolt of 1381* (London: HarperCollins, 2009).

On Richard II, the best starting point is the Yale biography, Saul, N., *Richard II* (New Haven, Conn. and London: Yale University Press, 1999). On his first Parliament and the continual councils, this was a useful article: Edwards, J.G., 'Some Common Petitions in Richard II's First Parliament', *Bulletin of the Institute of Historical Research*, 26 no. 74, 1953, pp. 200–13. There has been much attention given to the latter part of Richard's reign, his 'tyranny' in particular. For this, see Bennett, M., *Richard II and the Revolution of 1399* (Stroud: Sutton, 1999). This is best read alongside the excellent McHardy, A.K., trans. and ed., *The Reign of Richard II, From Minority to Tyranny 1377–97* (Manchester: Manchester University Press, 2012), and Given-Wilson, Chris, trans. and ed., *Chronicles of the Revolution, 1397–1400: The Reign of Richard II* (Manchester: Manchester University Press, 1993).

Also by Chris Given-Wilson is the best and most comprehensive biography on John of Gaunt's son, Henry IV. Given-Wilson, Chris, *Henry IV* (New Haven and London: Yale University Press, 2017).

John of Gaunt's will is published here: Nichols, J., *A Collection of all the Wills, now Known to be Extant, of the Kings and Queens of England* (London: printed by John Nichol, 1780).

Some printed or digitised primary sources:

Calendar of Entries in the Papal Registers Relating To Great Britain and Ireland: Volume 3, 1342-1362, ed. W.H. Bliss and C. Johnson (London: H.M.S.O., 1897).

Calendar of Inquisitions Post Mortem: Volume 13, Edward III, ed. A.E. Stamp, J.B.W. Chapman, M.C.B. Dawes (London, 1954).

Calendar of Letter Books, (London: J. E. Francis, 1899-1912). Also see the Plea and Memoranda rolls which highlight the efforts made by Londoners, online at https://www.british-history.ac.uk/search/series/plea-memoranda-rolls.

Collection des Chroniques Nationales Français, ed. J.A. Buchon, xxiii (Paris: Verdière, 1826).

Fawtier, R., *Hand-list of Additions to the Collection of Latin Manuscripts in the John Rylands Library, 1908-1920* (Aberdeen: University Press, 1921).

Froissart, Jean, *Chronicles of England France and Spain*, trans. and ed. Thomas Johnes (London: William Smith, 1844).

Froissart, Jean, *The Chronicles of England, France and Spain,* ed. Geoffrey Brereton (London: Penguin, 1968).

Froissart, Jean. *The Chronicles of England, France and Spain*, ed. Ernest Rhys (London: J.M. Dent & Co, 1906).

Gray, Thomas, *Scalacronica: The Reigns of Edward I., Edward II., and Edward III.* trans. Sir Herbert Maxwell (Glasgow: James MacLehose & Sons, 1907).

Hardyng, John, *Chronicle: Edited from British Library MS Lansdowne 204*, ed. James Simpson and Sarah Peverley (Kalamazoo, MI: Medieval Institute Publications, 2015).

John of Gaunt's Register edited for the Royal Historical Society from the original MS. at the Public Record Office by Sydney Armitage-Smith. Camden third series; vol. XX, XXI (London: Offices of the Society, 1911).

Knighton, Henry, *Knighton's Chronicle: 1337-1396*, ed. and trans. G.H. Martin (Oxford: Clarendon Press, 1995).

Le Bel, Jean, *The True Chronicles of Jean le Bel, 1290-1360*, trans. Nigel Bryant (Woodbridge: Boydell Press, 2011).

Parliament Rolls of Medieval England, ed. Chris Given-Wilson, Paul Brand, Seymour Phillips, *et al.* (Woodbridge: Boydell Press; London: National Archives, 2005), British History Online.

The Paston Letters, ed. Norman Davis (Oxford: Oxford University Press, 1999).

Walsingham, Thomas, *The Chronica Maiora of Thomas Walsingham, 1376–1422*, trans. David Preest (Woodbridge: Boydell Press, 2005).

Walsingham, Thomas, *The St Albans Chronicle: The Chronica Maiora of Thomas Walsingham*, ed. and trans. John Taylor, Wendy R. Childs, and Leslie Watkiss (Oxford: Clarendon Press, 2003–11).

The Register of Walter de Stapledon, Bishop of Exeter, A.D. 1307–1326, ed. F.C. Hingeston-Randolph (s.l.: George Bell & Sons, 1892).

The Westminster Chronicle 1381–1394, ed. L.C. Hector and B.F. Harvey (Oxford: Clarendon Press, 1982).

Notes

Chapter 1

1 Froissart, Jean, *The Chronicles of England, France and Spain*, ed. Geoffrey Brereton (London: Penguin, 1968), pp. 62–5.

2 The French Chronicle of London, in Rogers, Clifford J., *The Wars of Edward III, Sources and Interpretations* (Woodbridge: Boydell Press, 1999), p. 85.

3 MEC1586, National Maritime Museum, Greenwich, London. Caird Fund.

4 The news was delivered to the King in London by three of the Queen's maids; Amicia de Gloucestria, Alice de Betyngfeld and Margery de Semor. They were rewarded with £200, *CCR*, 1341–1343, p. 467.

5 Froissart, Jean, *The Chronicles of England, France and Spain*, p. 65.

6 Le Bel, Jean, *The True Chronicles of Jean le Bel, 1290–1360*, trans. Nigel Bryant (Woodbridge: Boydell Press, 2011).

7 Froissart, Jean, *The Chronicles of England, France and Spain*, ed. Ernest Rhys (London: J.M. Dent & Co, 1906), p. 18.

8 Foedera, vol. II, pp. 799–800, translated in *CCR*, 1330–1333, pp. 158–9.

9 Le Bel, 165–8, in Rogers, *Wars of Edward III*, p. 79.

10 Ormrod, W. Mark, *Edward III* (New Haven: Yale University Press, 2013), p. 214.

11 Armitage-Smith, S., *John of Gaunt* (s.l.: Constable, 1904), pp. 1–3.

12 C47/13/6/3. The National Archives, London.

13 Sumption, Jonathan, *The Hundred Years War, Volume 1: Trial by Battle* (London: Faber & Faber, 1990), p. 345.

14 Goodman, Anthony, *John of Gaunt: The Exercise of Princely Power in Fourteenth-Century Europe* (Harlow: Longman, 1992), p. 29.

15 *CPR*, 1343–1345, pp. 4–5.

16 *The Register of Walter de Stapledon, Bishop of Exeter, A.D. 1307–1326*, ed. F.C. Hingeston-Randolph (s.l.: George Bell & Sons, 1892).

17 Sub nomine aule scholarium Regine de Oxon (Foundation Charter, Magrath, i, 14; Cal. of Arch. iv, p. 732).

18 Ormrod, W. Mark, 'The Royal Nursery: a Household for the Younger Children of Edward III', *English Historical Review*, 120 no. 486, (2005), pp. 398–415, pp. 404–5.

19 Parliamentary Rolls (C65/5. *RP*, II.103–106).

20 Hardyng, John, *Chronicle: Edited from British Library MS Lansdowne 204*, ed. James Simpson and Sarah Peverley (Kalamazoo, MI: Medieval Institute Publications, 2015), p. 334.

21 Goodman, Anthony, *John of Gaunt: The Exercise of Princely Power in Fourteenth-Century Europe* (Harlow: Longman, 1992), p. 29.

22 Knighton, Henry, *Knighton's Chronicle: 1337–1396*, ed. and trans. G.H. Martin (Oxford: Clarendon Press, 1995), pp. 101–3.

23 Knighton, pp.101–3.

24 Thomas Walsingham, in *The Black Death*, ed. Rosemary Horrox (Manchester; New York: Manchester University Press, 1994), p. 154.

25 Palmer, Robert C., *English Law in the Age of the Black Death, 1348–1381: A Transformation of Governance and Law* (Chapel Hill, NC: University of North Carolina Press, 1993), p. 4.

26 Cantor, Norman F., *In the Wake of the Plague: The Black Death and the World it Made* (New York: Simon & Schuster, 2001), p. 6.

Chapter 2

1 Cushway, Graham, *Edward III and the War at Sea: The English Navy, 1327–1377* (Woodbridge: Boydell Press, 2011), p. 157.

2 Le Baker, Geoffrey, *The Chronicle of Geoffrey Le Baker of Swinbrook*, trans. David Preest, ed. Richard Barber (Woodbridge: Boydell, 2012), p. 94.

3 Ibid., p. 95.

4 Froissart, Jean, *Chronicles of England France and Spain*, trans. and ed. Thomas Johnes (London: William Smith, 1844), p. 198.

5 Le Baker, *Chronicle of Geoffrey le Baker*, p. 60.

6 Froissart, Chronicles (1844), pp. 198–9.

7 8 September 1350, Rotherhithe, William, son of William de Radeclif, was pardoned for burning the grange of Roger de Atherton and the deaths of three men, for good service against the Spanish at Sea. *CPR*, 1350, Public Record Office, p. 562.

8 *Black Prince's Register*, 1352, p. 54.

9 Newton, Stella M., *Fashion in the Age of the Black Prince: A Study of the Years 1340–1365* (Woodbridge: Boydell, 1980).

10 Fawtier, R., *Hand-list of Additions to the Collection of Latin Manuscripts in the John Rylands Library, 1908–1920* (Aberdeen: University Press, 1921), pp. 11–13.

11 *CCR*, Edward III, Vol. 9 1349–1354, pp. 248–54, reference to extensive payments being made for the running costs and garden maintenance in 1350, this is around £200 per week today.

12 *Black Prince's Register*, Vol. 2, p. 9.

13 Le Bel, *True Chronicles*, p. 207.

14 Le Baker, *Chronicle of Geoffrey le Baker*, p. 125.

15 Le Bel, *True Chronicles*, p. 212.

16 Grummitt, David, *The Calais Garrison: War and Military Service in England, 1436–1558* (Woodbridge: Boydell Press, 2008), p. 1.

17 Avesbury, pp. 429–31, in Rogers, pp. 151–2.

18 *Knighton's Chronicle*, p. 137.

19 Le Bel, *True Chronicles*, p. 119.

20 *Knighton's Chronicle*, p. 137.

21 Ibid., p. 139.

22 *CPR*, Edward III, 1327–1377, p. 543.

23 Walsingham, Thomas, *The Chronica Maiora of Thomas Walsingham, 1376–1422*, trans. David Preest (Woodbridge: Boydell Press, 2005), p. 123.

24 Froissart, *Chronicles* (1968), p. 169.

Chapter 3

1 Turner, Marion, *Chaucer: A European Life* (Princeton, New Jersey: Princeton University Press, 2019), p. 48.

2 *CPR*, 1358–1361, p. 488.

3 'Regesta 234: 1359', in *Calendar of Entries in the Papal Registers Relating to Great Britain and Ireland: Volume 3, 1342–1362*, ed. W.H. Bliss and C. Johnson (London: H.M.S.O., 1897), pp. 603–9.

4 Constitutions of Richard de Marisco, Bishop of Durham, at the Council of Durham, 1220, in Scott, A.F., *Everyone a Witness: The Plantagenet Age, Commentaries of an Era* (New York: Thomas Y. Crowell Co., 1975), p. 55.

5 *CCR*, 1354–1360, membrane 28, p. 36. Auditors of the account of the King's clerk requested to 'pay £226, 11s and 7.5d for wax, spidery, napery, linen, cloth of gold and silk for the marriage of John of Gant, Earl of Richemunde, celebrated at Redynges.'

6 Holinshed, *Chronicles of England, Scotland and Ireland Vol. 2* (Delhi: Pranava Books, 1965–2007), p. 671.

7 Previously, Londoners had loaned Edward a sum of £130,000 to finance his military ventures in France. Not only this, they also donated soldiers to the

war effort, see the *Calendar of Letter Books*, ed. Reginald R. Sharpe (London: J.E. Francis, 1899–1912). Also see the Plea and Memoranda rolls which highlight the efforts made by Londoners, online at https://www.british-history.ac.uk/search/series/plea-memoranda-rolls.

8 *Knighton's Chronicle*, p. 169.

9 *CCR*, Edward III, 1354–1360, mb.14, 'the King is about to cross the sea with his army for the furtherance of his French war.'

10 *Anonimalle Chronicle*, pp. 44–5.

11 Turner, *Chaucer*, p. 79.

12 *Knighton's Chronicle*, p. 173.

13 Edward managed to negotiate a three-year truce for 200,000 florins at Burgundy: Gray, Thomas, *Scalacronica: The Reigns of Edward I., Edward II., and Edward III.*, trans. Sir Herbert Maxwell (Glasgow: James MacLehose & Sons, 1907), pp. 148–59.

14 Ambühl, Rémy, *Prisoners of War in the Hundred Years War* (Cambridge: Cambridge University Press, 2013), p. 3.

15 Turner, *Chaucer*, p. 70. £16 equates to around £8,000 today.

16 *Knighton's Chronicle*, p. 177.

17 *Scalacronica*, pp. 148–59.

18 *Scalacronica*, pp. 148–59, in Rogers, *The Wars of Edward III*, pp. 176–80.

19 *Knighton's Chronicle*, p. 177.

20 Froissart, *Chronicles* (1844), p. 283.

21 'Regesta 240: 1359–1360', in Bliss and Johnson, eds., *Calendar of Papal Registers*, pp. 628–32.

22 King Jean's [John's] Letter on the Treaty of Brétigny, in Rogers, *The Wars of Edward III*, p. 183.

23 Ormrod, *Edward III*, p. 407.

24 Foedera, pp. 487–94.

25 Hallam, E.M., *Capetian France 987–1328* (London: Longman, 1983), p. 74.

26 *CPR*, 1358–1361, p. 375. John of Gaunt was granted Hertford Castle 20 May 1360.

Chapter 4

1 Statutes of the Realm, Vol. 1, pp. 366–7.

2 *Knighton's Chronicle*, p. 185.

3 Fowler, Kenneth, *The King's Lieutenant: Henry of Grosmont, First Duke of Lancaster, 1310–1361* (London: Elek, 1969), pp. 209–21.

4 *Knighton's Chronicle*, p. 183.

5 Ibid., p. 185.

6 Somerville, Robert, *History of the Duchy of Lancaster* (London: Chancellor and Council of the Duchy of Lancaster, 1953), pp. 1–25.

7 Bothwell, J.S., 'The Making of the Lancastrian Capital at Leicester: The Battle of Boroughbridge, Civic Diplomacy and Seigneurial Building Projects in Fourteenth Century England', *Journal of Medieval History*, 38 no. 3, 2012, pp. 335–57.

8 Walker, Simon, *The Lancastrian Affinity 1361–1399* (Oxford: Clarendon, 1990), p. 8.

9 Extract from the will of John of Gaunt, 1398: '*Je ly devise un fermail d'or del veil manere, et escript les noms de Dieu en chascun part de icel fermail, la quel ma treshonoré dame et miere la Roigne*'. Gaunt's original will, dated 3 Feb 1399, was probably left at Lincoln Cathedral. A near-contemporary copy is written into the register of Bishop Henry Beaufort (at Lincoln, 1397–1405): DIOC/REG 13, fols 13v–18r.

10 See Mortimer, Ian, *The Fears of Henry IV: The Life of England's Self-Made King* (London: Vintage, 2008), Appendices Seven: The Lancastrian Esses Collar.

11 Sumption, Jonathan, *The Hundred Years War, Volume 3: Divided Houses* (London: Faber & Faber, 2009), p. 274.

12 Goodman, p. 45.

13 Chandos Herald, *Life of the Black Prince by the Herald of Sir John Chandos*, ed. Mildred K. Pope and Eleanor C. Lodge (Oxford: Clarendon Press, 1910), p. 148.

14 Jones, Michael, *The Black Prince* (London: Head of Zeus, 2017), p. 271.

15 Ayala, pp. 393–4, in Villalon, L.J. Andrew, 'Spanish Involvement in the Hundred Years War and the Battle of Nájera', in *The Hundred Years War: A Wider Focus*, Part 1, ed. L.J. Andrew Villalon and Donald J. Kagay (Leiden: Brill, 2005), p. 7.

16 The Chronicler Pero Lopez Ayala does a fine job in enhancing Pedro's reputation as a villain, whereas Chaucer sympathises with him in *A Monk's Tale*, see Estow, Clara, *Pedro the Cruel of Castile: 1350–1369* (Leiden: Brill, 1995), pp. xx–xxi.

17 Vernier, Richard, *The Flower of Chivalry, Bertrand du Guesclin and the Hundred Years War* (Woodbridge: Boydell Press, 2003), p. 85.

18 Villalon, 'Spanish Involvement in the Hundred Years War', p. 6.

19 *JGR*, 1371–1375, vol. I, no. 748 f.103b, p. 276.

20 Chandos Herald, *Life of the Black Prince by the Herald of Sir John Chandos,* ed. Mildred K. Pope and Eleanor C. Lodge (Oxford: Clarendon Press, 1910), p. 153.

21 Kempe, Margery, *The Book of Margery Kempe*, trans. Anthony Bale (Oxford: Oxford University Press, 2015), p. 97.

22 *JGR*, 1372–1376, vol. I, nos. 60, 73, p. 45.

23 Chandos Herald, in Jones, *The Black Prince*, p. 307.

24 Villalon, 'Spanish Involvement in the Hundred Years War', p. 34.

25 Ibid., p. 37.

26 Ayala, 562–3, in Villalon, 'Spanish Involvement in the Hundred Years War', p. 48.

27 Rigg, A.G., *A History of Anglo-Latin Literature, 1066–1422* (Cambridge: Cambridge University Press, 1992), p. 277.

Chapter 5

1 Turner, *Chaucer*, p. 132.

2 Ibid., pp. 132–43.

3 Green, David, *Edward the Black Prince* (Harlow: Longman, 2007), p. 8.

4 Sumption, Jonathan, *The Hundred Years War, Volume 2: Trial by Fire* (London: Faber & Faber, 1999), p. 1016.

5 *Anonimalle Chronicle*, pp. 59–61, in Rogers, *The Wars of Edward III*, p. 187.

6 Ibid., p. 187.

7 Quatre Premiers Valois, pp. 200–5, in Rogers, *The Wars of Edward III*, p. 186.

8 Ibid., p. 186.

9 Jones, *The Black Prince*, p. 358.

10 Ibid., pp. 365–7.

11 Jones, p. 367.

12 C47/28/9/15: Chancery Miscellanea, diplomatic documents; Return by John, Duke of Lancaster, as to the custody of La Roche-sur-Yonne since 1370, National Archives, London.

Chapter 6

1 *JGR*, 1371–1375, vol. II, nos. 1661, 1662, pp. 298–302.

2 *JGR*, 1371–1375, vol. I, no. 409, p. 169.

3 *JGR*, 1371–1375, vol. II, no. 969, pp. 47–8.

4 Stamp, A.E., Chapman, J.B.W., Dawes, M.C.B., *et al.*, 'Inquisitions Post Mortem, Edward III, File 229', in *Calendar of Inquisitions Post Mortem: Volume 13, Edward III* (London, 1954), no. 204, pp. 163–78.

5 Ibid., no. 204, pp. 163–78.

6 *JGR*, 1379–1383, vol. II, no. 963, p. 302.

7 *JGR*, 1371–1375, vol. II, no. 1056, p. 82.

8 Turner, *Chaucer*, pp. 50–1.

9 *JGR*, 1379–1383, vol. I, no. 327, pp. 111–12.

10 *JGR*, 1371–1375, vol. I, no. 409, p. 169.

11 *JGR*, vol. II, no. 1607, p. 279.

12 Calendar of Papal Registers Relating to Great Britain and Ireland: Volume 4, 1362–1404, Kal. Sept. St. Peter's, Rome (f.232d.).

13 Walsingham, Thomas, *The St Albans Chronicle: The Chronica Maiora of Thomas Walsingham*, ed. and trans. John Taylor, Wendy R. Childs and Leslie Watkiss (Oxford: Clarendon Press, 2003–11), p. 13.

14 Thornbury, Walter, 'The Savoy', in *Old and New London: Volume 3* (London, 1878), pp. 95–100. The Savoy Hotel is built on the same site as the original palace.

15 Loftie, W.J. and White, H., *Memorials of the Savoy, the Palace, the Hospital, the Chapel* (London: Macmillan and Co., 1878), p. 25.

16 *JGR*, 1372–1376, vol. II, no. 994, p. 58.

17 *JGR*, 1372, nos. 912, 913, 914, pp. 21–22; and nos. 925, 926, 927, p. 28.

18 *JGR*, vol. II, no. 217, p. 95. In 1372, John was running a large part of the King's administration.

19 Sumption, *Divided Houses*, p. 171.

20 National Archives, C47/30/8/1.

21 Holmes, George, *The Good Parliament* (Oxford: Clarendon Press, 1975), p. 1. The records produced for the Good Parliament that still survive to this day include 40 large folio pages.

22 *Walsingham, St Albans Chronicle* vol. I, p. lxxv.

23 Tompkins, Laura, '"Said the Mistress to the Bishop": Alice Perrers, William Wykeham and Court Networks in Fourteenth Century England', in *Ruling Fourteenth-Century England*, ed. Rémy Ambühl, James Bothwell, and Laura Tompkins (Woodbridge: Boydell Press, 2019), pp. 205–26.

24 Holmes, *The Good Parliament*, p. 103.

25 From 1314, the Crown required all wool for export to be traded at a designated market, called 'the Staple'. This allowed the Crown to monitor the trade and levy tax on exports.

26 The Staple – the centre of the wool trade administration – was removed from Calais, meaning that the merchant community which thrived in Calais no longer separately funded its defence as a garrison. Whilst the Staple was in Calais, the merchants relied on the soldiers for safety. They paid their wages, not the Crown. When the Staple was removed, the Crown was forced to pay the Calais soldiers.

27 Ormrod, W. Mark, 'The Trials of Alice Perrers', *Speculum*, 83, no. 2, 2008, pp. 366–96.

28 Walsingham, *The St Albans Chronicle*, p. 47.

29 Ibid., pp. 43–5.

30 Thomas Walsingham in Jones, *The Black Prince*, p. 379.

31 Ibid., p. 379.

32 *JGR*, 1372–1376, vol. II, pp. 353–355. From 1376–1377, John of Gaunt was largely based at the Savoy Palace. This indicates a highly active role at court on behalf of the King.

33 Walsingham, *The St Albans Chronicle*, p. 63.

34 *JGR*, 1371–1375, vol. II, no. 1806, p. 352. Letter to the chancellor, John Kynvett, to help the people of Havering pay for the repair and preservation of property, otherwise they would fall into the hands of private landowners. 17 August 1376.

35 E42/3 & SC8/223/11132: Special Collections, Ancient Petitions: Gaunt's complaint to Edward III that the manors exchanged for the Earldom of Richmond were 'ruinous and wasted'. National Archives, London. In 1377, there was an ongoing row over Richmond lands which Gaunt had exchanged for Yorkshire lands that had proved to be less lucrative. Parliament were refusing to return land to him. Indicates animosity between Gaunt and Parliament at this stage.

36 Wedgewood, Josiah C., 'John of Gaunt and the Packing of Parliament', *The English Historical Review*, 45 no. 180, 1930, pp. 623–5.

37 McKisack, May, *The Fourteenth Century 1307–1399* (Oxford: Clarendon Press, 1959), p. 394.

38 *JGR*, 1371–1375, vol. II, no. 932, p. 31.

39 British Library, CH 71913, confirmation of the sale of Kirkby Mallory manor to St Mary's Abbey in Leicester.

40 C143/367/3: Chancery, Inquisitions Ad Quod Damnum; 'John Duke of Lancaster, to grant the manor of Landbeach, with the advowson of its church, and messuages and land in Cambridge, Barnwell Grantchester and Coton, to the master and scholars of Corpus Christi College Cambridge', 43 Edward III, 1369–70, National Archives, London.

41 *JGR*, 1371–1375, vol. I, nos. 686, 687, pp. 252–3. Grants given to Carmelite confessor, Walter Disse.

42 *JGR*, 1371–1375, vol. II, no. 1738, p. 323.

43 Walsingham, *The St Albans Chronicle*, p. 83.

44 Ibid., p. 83.

45 McKisack, *The Fourteenth Century*, p. 397.

46 SC1/43/81: Special Collections, Ancient Correspondence; Maud, former nurse of Philippa, his daughter, to John of Gaunt, Duke of Lancaster: report of evil report put out against him by friars minor and friars preachers. 1376–1377, National Archives, London.

Chapter 7

1 Ormrod, *Edward III*, p. 577.

2 *CCR*, 1377–1381, 1–7.

3 National Archives, C54/217, m. 45.

4 National Archives, SC8/146/7271.

5 *The Westminster Chronicle 1381–1394*, ed. L.C. Hector and B.F. Harvey (Oxford: Clarendon Press, 1982), pp. 414–16.

6 Throsby, J., *Select Views in Leicestershire, from Original Drawings: Containing Seats of the Nobility and Gentry, Town Views and Ruins, Accompanied with Descriptive and Historical Relations*, Volume 2 (Leicester: J. Throsby, 1790), p. 84.

7 The cellar, known now as 'John of Gaunt's Cellar', is still in existence underneath part of De Montfort University. The site also includes the original hall, which was in existence in John of Gaunt's time.

8 Walsingham, *The St Albans Chronicle*, p. 165.

9 *John of Gaunt's Register, 1379–1383*, ed. Eleanor C. Lodge and Robert Somerville (London: Offices of the Royal Historical Society, 1937) *Camden Third Series, 56*, 1–233. p. 205, note 1.

10 Parliamentary Rolls, Richard II, October 1377 (C65/32. *RP*, III.3–29. *SR*, II.1–5).

11 Ibid.; Saul, Nigel, *Richard II* (New Haven, Conn. and London: Yale Univ. Press, 1999), p. 28.

12 Edward III was fourteen when he inherited the throne in 1327, however, his guardian, Roger Mortimer, was a de facto ruler rather than official regent.

13 Saul, *Richard II*, p. 28.

14 Ibid., p. 2; Holmes, *The Good Parliament*, p. 105.

15 Edwards, J.G., 'Some Common Petitions in Richard II's First Parliament', *Bulletin of the Institute of Historical Research*, 26 no. 74, 1953, pp. 200–13.

16 *CPR*, Richard II, 1377–1381, p. 7.

17 Ibid., p. 7.

18 National Archives, SC8/122/6051.

19 Parliamentary Rolls, Richard II, October 1378, (C65/33. *RP*, III.32–49. *SR*, II.6–11).

20 Ibid.

21 Ibid.

22 McKisack, *The Fourteenth Century*, pp. 404–5.

23 Parliamentary Rolls, Richard II, October 1378 (C65/33. *RP*, III.32–49. *SR*, II.6–11. 13).

24 Parliamentary Rolls, Richard II, November 1380, C65/36. *RP*, III.88–97. *SR*, II.16.

25 Ibid.

Chapter 8

1　As civil war took over important trading centres such as Ghent, cloth makers moved out of the towns and cities and began to trade elsewhere, compromising, even destroying trade with the English, for there was little demand for English wool. Lloyd, T.H., *The English Wool Trade in the Middle Ages* (Cambridge: Cambridge University Press, 2005), p. 225.

2　Parliamentary Rolls, Richard II, November 1380, C65/36. *RP*, III.88–97. *SR*, II.16.

3　Ibid.

4　*JGR*, 1379–1383, vol. II, no. 1185, p. 374.

5　*JGR*, 1379–1383, vol. I, nos. 31 & 32, p. 18.

6　*JGR*, 1379–1383, vol. I, nos. 493–8, p. 161.

7　Dobson, R.B., ed., *The Peasants' Revolt of 1381* (London: Macmillan, 1970), p. 155.

8　Coulton, G.G., *Medieval Panorama, the English Scene from Conquest too Reformation* (Cambridge: Cambridge University Press, 1943), pp. 69–80.

9　*Anonimalle Chronicle*, in Dobson, *The Peasants' Revolt*, p. 127.

10　Ibid., p. 127.

11　There is speculation over the involvement or even existence of Jack Straw, but Walsingham states that he came from Bury St Edmunds in Suffolk.

12　*Anonimalle Chronicle*, in Dobson, *The Peasants' Revolt*, p. 127.

13　Ibid., p. 127.

14　*JGR*, 1379–1383, vol. I, no. 529, p. 170.

15　Walsingham, *The St Albans Chronicle*, p. 419.

16　Around thirty rebels died in the cellars of the Savoy, *Knighton's Chronicle*, in Dobson, *The Peasants' Revolt*, p. 184.

17　Walsingham, *The St Albans Chronicle*, p. 427.

18　*JGR*, 1379–1383, vol. I, no. 551, p. 177.

19　*Knighton's Chronicle*, p. 227.

20　Ibid., p. 233.

21　*JGR*, 1379–1383, vol. I, no. 535, p. 173.

22　According to Henry Knighton, John of Gaunt believed that he had been punished by God for his ongoing relationship with Katherine. *Knighton's Chronicle*, p. 237.

23　Walsingham, *The St Albans Chronicle*, p. 567.

24　*JGR*, 1379–1383, vol. I, no. 688, pp. 221–2. In February 1382, John of Gaunt sent Katherine ten barrels of wine from Gascony as a gift.

25　Ibid., no. 553, p. 177.

26　*Knighton's Chronicle*, p. 231.

27　Ibid., p. 231.

28 *JGR*, 1379–1383, vol. I, no. 564, p. 185.

29 *CPR*, 1381–1385, p. 30.

30 *Knighton's Chronicle*, p. 289.

31 *CPR*, 1381–1385, p. 35.

32 Saul, *Richard II*, p. 108.

Chapter 9

1 Parliamentary Rolls, Richard II, November 1381 (C65/37. *RP*, III.98–121. *SR*, II.17–23).

2 In September 1381, John of Gaunt was at York Castle as part of a judicial commission, representing the King regarding the crimes committed during the uprising. National Archives, Kew, E42/303–11758189.

3 *CPR*, 1381–1386, p. 224.

4 *Knighton's Chronicle*, p. 239.

5 Walsingham, *The St Albans Chronicle*, p. 569.

6 *CPR*, 1381–1385, pp. 125–6.

7 *JGR*, 1379–1383, vol. I, no. 714, pp. 229–230.

8 Parliamentary Rolls, Richard II, November 1381, (C65/37. *RP*, III.98–121. *SR*, II.17–23).

9 Ibid.

10 Jean Froissart, in *The Reign of Richard II, From Minority to Tyranny 1377–97*, ed. and trans. A.K. McHardy (Manchester: Manchester University Press, 2012), pp. 95–6.

11 *The Westminster Chronicle*, pp. 27–9.

12 Parliamentary Rolls, Richard II, October, 1382, (C65/39. *RP*, III.132–143. *SR*, II.26–30).

13 Ibid.

14 Walsingham, *The St Albans Chronicle*, p. 493.

15 *Knighton's Chronicle*, p. 325.

16 *The Westminster Chronicle*, p. 39.

17 Sumption, *Divided Houses*, p. 504.

18 *Knighton's Chronicle*, p. 335.

19 Sumption, *Divided Houses*, p. 519.

20 *The Westminster Chronicle*, p. 69.

21 Ibid., p. 69.

22 Walsingham, *The St Albans Chronicle*, p. 725.

23 Ibid., p. 217.

24 Walsingham, *The St Albans Chronicle*, p. 727.

25 *The Westminster Chronicle*, p. 113.

26 Ibid., p. 113.

27 Ibid., p. 115.

28 Walsingham, *The St Albans Chronicle*, p. 757.

29 *The Westminster Chronicle*, p. 123.

30 There were around 14,000 men and archers on the march to Scotland, Sumption, *Divided Houses*, p. 548.

31 Walsingham, *The St Albans Chronicle*, p. 763.

32 Adhering to the Anglo–Portuguese treaty of 1373, English longbowmen were dispatched to aid the Portuguese in the battle.

33 The crusade was made public at Saint Paul's Cathedral on 18 February 1386, *Calendar of Papal Letters, IV (1362–1404)*.

34 Parliamentary Rolls, Richard II, October 1385, (C65/44. *RP*, III.203–214. *SR*, II. 36–7).

35 *Knighton's Chronicle*, p. 343.

36 Dawes, M.C.B., Devine, M.R., Jones, H.E. and Post, M.J., 'Inquisitions Post Mortem, Richard II, File 43', in *Calendar of Inquisitions Post Mortem: Volume 16, Richard II* (London, 1974), pp. 126–31. no. 351.

37 Froissart, Jean, *Chroniques*, ed. S. Luce, vol. 12 (Paris: SHF, 1869–1919), p. 297.

Chapter 10

1 *CCR*, Richard II: Volume 3, 1385–1389, pp. 66–70.

2 National Archives, Kew, SC1/51/26.

3 National Archives, Kew. Letter to Thomas Percy under John of Gaunt's privy seal, SC1/51/26.

4 British Library. Detail of a miniature of the storming of Corunna by Broadas, from *Poems and Romances* (the 'Talbot Shrewsbury book'), France (Rouen), *c.*1445, Royal 15 E. vi, f. 207r.

5 Russell, P.E., *The English Intervention in Spain and Portugal in the Age of Edward III and Richard II* (Oxford: Clarendon Press, 1955), p. 432.

6 Froissart, *Chronicles* (1968), p. 328.

7 Ibid., pp. 328–9.

8 *Calendar of Inquisitions Post Mortem*, Vol. 16, Richard II. No. 497.

9 Froissart, *Chronicles* (1968), p. 331.

10 Sumption, *Divided Houses*, p. 334.

11 *JGR*, 1379–1383, vol. II, no. 1233, p. 406. The safe conduct was granted for a period of five days from 20–25 May.

12 *Knighton's Chronicle*, p. 343. This was the second payment from Juan Trastámara to Gaunt.

13 Sumption, *Divided Houses*, p. 619.

Chapter 11

1 *The Westminster Chronicle*, pp. 206–12.

2 Scott, Sir Walter, ed., *A Collection of Scarce and Valuable Tracts, on the Most Interesting and Entertaining Subjects: But Chiefly Such as Relate to the History and Constitution of These kingdoms: Selected from an Infinite Number in Print and Manuscript, in the Royal, Cotton, Sion, and Other Public, as Well as Private, Libraries: Particularly that of the Late Lord Somers, Volume 1* (London: T. Cadell and W. Davies, 1809), p. 21.

3 *The Westminster Chronicle*, pp. 212–14.

4 Walsingham, *The St Albans Chronicle*, p. 823.

5 Ibid., p. 837.

6 *Knighton's Chronicle*, pp. 420–4.

7 Walsingham, *The St Albans Chronicle*, p. 839.

8 C65/47, m.8.

9 National Archives, DL 28/3/2.

10 Eulogium, pp. 366–7 in McHardy, *The Reign of Richard II*, p. 212.

11 Goodman, *John of Gaunt*, p. 144.

12 Parliamentary Rolls, Richard II, January 1390, (C65/49. *RP*, III.257–273. *SR*, II.61–75).

13 Gaunt visited Aquitaine in 1390 to deal with the concerns of Gascons over the separation of Gascony from the English crown, and to manage some of the administration himself, National Archives SC8/176/8790.

14 Turner, *Chaucer*, p. 414.

15 Edinburgh University Library, MS 183/f. 135v[1] dated 5 March, 1391/92 at Lincoln.

16 South of the Dordogne, Charles VI was willing to restore all the land originally surrendered at Brétigny, except for Quercy. North of the river, Charles VI offered Péigord, southern Saintonge and the county of Angoulême. Sumption, *Divided Houses*, p. 783.

17 Froissart, in McHardy, *The Reign of Richard II*, no. 132, p. 259.

18 *The Westminster Chronicle*, p. 451.

19 Ibid., p. 457.

20 *Knighton's Chronicle*, p. 545.

21 Froissart, *Chronicles* (1968), p. 394.

22 Ibid., pp. 395–6.

23 Given-Wilson, Chris, *Henry IV* (New Haven and London: Yale University Press, 2017), p. 77.

24 The National Archives, Kew, E364/36 rot.H.

Chapter 12

1 *CPR* 1391–1396, p. 688; *CCR*, 1392–1396, pp. 518–27.

2 Issues of the Exchequer, trans. Devon, 259; adapted. In McHardy, *The Reign of Richard II,* no. 159, p. 304.

3 BL Harley MS, 3988 ff39r-40d.

4 Parliamentary Rolls, Richard II, January 1397, C65/56. *RP*, III.337–346. *SR*, II.92–94.

5 Ibid. On 4 February 1397, the Beauforts were legitimised in Parliament.

6 Froissart, *Chronicles* (1874), pp. 638–40.

7 *Rotuli Parliamentorum, vol. iii*, pp. 378–9.

8 The Monk of Evesham, *Vita Ricardi Secundi,* 137–51, in *Chronicles of the Revolution, 1397–1400: the Reign of Richard II,* trans. and ed. Chris Given-Wilson (Manchester: Manchester University Press, 1993), p. 54.

9 Ibid., p. 58.

10 'Richard II: September 1397, Part 2', in *Parliament Rolls of Medieval England,* ed. Chris Given-Wilson, Paul Brand, Seymour Phillips, *et al.* (Woodbridge: Boydell Press; London: National Archives, 2005), British History Online.

11 Given-Wilson, *Chronicles of the Revolution,* p. 109.

12 Ibid., p. 110.

13 Traison et Mort (trans. B. Williams), 117–27, 146–9, in Given-Wilson, *Chronicles of the Revolution,* p. 104.

14 Froissart, *Chronicles* (Paris: Mme Ve. J. Renouard, 1873) p. 663.

15 Bennett, M., *Richard II and the Revolution of 1399* (Stroud: Sutton, 1999), p. 132.

16 McNiven, Peter, 'The Problem of Henry IV's Health, 1405–1413', *The English Historical Review,* 100 no. 397, 1985, pp. 747–72; Skelton, John, *A Treatise on the Venereal Disease and Spermatorrhœa* (Leeds: Samuel Moxon, printer, 1857), p. 12.

17 Froissart, *Chronicles* (1873), p. 676.

18 Given-Wilson, *Chronicles of the Revolution*, p. 122.

19 Kirkstall Chronicle, 121–5, in Given-Wilson, *Chronicles of the Revolution*, pp. 132–5.

20 *Translation of a French Metrical History of the Deposition of King Richard the Second*, ed. and trans. John Webb, 55–176; *Collection des Chroniques Nationales Français*, ed. J. A. Buchon (Paris: Verdière, 1826), 341–415, in Given-Wilson, *Chronicles of the Revolution*, p. 139.

21 Adam Usk, 174–86, in Given-Wilson, *Chronicles of the Revolution*, p. 157.

Index

Author photo © George Naylor

HELEN CARR is a historian, writer and history producer. She has produced documentaries for the BBC, SkyArts, Discovery, CNN and HistoryHit TV and has previously worked for BBC Radio 4's weekly programme *In Our Time*. Helen is a regular features writer for *BBC History Magazine* and has contributed to the *New Statesman*, *History Today* and *History Extra*. She now runs her own podcast, *Hidden Histories*, available on iTunes. She tweets at @HelenhCarr.